INFORMATION TECHNOLOGY
FOR
MANUFACTURING

Reducing Costs and
Expanding Capabilities

INFORMATION TECHNOLOGY FOR MANUFACTURING

Reducing Costs and Expanding Capabilities

Kevin Ake
John Clemons
Mark Cubine
with Bruce Lilly

S^t_L

ST. LUCIE PRESS

A CRC Press Company
Boca Raton   London   New York   Washington, D.C.

Library of Congress Cataloging-in-Publication Data

Information technology for manufacturing : reducing costs and expanding capabilities / Kevin Ake...[et al.]
    p. cm.
Includes index.
ISBN 1-57444-359-3 (alk. paper)
    1. Computer integrated manufacturing systems. 2. Manufacturing processes--Automation. 3. Manufacturing industries--Information technology. I. Ake, Kevin.

TS155.63.I44 2003
670′.285—dc22   2003061062

Visit the CRC Press Web site at www.crcpress.com

© 2004 by EnteGreat, Inc.
St. Lucie Press is an imprint of CRC Press LLC

No claim to original U.S. Government works
International Standard Book Number 1-57444-359-3
Library of Congress Card Number 2003061062
Printed in the United States of America   2 3 4 5 6 7 8 9 0
Printed on acid-free paper

TABLE OF CONTENTS

FOREWORD

The dynamics of manufacturing strategy have changed. Over the last 10 years, manufacturers of all sizes have been moving from a "supply-push" drive for manufacturing efficiency to a "demand-pull" focus on customer fulfillment and predictable quality. Quite simply, this change means that manufacturing must play its part in delivering to plan, if the supply chain is to meet its goals profitably at the customer face. To this end, all forms of variability are the common enemy of manufacturing.

Manufacturers of all types — "make to stock," "make to demand," and "make to order" — are grappling with the challenge to transition culturally and operationally to a world where manufacturing is both a core part of the customer fulfillment process and a critical element of the extended supply chain, which includes both suppliers and customers. In this process, the "perfect order" benchmarking metric is as much a manufacturing improvement opportunity as a traditional customer-facing service measure. Meeting the customer's needs without a supply shortfall, whether in discrete or process manufacturing operations, is the ultimate "moment of truth" for a business, but this is a capability that takes years to build. To achieve this end and sustain the changes, four cornerstone business capabilities must emerge: demand visibility, business process integration and synchronization, information-enabled performance management, and collaboration.

The change process of retooling and refocusing manufacturing requires core differentiating capabilities that eliminate waste, reduce variability, meet production schedules, enforce regulatory compliance, and optimize cycle and lead times. All of this is necessary for manufacturing to play its role in customer service and responsiveness. The transition is not trivial and requires a new brand of change leader: a bridge builder that fuses the traditional factions and silos of business functions, information technology, engineering, and quality and drives them to a common business agenda.

Until now, information technology (IT) has had limited success, because the benefits it brings to manufacturing are seldom measured in supply chain terms. However, information technology isn't a "silver bullet," thus making people and readiness fundamental success factors. Today, IT is playing an increasing role in supporting business change, sustaining best practices, driving performance improvements, and enabling business scale. This *must* be the agenda of the new manufacturing strategy. A book that proposes the ground rules for this change is long overdue. Who better to deliver it than a company that differentiates itself by way of its broad manufacturing IT integration experience, namely EnteGreat.

Roddy Martin
VP Industry Strategies
AMR Research
Boston, MA

ACKNOWLEDGMENTS

A book such as this is the result of the efforts of many different people. The ideas contained in this book were generated while we served as consultants to manufacturing companies around the world. We are grateful to all of the people at those companies who gave us the opportunity to work on projects with them and who patiently taught us the many intricate details of their businesses. During this time, we have had the honor of working with an exceptional group of partners and co-workers at Ente-Great. Their skills, professionalism, and dedication have been and continue to be the keys to our collective success, and this book would not have been possible without them. We would especially like to thank EnteGreat's President and CEO, Rob Gellings, for giving us the support and encouragement necessary to complete this book. We would also like to thank Roddy Martin of AMR Research for encouraging us to undertake this project. We hope that we have done this subject justice, and we appreciate his guidance and advice over the years. Additionally, we would like to thank Bruce Lilly, who contributed a great deal to the process of writing *Information Technology for Manufacturing*, for his tireless efforts, creativity, and patient work with us to put the book together. Finally, we owe a tremendous debt of gratitude to our families. Without their unflagging support, we would never be able to endure the thousands of miles of travel and the countless nights away from home that are required to do our jobs well.

ABOUT THE AUTHORS

Kevin Ake, John Clemons, and **Mark Cubine** are three of the five founders of EnteGreat, a leading manufacturing and supply chain consulting and systems integration company serving primarily Fortune 500 manufacturing companies across North America. Each has extensive experience across the entire range of technologies employed in manufacturing, from control systems to ERP.

Kevin Ake: Kevin's 15 years in manufacturing have been spent in the Food & Beverage, Discrete Electronics, Government, and Consumer Products industries. A graduate of Florida State University's School of Engineering, he has worked for industry leading manufacturing companies and consulting firms, including General Dynamics, Rust International, and Raytheon Consulting and Systems Integration (CSI). As the National Director of Manufacturing IT and Technology for CSI, he managed multiple office locations consisting of technical staff supporting the company's consulting business. Earlier, Kevin's entrepreneurial spirit led him to found Computer Concepts, Inc., a software company that specialized in the sales of educational and vocational software solutions. At CCI, he was in charge of software development.

John Clemons: John has worked in manufacturing for over 23 years and has experience in many industry segments (Food & Beverage, Consumer Products, Pulp & Paper, Steel, Specialty Chemicals, Pharmaceuticals, and Biotechnology). A graduate of Samford University, Birmingham Southern College, and Southern Methodist University, John has spent his career working for industry-leading systems integrators and consultants, including Rust International and Raytheon Consulting and Systems Integration (CSI), and he has done consulting work almost exclusively for Fortune 500 Companies. By authoring papers and industry press articles, and as the leader of many technical sessions, he has helped industry leaders, managers, and engineers gain a firmer grasp of many critical IT issues in manufacturing.

Mark Cubine: During his 24 years in manufacturing, Mark has worked in multiple industry segments (Food & Beverage, Consumer Products, Pulp & Paper, Steel, Specialty Chemicals/Fibers/Films, Printing, Pharmaceuticals, Biotech, Automotive, and Electronics). Upon graduating from Vanderbilt University's School of Engineering, Mark's career took him to industry leading technology suppliers & consultants, including Honeywell, Hewlett-Packard, Measurex, Rust International, and Raytheon Consulting and Systems Integration (CSI). His papers, industry press articles, and technical sessions have helped people throughout the industry gain a better understanding of the integration of Manufacturing Systems within the Enterprise IT environment and the implications for using commercial off-the-shelf applications in manufacturing plants.

INTRODUCTION

Veins of gold run throughout manufacturing plants. Take a good map, gather up the right tools, follow some tried and true methods, and this gold can be yours. This book is both the map and the manual that describes the tools and methods you will need. The gold comes in the form of lower costs and valuable new capabilities. Cutting-edge information technology provides the tools; the methods come from firsthand observations of what works and what does not. Drawing upon our many years of experience in this field, we can show you where the gold lies and we can explain to you how to go about mining it. That is the purpose of this book.

Simply stated, the premise of everything that follows is that *the intelligent use of manufacturing information technology brings a solid and substantial return on the investment made.* Skeptics may ask why this gold has not been mined already. That is an entirely valid question. In fact, many companies have mined this gold; that is how we know it can be done. But it is not easy to do, and that is why so many other companies still have not done it. It is difficult for a variety of reasons and to explain them we must look at the history of information technology (IT) in manufacturing companies.

In Chapter 1, we look at the tremendous amount of change that has occurred in manufacturing in recent decades. Not only has manufacturing changed immensely, but the rate of change today is faster than ever and continues to accelerate. The result is that some segments of manufacturing are essentially extinct in North America, and many others have witnessed a radical transformation of their business models.

When you survey the change in manufacturing, a few major themes emerge:

- Consumers and retailers have more power than ever, which forces manufacturing companies to develop higher and higher levels of flexibility and responsiveness.
- Quality and safety failures have the potential to be devastating, so more and more resources are spent ensuring that such calamities are avoided.
- Regulatory compliance has dramatically increased the risk faced by companies. The trend is toward more intrusive and more intensive governmental oversight.
- Consolidations and mergers have skyrocketed, and the pressure keeps mounting to show cost and efficiency improvements as a result.
- The supply chain has tightened, forcing companies to develop increasingly collaborative and complex relationships with customers and suppliers.

The final theme that ties all of the other themes together is that IT is playing a bigger and bigger role in every aspect of manufacturing. If you want to make an effective response to the pressures brought about by any or all of these changes, you need the right computer software systems. IT has driven many of the productivity gains in recent years, and there is every reason to expect it to continue in this role.

Although computer technology is only a few decades old, a lot of ground has been covered in that time and we explore this history in Chapter 2. In manufacturing companies, the use of computers developed along two independent paths. Computers were being used both by plant engineering and corporate management, and the visions, goals, priorities, and approaches of the two groups were vastly different.

At first, the two groups worked independently of each other in peaceful coexistence. However, as the technology grew more sophisticated, its use by each group expanded and conflicts arose over vision, strategy, and tactics. Engineers attempted to create a unified concept of how a manufacturing company could integrate IT into every level of the organization, but ultimately these attempts failed. In the end, the corporate side asserted control over most aspects of IT throughout the organization.

This development had serious consequences, which go to the heart of this book. In too many cases, the strategies developed by people at the corporate level neglected to address the IT needs of the plant. Ideas about using IT to improve the way the plant operates were largely ignored. Although the ideas were ignored and continue to be ignored all too often, computer technology has continued to become more sophisticated. This is why we say that there is gold in manufacturing plants. Opportunities abound for the intelligent use of IT in the plant.

These opportunities have been ignored because people making the decisions at the corporate level about the use of IT have been focused on other areas. The most prominent evidence of this is the way budgets have been dominated by massive, corporate-wide software systems known as Enterprise Resource Planning (ERP) systems. This trend started in the 1990s, and it was accompanied by the Y2K fears and the dot-com mania at the end of the decade. All of these combined to create an environment in which little attention was given to finding better ways of using IT in manufacturing plants.

Where does all of this leave us today? Chapter 3 provides answers to that question. ERP was not only wildly successful at revolutionizing the way companies manage their business, it also had some serious negative consequences for manufacturing plants. In the case of ERP, the problems for the plant go beyond simply causing a diversion of IT resources. In many situations, ERP's reach into the plant actually made matters worse.

This happened because ERP was designed from the perspective of how *corporations* can be run more efficiently, not from the perspective of how *plants* can be run more efficiently. This clash of perspectives is the same one that existed at the start of the computer era. The gulf that developed between the vision of the plant engineers and the vision of the corporate IT department has left a damaging legacy that haunts us still. ERP failed to help plants because it failed to acknowledge essential elements of the manufacturing process. It didn't understand that the amount of materials needed to produce a product can vary; it didn't understand that scheduling must be dynamic, not static; and it didn't understand that quality, instead of always being black or white, can be a matter of degree.

One outcome of the corporate focus on ERP systems to the exclusion of applications that center on plant functions is that Microsoft®'s Excel and Access programs have become the most prevalent software packages in manufacturing plants today. While there can be no question that these two programs are valuable office tools, their pervasive use for a variety of important manufacturing functions puts the entire situation in bold relief. As useful as they may be in the office, such generic software tools are weak substitutes for the software products specifically designed for manufacturing companies. If more attention had been paid to addressing the IT needs of the plant, Excel and Access would have far less presence there.

Some people may argue that ERP's failures in the plant pale in comparison to its benefits for the corporation overall. We will let others settle that debate, but one thing no one dares to dispute is the fact that ERP costs a bundle. Implementations started big and became gargantuan, as consulting fees increased exponentially and deadlines crept ever onward into the future.

We bring this budgetary aspect of ERP into our discussion because it is an important element of where things stand today. There are great opportunities for using IT in the plant, but nothing will happen if your project doesn't get funded. It's critical that you understand how the funding of IT projects has changed in ERP's wake. We have seen the end of the days of buying on faith, buying on the basis of vendors' promises, or buying because it's the hottest new trend. Every IT project must be able to firmly demonstrate that a definite payback or the funds will not be forthcoming. IT proposals are scrutinized like never before.

The task of providing hard justification for projects leads us to the next essential question: Exactly where does all of this gold lie? The specific answers to this question must be multifaceted, because manufacturing is highly diverse. The tools and methods used to mine the gold in a pharmaceutical plant are not the same as those used in an automotive plant. Nevertheless, there are two fundamental ways that manufacturing companies can use IT to their advantage: to cut costs and to add valuable new capabilities. Chapter 4 presents a thorough description of how this can be done.

Time after time, we've seen companies attack their waste streams by using such IT applications as real-time data collection and analysis, supplier integration, and quality management. As a result, they reap substantial reductions in labor costs, materials costs, and asset utilization costs. Likewise, we've seen companies become more competitive by adding valuable new capabilities such as a broadened product line, sharply improved customer responsiveness, and better use of raw materials. In addition to these, some companies have used IT to obtain dramatic improvements in regulatory compliance.

It turns out that in most cases, companies find that they improve in more than one area at once. The steps they take to improve a manufacturing process give them new capabilities while simultaneously reducing costs. The reality is that, through the intelligent use of manufacturing IT, savvy companies are saving millions of dollars, becoming much more competitive, and avoiding millions of dollars in fines from regulatory agencies. The benefits are impressive.

There may be gold in *your* plants waiting to be mined, but to get this gold out, you need the right tools. Finding the right tools may be the most challenging task you face. Our description of the tools needed may be the most vital part of this book. The reason finding the right software can be so difficult is that there is no single source of information about manufacturing IT as it exists today. There's plenty of information available, but it is fragmented and much of it comes from sources that have a vested interest in the decisions you make.

In Chapter 5, we offer you an unbiased and comprehensive look at five major areas where IT systems can play a pivotal role in improving your company's manufacturing processes. These five areas and the corresponding IT systems are:

- Manufacturing Execution – Manufacturing Execution Systems (MES)
- Product Management – Product Lifecycle Management (PLM) Systems
- Data Collection and Analysis – Decision Support Systems (DSS)
- Planning and Scheduling – Advanced Planning and Scheduling (APS) Systems
- Maintenance Management – Computerized Maintenance Management Systems (CMMS)

These tools can help you reduce costs and add new capabilities. Our goal is to provide you with a thorough understanding of how these tools can benefit your company.

To bring the message home, we devote all of Chapter 6 to stories showing how manufacturing companies have used these IT systems successfully. This book isn't just about theory. There can be a real payback on manufacturing IT investments. We have ample proof and we present it to you here.

But even if you can see the opportunities in your company and you have an understanding of the tools that are available, many daunting challenges still lie ahead. Using information technology in manufacturing plants is difficult, make no mistake about it. Making use of the best methods available is critical for success. By observing scores of IT projects in all types of manufacturing plants, we have gained insights into the secrets of success.

Above all else, understand that IT projects have a distinct lifecycle that goes through four stages: strategy, framework, implementation, and support. Through an examination of these four stages in Chapter 7 to Chapter 10, plus some important warnings concerning pitfalls in Chapter 11, we lay bare our collective wisdom about bringing new information technology into manufacturing companies. By following the methods we put forth, which have been put to the test time and time again, you can ensure that the IT projects at *your* company will be successful.

The use of information technology has come a long way. Today, the tools are there to do almost anything you can imagine wanting to do in a manufacturing plant. Unfortunately, much of this potential goes untapped, and the gold just sits there waiting to be mined. If you think that the plants in your company could benefit from better use of IT systems, you're probably right. Read on and see if the ideas and examples we present could help you mine some gold of your own.

1

MANUFACTURING CHANGES IN RECENT DECADES

Imagine that the legendary Rip Van Winkle was the CEO at a large manufacturing company and he's just now waking up from his 20-year nap. Jack Rogers, the COO and Mr. Van Winkle's most trusted advisor, is given the task of bringing the crusty old man up to date on all that has transpired in manufacturing over the last two decades.

"Rip, there've been a few changes while you were sleeping."

"Of course there have been. Things always change. I bet the Japanese own everything by now."

"Actually, the Japanese economy is suffering a long-term recession. But, before we talk about that, let's focus on some of the major changes in North America. For one thing, the textiles industry here has been decimated."

"What happened? Aren't people wearing clothes anymore?"

"Relax, Rip, people are still wearing clothes."

"Then who's making the clothes and why are they so successful?"

"Remember what you always told me — 'Cost is relative.'"

"I knew it would happen. Labor costs have skyrocketed, I bet."

"Actually, the real issue in textiles is not that labor costs have increased so dramatically here, but that cheap labor abroad became so readily accessible."

"Hmm, that could be a problem. But how much cheaper is this labor anyway?"

"A lot. In many places maybe less than a tenth of what it is here."

"Less than a tenth? No wonder they've left town. Do we make anything here anymore?"

"Of course, Rip. The cheaper labor overseas involves unskilled work, so we can still compete in industries requiring skilled labor."

"But what about steel? When I fell asleep in the early 80s, American steel was dying fast. I bet it's gone now."

"No, with the rise of minimills, steel has taken some positive steps forward."

"I see. Jack, this is a lot to swallow. Tell me this, we do still make cars, don't we?"

"Yes, Rip, we do, but the automotive industry has seen some pretty big changes as well. For starters...."

Listening in on Rip's conversation with Jack serves two purposes. It begins a review of some of the changes that have occurred in manufacturing in the last 20 years. It also helps to emphasize how much has changed. Huge portions of the North American manufacturing base have packed their bags and left the country. The plants still successful here generally are engaged in complex and hybrid types of manufacturing, which means that they employ highly skilled workers. The cheap, unskilled labor available in developing countries holds no particular advantage to these companies. Also, in many cases, there's an issue of being close to either a source of raw materials or to customers. The need to be close to raw materials or to customers can trump any efforts to relocate a plant. In the end, regardless of whether industries have moved their plants abroad or stayed put, the amount of change overall has been massive.

Figures 1.1 and 1.2 show dramatic examples of the ways manufacturing is evolving. In the past decade, we've seen manufacturing output increase

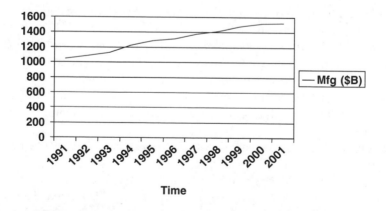

Figure 1.1 Changes in Manufacturing: Size of the Industry (Source: U.S. Department of Commerce, Business Economic Analysis.)

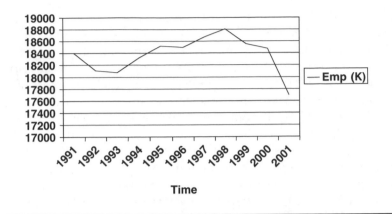

Figure 1.2 Changes in Manufacturing: Employment within the Industry (Source: U.S. Department of Commerce, Business Economic Analysis.)

by more than $1 billion, while at the same time, jobs have been evaporating. There's been a net loss of more than 1 million jobs since 1998, which means that the labor needed to fuel growth has declined significantly. Companies are expanding their production through increases in capital expenditures, not through increases in labor. They are accomplishing more with fewer people on board.

If you lived through the changes and saw them happen gradually, you may have failed to fully appreciate their magnitude. By looking at all of the changes through the eyes of someone like Rip, who didn't see it happen, we get a clearer perspective on all that transpired. Rip and Jack touch on steel and textiles, but there's more to say about each of those industries. After that we will go on to consider a few other industries — automotive, pulp and paper, and food and beverage — all of which have seen big changes.

TEXTILES

Mention the textile industry and many people instantly think of what is technically known as the apparel industry. In broad terms, the best way to distinguish one from the other is that the textile industry makes cloth and yarn, which is used by the apparel industry to make clothing. For our purposes, the distinction becomes meaningless because both industries have been devastated in this country by the availability of cheap labor in developing countries. Labor costs have always been a huge component of the overall costs for both industries, even though the work doesn't require a high level of skill. Major apparel makers, such as Levi-Strauss and Fruit of the Loom, have shut down the better part of their domestic operations and moved production overseas, but it's not that they really wanted to leave. Most manufacturers prefer to be as close to their markets as possible. Moving overseas means a rise in both shipping costs and inventory costs, because the supply chain is lengthened. It also complicates production. In order to stay competitive, any apparel manufacturer wants to be able to make quick adjustments to the demands of retailers. This is far easier to do if your plant is in South Carolina than if it's in South Asia. But the cost advantages in terms of labor trumps all other considerations.

And the trend is expected to continue. The Bureau of Labor Statistics predicts that employment in the *apparel* industry will decrease by more than 15% between 2000 and 2010, which translates into the loss of over 100,000 jobs, a greater decline than is predicted for almost any other industry. Except perhaps the *textile* industry. One of the problems for textiles is that the U.S. apparel industry is its major customer, so the domino effect will be felt. But that's only one of its problems.

The textile industry is truly global. Both the raw materials required and the machinery used to transform those materials into cloth are available all over the globe. Both the finished products and the raw materials are nonperishable and easy to ship. There is no compelling reason for a textile plant to be in any particular spot — other than the reason that labor costs are lower there. And labor costs are certainly not low in the U.S.

Labor costs alone have hit the industry hard, but there have been other problems recently. Much of the competition has come from Asia. For several years the dollar has risen steadily against Asian currencies. This results in cheaper prices for fabric produced in Asia vs. the same fabric made here. The results of all this are some grim numbers: From 1997 to 2002, almost 200,000 textile jobs were lost in North and South Carolina alone and almost 250 textile plants were closed nationwide. The textile and apparel industries have gone global on a massive scale and there's little reason to expect this to change.

STEEL

The American steel industry dominated the world at the end of World War II, but its share of the world market has been in decline ever since. The output of U.S. steel companies accounted for over 60% of the world total in 1945, but by 1985, its share had fallen to just over 10%. Of course, statistics are tricky and must be watched carefully. Given that overall production increased steadily in response to the worldwide rise in demand, losing share in the world market doesn't translate directly into the same loss of production by American companies. Yet there *has* been a real loss in production. The 1970s saw U.S. production of unfinished steel drop by more than 12%. During the same decade, capacity declined by 25% as companies downsized and closed plants.

The story since the 1980s is not as bleak, and it illustrates some of the general changes affecting American manufacturing. While the number of wage and salary jobs was cut in half between 1980 and 2000, only part of this was due to cutbacks in production. American steel isn't about to dominate the world market anytime soon, but the industry has made significant gains in efficiency and worker productivity and is both competitive and profitable. The Bureau of Labor Statistics estimates that employment will decrease by more than 20% in the first decade of this century, but improved technology is the central reason given for this expected decline in jobs. Capital investments in labor-saving technologies and machinery have increased dramatically.

A huge part of the changes in steel revolve around the ascendancy of the minimill. Steel plants involve huge capital outlays, which means that there is a high fixed cost. Minimills have the appeal of lower startup costs, lower maintenance expense, and lower energy costs. But that's only the beginning of their advantages. Another huge factor is the use of scrap by minimills, such as old bridges and cars. In contrast to the traditional integrated mills, which use blast furnaces to process iron ore into pig iron and then oxygen furnaces to transform the pig iron into steel, minimills use scrap and turn it into steel quicker. The steel produced by minimills is generally much less expensive.

Not only is scrap cheaper, the high transportation costs for the iron ore used by integrated mills makes it important for those mills to be close to their raw materials source. But the transportation costs for the finished product are also high. Given that scrap is available virtually everywhere, minimills can be located nearer to the customer or a transportation hub, and that can save money. It also turns out that several minimills have been built in rural areas to make use of the lower labor costs.

One important change affecting manufacturing is environmental regulations. Once again, minimills have the advantage. Integrated mills need coal to be converted to coke for use in the blast furnaces. This is done by heating the coal in coke ovens to remove impurities and leaving almost pure carbon. But where do those impurities go? The Clean Air Act sets strict standards on emissions, which means one of two things for the integrated mills. Either they have to spend loads of money modifying their coal processing facilities to reduce the amount of pollution being released into the air or they have to shut down. The steel made by integrated mills is already more expensive, and the capital expenditures needed to comply with environmental laws only pushes prices higher.

Another key factor here is *flexibility*, one of the watchwords for manufacturing today. Competition has produced specialization. More steel companies are targeting niche markets. With their inherent ability to be more adaptable, minimills have led the way in this effort to produce customized products for certain industries. The overall impact of the move toward specialization has been to prod companies to seek greater flexibility and adaptability in terms of their technology and the skills of their workers. The American steel industry may never regain its world dominance, but it has made some important adjustments to the changes facing manufacturing today.

AUTOMOTIVE

When Japanese cars started coming to North America by the boatloads, people here eventually decided to import some Japanese business ideas to boot. That is where JIT — *just in time* — comes in. Previously, car manufacturers would stockpile huge inventories of parts from their suppliers. The plant manager knew that causing the assembly line to shut down was a good way to lose his job, so having a good supply of components took high priority. The Japanese auto manufacturers developed a different approach. They worked more closely with their suppliers, so that the parts could be delivered just in time for the plant to use them. Guess who catches the heat now if the assembly line goes down due to the lack of a component? That's right; it's the suppliers that have to worry and that means that they are shouldering more of the burden of inventory costs.

Just because the original equipment manufacturer (OEM) sheds the cost of huge inventories, inventory costs don't disappear from the supply chain. Everyone understands that if the suppliers have to shoulder additional inventory costs, they will also have to either increase their prices or find other ways to reduce costs — or both. But the JIT system is more efficient, and it does reduce the overall product cost. It forces cost accountability on more parts of the supply chain, which means that there is greater scrutiny of the entire production process. Increased efficiency and decreased costs are squeezed out of every place possible.

Quality accountability for suppliers has become more critical as well. Car manufacturers began to ask this question: "If we have to pay for a warranty repair that involves the failure of a supplier's component, shouldn't the supplier be held accountable?" The obvious answer is "Yes," and more and more automakers are demanding that their suppliers participate in the total lifecycle costs of the cars and trucks being sold. This means that suppliers are seeing charge-backs from OEMs on warranty claims.

JIT wasn't the only thing we grudgingly learned from our Asian competitors. American car companies were getting beat on quality, innovation, and market response. Consumers vote with their dollars and American cars started coming in second and third or worse.

The rise of foreign car manufacturers is one part of how the world economy changed in the last few decades. Prior to 1970 nobody in this country gave a second thought to imported cars, apart from the luxury and high-end sports car markets. Americans drove American-made cars. Detroit was the auto industry. That all changed when the Japanese beat us at our own game. They started making better cars and selling them for less. As patriotic as many Americans are, in this case, the deals were too good to pass up.

As the Japanese economy boomed and as other developing countries, such as South Korea, became successful in manufacturing, huge sums of money started pouring into these countries. More money in the pockets of the Korean populace meant more money to be spent on consumer goods, including automobiles. American companies began to see huge new potential markets for their products. Car manufacturers sought to design a "world car" that would share components from around the world and only have minor cosmetic changes to allow for the local style preferences.

As international trade blossomed, other issues arose. Trade deficits became a more pressing issue for many countries. Also, as manufacturing plants moved around the globe in an effort to find the cheapest labor, the best tax structure, or the least stringent regulatory oversight, countries started looking for ways to protect local jobs. These pressures gave birth to "local content laws," which required as much as 80% of a product, such as an automobile, to be assembled from locally supplied parts.

This gave auto manufacturers a new reason to relocate their plants; they started putting them where the buyers lived and they told suppliers to move nearby. They had to do this to avoid being shut out of some increasingly lucrative markets. Building plants overseas has accelerated the globalization of auto manufacturers and, at the same time, has pushed many suppliers toward greater globalization.

As the largest market for automobiles in the world, the U.S. provides an instructive window on the globalization of the automotive industry. Prior to 1970, if you drove a "foreign" car, you knew that you were in possession of something that was manufactured abroad and imported. So there was some logic behind the idea of buying American in order to preserve domestic jobs and support the economy. That all started to change in 1978 when a Volkswagen assembly plant in Pennsylvania, which was acquired two years earlier, began turning out VW Rabbits. By 1983, Nissan was producing trucks in Tennessee. Two years later at another plant in the same state, Nissan was making the Sentra, its most popular model. Today, there are Honda, Toyota, Mercedes-Benz, and BMW plants scattered across the land, and they do not only make cars to be sold here. The largest exporter of assembled cars isn't GM and it isn't Ford; it's BMW. A BMW plant in South Carolina sends 60% of its Z3 roadsters to over 120 countries around the world.

So "Buy American" isn't such a simple equation anymore. In fact, it's complicated in one other major way — mergers and partnerships. American companies started buying interests in foreign companies as early as 1979, when Ford acquired a stake in Mazda. GM followed by buying a stake in Suzuki in 1981, and 5 years later GM entered into a joint effort with the Japanese company to build small cars and sport utility vehicles in Canada. It was only 2 years after that, in 1988, that Ford and Nissan agreed to design and build minivans together. In the same year, Chrysler and Mitsubishi started building cars together in Illinois. It has only continued since then, and no one can say where it will all end. GM now owns Saab, and the biggest change of all is that Daimler-Benz AG merged with Chrysler to become DaimlerChrysler. What is an American car company? What is a foreign car company? The distinction is losing any meaning.

PULP AND PAPER

Changes in this industry have occurred more recently, but don't think that means there haven't been big changes. For most of the 20th century, the pulp and paper industry followed a fairly predictable supply and demand cycle every 7 to 8 years. While demand steadily increased year after year, managing supply was no simple matter. Paper mills employ huge machines that cost hundreds of millions of dollars. When demand appeared to be exceeding capacity, paper companies would willingly spend the large sums of capital required for purchasing the equipment needed to increase production. But after the new machines were up and running, supply would outstrip demand. Eventually, demand would catch up again, and more money would be spent on increasing capacity, and the cycle just continued.

Companies didn't become overly concerned with costs, because they knew that they could sell all of the paper that their mills could roll out, regardless of the cost. It was an enviable situation, but it didn't last. In the mid- to late-1990s, demand fell and this was a literal decline, not just a slowing down of the rate of increase in demand. For most grades of paper, there was a gross drop in the total amount being sold. This was a real change, because demand had consistently grown for a long time. The *rate* of growth may have waxed and waned, but overall growth had always kept increasing.

So why the drop in demand? It can't actually be pinned to any one development. Rather, it's the result of all kinds of factors coming into play at the same time. We may not have the paperless office yet, but technology has certainly reduced paper use in some areas. There are competing theories about the reason for the decline in newspapers, but no one disputes that circulation continues to shrink. And consider this: Every time you bring your groceries home in plastic bags, you are reducing the demand for paper. Regardless of the reasons, demand clearly fell.

To make matters worse, demand fell just after capacity had increased. Almost every segment of the industry — every specialty or grade of paper — has too much capacity. The result is an industry turned on its head. Any plans for capital expenditures to add capacity have been eliminated, and many mills, especially older and less efficient ones, have been closed. If a paper mill hasn't been modernized and upgraded, there is a good chance its doors are shut now. Plus, like the steel industry, pulp and paper has felt the effects of the Clean Air and Clean Waters Acts. Money that might have been used to upgrade more mills has been siphoned off to make the already modernized mills less dirty.

When mills close, jobs are lost, and there has been wave after wave of layoffs to match the mill closures. In 2001, for example, North American paper manufacturers reduced capacity by almost 6.8 million tons and laid off over 10,000 employees. Now with surplus capacity, paper companies are merging just so they can consolidate production and eliminate unprofitable capacity. In fact, if the merger trend continues much longer, there will be only a handful of players left in the industry when all of the dust settles.

As demand fell, companies were forced to find new ways to compete. Quality and consistency became competitive tools. There was a time not long ago when the customer took whatever the mills produced, but not anymore. "Are you having problems with paper jams in your office equipment? Then switch to our paper. We guarantee it to be jam-free." A jam-free paper may not exist, but it was certainly possible to improve the quality and consistency of office papers substantially. Some companies did exactly that and forced the others to follow suit. On top of this, more specialty papers were developed — copier paper, laser printer paper, fax paper, etc. The paper industry has become consumer driven to a degree never known before.

FOOD AND BEVERAGE

Breakfast cereals are a simple, stable food product — right? Wrong. The humble breakfast cereal provides a good window into the dynamic changes in the food industry. Some cereal companies plan to introduce four new cereals each year, essentially one every quarter. They accept that half of these cereals are likely to be utter failures, but they hope that 1 of the 4 will survive on the shelves for at least 18 months. Then they hope that 1 out of 10 or 1 out of 20 will have a run of 2 to 3 years. Finally, the goal is to eventually strike gold by hitting upon the right item that gains a permanent place in the homes of consumers. *They would be happy if this happens with 1 out of every 100 new cereals they create.*

This illustrates a variety of changes. One is that consumers are more demanding. They want new products and they want all kinds of specific options: sugar-free, caffeine-free, extra caffeine, low-fat, fat-free, and more. Then they want all different size options: soft drinks in 8-oz., 12-oz., 14-oz., 16-oz., 1-l., 2-l., 3-l. containers. They don't just want plain cheese crackers anymore, they also want specialty flavors, such as white cheddar or spicy. Go into a store and see how many different types of potato chips there are today. The choices are overwhelming. For manufacturers, this causes something called SKU (stock-keeping unit) proliferation. Each different flavor and size requires a specific SKU, so that it is clear how many cases of caffeine-free, sugar-free, 12-oz. cans of cola are in stock vs. the number of cases of caffeine-free, 12-oz. cans of cola that do have sugar. There are an amazingly high number of different products to produce, sort, and track today.

The effort to create one lasting cereal also exhibits the recognition of the power of brands. Companies have learned how important it is to build and preserve a brand name. Consumers tend to develop intense brand loyalties, and as a result, certain brands become household names. They dominate their respective markets and become firmly associated in the public's mind with a certain product. In some ways, this can actually be a problem. What if you're known far and wide for cheese, but you see that Mexican food is becoming more and more popular? Do you start marketing salsa under your cheese brand name? Probably not, because no one associates your brand with salsa. A better idea is to either license a brand that's already well-known or to engage in an advertising campaign to establish a new brand. Brands have tremendous power and this fact drives the industry more than ever.

Although many brand names have been with us for many years, few of them are independent anymore. Years ago there were all sorts of different companies and they specialized in different things. Originally, the companies making cheese only made cheese, the cereal companies only made cereal, the hot dog companies only made hot dogs, and so on. But then they started expanding their lines of products. The cheese companies started making a wider variety of cheeses. Perhaps they came out with or bought a different brand that was marketed as a "premium" cheese. Cereal companies started trying to invent new cereals. Hot dog companies started selling cold cuts. Then all of this expansion went into hyper-drive with an intense period of mergers and consolidations. If you took all of the products lining the shelves in your local grocery stores and grouped them according to manufacturer, you would have a few really large piles of merchandise and a small assortment of other products to the side.

The impact of mergers and acquisitions on the industry has been huge and much of it has been good. Efficiency is up, as the companies that cannot keep up with production standards have been shaken out. The big food companies are now better able to concentrate on real value, such as adjusting to the new production trends and new consumer trends.

On the production side, this means consolidating the manufacture of some products. Cereal doesn't weigh a lot, it has a long shelf life, and the raw materials can be shipped in easily. Instead of having several different plants that make your company's best-selling brand of breakfast cereal in different regions, why not make it all at one plant and then ship it all over the world? Extra manufacturing costs usually dwarf the additional transportation costs that are brought on by consolidating all production to one location. Plus, with most regional brands going national (if not international), there is more opportunity to consolidate production than ever before.

On top of all this, food styles have changed, dietary theories have changed, and the food companies have been forced to keep pace. For example, the nutritional value of food plays a significant role today. In the past, the general consensus was that price, taste, and convenience sold food, not nutrition. A simple glance at a handful of the fat-free food items available today makes it clear that nutritional content has become both a central factor for consumers and a competitive tool for manufacturers. Further evidence of this trend is the mandatory food labeling law that went into effect in 1993. In 2003, the Food and Drug Administration announced a major change to nutrition labeling, which will require food labels to identify the amount of trans fatty acids. Calories, fat (both saturated and unsaturated), sodium, vitamins and minerals, sugar, protein, and more are given on the side of every food item sold in this country today. Consumers are more informed and also more discriminating.

While nutrition has become more central, price, taste, and convenience still matter, especially convenience. People always love to eat, but they don't always relish the chore of preparing meals. Today, if you want to serve your family a Chinese-style chicken and vegetable stir-fry dish for dinner, you can do so with much less work than before. Just purchase a bag of assorted vegetables that are already chopped to the necessary size and get some skinned, boneless, chopped, marinated pieces of chicken breast. At home, all you need to do is fry everything quickly in the skillet, add your seasonings, and your meal is ready to serve in record time. Even that is too much work for many people. Grocery stores face stiffer and stiffer competition from restaurants. Fast food, besides living up to its name, is also competitively priced and pleases the palettes of millions. But it's not only fast food restaurants that draw patrons. More and more people choose to spend more and more of their income on eating out at all kinds of dining establishments.

THE BIG PICTURE

What does all of the change from the last few decades mean to the manufacturing industry? Here are some major themes to consider.

The Rate of Change Has Increased and Continues to Accelerate

Ever since the industrial revolution, manufacturing has been evolving. In other words, change itself has always been a constant. Furthermore, some of the standard drivers for change that have been with us all along are still there — everyone tries to cut costs, increase productivity, and improve quality. The difference today is the very rate of change itself. The globalization of markets and production, advances in technology, and the increasing sophistication of consumers have combined to provide both the means and the motivation for companies to change more quickly than ever before.

Global markets mean both new opportunities and new competition. The playing field is larger and more companies are hustling to get into all of the new markets that have opened. This expansion of opportunity and competition speeds things up by itself, but it is helped along by technological advances that keep coming at a remarkable rate. Plants are more automated than ever, and this is having a big impact on labor strategies.

Gone is the trend toward unskilled labor, which had the obvious appeal of low cost. Fewer and fewer manufacturing plants in North America today still use unskilled labor. For the most part, the unskilled labor jobs have left for foreign shores. Products that require more processing, such as processed cheese or breakfast cereal, bring with them the need for more highly skilled workers. While highly skilled workers are paid more, don't forget that there are hidden costs to unskilled labor, one prime example being an unusually high turnover rate. Companies now see the value in using highly skilled, highly trained, self-directed employees. There is a term for this approach; it's called high performance work systems (HPWS). Companies are embracing HPWS because they are getting a good return on their investment.

A trend like this accelerates change by being very technology driven. In today's world, no one stays "highly trained" for very long without additional training. How old is the computer you use in your home or office? How old is the software? If either are more than a year old, you probably wish you could buy an upgrade right now. Workers have to constantly keep up with the technological changes in their industries, and their bosses have to do so as well. Using highly skilled workers pays off, but one of the prices is a faster pace for everyone — labor and management.

The globalization of the economy means not only global markets, but also global production. Manufacturing plants are moving all over the world, and for all kinds of reasons. We already discussed the movement of auto plants to other countries in order to qualify for laws concerning local content, but that's just one example. Lower labor costs, more lax regulatory control, less burdensome tax structures, and cheaper sources of raw materials are some of the major factors that dictate where new plants are built.

If you're a pharmaceutical company, you might build a plant in Puerto Rico, because taxes are lower there, labor is less expensive, and shipping costs for pills are negligible. If you're a clothing company, you might build a plant in Singapore, where labor costs are low. If environmental concerns are an issue, you might build a plant in South America or Africa, where countries favor industrial investment over pollution control. If you're making cheese, then milk is one of your highest cost items, making up anywhere from 50% to 75% of your total cost. So you want to have the simplest, least expensive access to milk that you can get and you build your plant near the cows.

This mobility of production accelerates change by forcing entirely new worlds on manufacturing companies. There's a lot to learn when you plan to start producing goods with a workforce that doesn't speak your native language. And that's after you have done all of the work learning the local laws and arranging to have the plant constructed. The amount of knowledge required to deal with the global nature of business today is overwhelming. But the competition is keeping pace, so you have to get up to speed or be left behind.

The consumer electronics industry provides another example of the rapid rate of change. Everything in electronics is disposable now, making electronic repair a totally dead industry. Items are not designed to be repaired for several reasons. There's no profit in doing the repairs (so there's no point in stocking parts), and new models are being produced so quickly that the whole process of repairing becomes obsolete quickly. Technological advances and competition are driving this. Why bother to repair something when you can spend almost the same amount of money and get the next generation model?

Another way that competition is accelerating the pace of change concerns the increasing sophistication of consumers. But this deserves a focus of its own.

The Market Has Changed in Response to the Demands of Consumers

The demands of consumers have more impact on the marketplace today than ever before. There was a time when you bought oatmeal because it was there. A company decided that oatmeal was a good product to sell, so it made it. Certainly you had the choice of whether to buy it or not, but what you didn't have was the choice of whether to buy regular, quick, 1-minute, or instant oatmeal. You also didn't have the option of individual serving packets or flavored oatmeal, such as honey, cinnamon, and apple. Companies didn't care so much about what consumers wanted, but today they are working proactively to find out. The number of new cereals created each year is a prime example.

Times have changed. It may sound trite, but it's true in a million different ways. Consumers today are more informed and more demanding. They read the nutritional labels on the side of food packages. For example, a brand of cheese-flavored popcorn made national news because someone discovered that it had misrepresented its fat content. This product was making a huge splash because everyone thought the taste was remarkable for such a low-fat snack, but it turns out that it wasn't so low-fat after all. The point is that people were being highly conscious of the fat content listed on the nutritional label on the side of this bag of popcorn.

Buying patterns have changed. Convenience is a big selling point. Superstores are ubiquitous because they provide the convenience of one-stop shopping. Say you get a call at the office from your spouse and on the way home you're supposed to get a loaf of bread, a dozen eggs, some printer paper, and film for a camera, so you stop at a superstore and get everything. Once there, you remember you need toothpaste, then see underwear on sale and a cool, new car stereo on display. You can get all of your needs met in one place.

One of the reasons that the car stereo you saw seems so cool is that it incorporates all of the latest technology. Product lifecycles have shortened dramatically. By producing new products, companies not only attempt to satisfy the specific desires of consumers, but they also compete for market share and shelf space. The overall impact is to force companies to be more streamlined. The pace of change is accelerating and there's no end in sight. More and more products are brought to the market each year. Consumers keep up and want the latest and best products.

They also demand high quality and complete safety, which brings us to the next point.

Companies Have Learned That Intense Efforts Must Be Made to Provide Consumers with Quality and Safety

Failures in These Areas Can Be Devastating

Think of this as the "*Wall Street Journal* issue." Many companies have learned the hard way how much damage can result from a front page article in the *Journal* detailing a product recall or some other product problem. Consumers have become more quality conscious and more informed than ever.

Consider the impact of the Tylenol tampering incident years ago. This changed the entire industry. It has been long enough now that we just take all of the tamper-evident seals for granted, but this was an earthquake of the highest magnitude for manufacturing. Today, even bottles of shampoo at a hotel have tamper-evident seals. The person behind this incident created more manufacturing jobs in a shorter period of time than any other single individual in history. And the entire effort to put seals on bottles was consumer driven.

Auto manufacturers used to say "Safety doesn't sell." Talk to a Ford car dealer about the effect of the Firestone tire and Ford Explorer debacle and you are likely to hear a different story. Any time a fatality happens as a result of a product failure, the impact can be massive — in the millions or hundreds of millions of dollars. This is why companies are trying harder than ever to prevent product recalls in the first place, and to manage them more effectively when they do occur.

Any negative news in the *Wall Street Journal* can have far-reaching results. One article can cost a company millions of dollars through a drop in the company's stock price. For this reason, companies have become willing to take whatever steps are necessary to ensure that they avoid this type of calamity.

Retailers Wield More and More Power

When it comes to choosing which products will be made readily available to consumers, retailers call the shots. Suppose you're a rice farmer who has been selling rice through a mega-retailer chain, and suddenly for some reason unknown to you, your product is dropped from its shelves. Maybe sales weren't down at all — they could even have been up — but perhaps the retailer wanted the shelf space for some other product. You're still making a good product and consumers still want it, but access to your product has been cut off in hundreds of stores across the country. And the fact is, most people don't want to go searching around at different stores to find your product somewhere else. If the big store doesn't have it, people will buy whatever the big store does have. The whole matter is completely out of your control. You are totally at the mercy of the retailer. Maybe it made a good decision for its stores, or maybe not, but either way, you weren't consulted and you simply have to live with it. A simple decision like this can put you out of business. On the other hand, if the retailer suddenly decides to double your shelf space and promote your product by placing it more strategically for better visibility, you may find yourself with more orders than you can fill.

Product selection and shelf space are not the only way retailers exert their will on manufacturers. By commanding such a dominant market share, the mega-retailers can lay down the laws about matters such as order cycle times. Right now, it's not unusual for a major retailer to demand that orders for many products arrive within three or four days. There's no indication that lead times will do anything other than tighten even more in the future. This puts even greater pressure on manufacturers to coordinate with their suppliers so goods can be produced *just in time* to meet the orders of the retailers.

Regulatory Compliance Has Become a More Pressing Issue

Gone are the days when the worst case scenario for breaking a government regulation was a small to moderate fine. Both fines and enforcement have increased dramatically, and it's no longer out of the question for jail time to be a possibility. This trend is still increasing and it's not expected to change. Twenty years ago, regulatory agencies had much less influence and power than they do today.

Compliance has become a competitive issue. Automakers are producing vehicles that are ahead of government deadlines for emission standards, and they advertise this fact in order to appeal to environmentally conscious consumers.

Regulations can affect where new plants are built. Think about building a new steel plant in the U.S. How long would it take? Probably 3 years to find a place to build it, another 3 years to obtain all of the permits, 2 years to get it designed, 3 years to get it built, and a year to get it up and running. That means going from idea to reality could take you 12 years! In contrast, if you want to put a steel plant in South America, you could probably break ground in a month and be up and running in about 2 years. Where would you build the steel plant?

Here are other examples of how regulations affect companies. A few years ago, for the first time, the pharmaceutical industry in the U.S. was given guidance on how to report their regulatory compliance electronically to the Food and Drug Administration (FDA). It's important to realize that legislative documents that address industry regulation come first and the specific rules come later. After legislation is passed, government officials sit down and spell out the detailed regulations in what is known as the Code of Federal Regulations (CFR). Pharmaceutical companies look to Section 21 of the CFR, Subsection Part 11, or 21-CFR-11, to learn about many of the issues addressing their industry. Conforming to government rules means extensive effort to keep detailed records, and prior to the new guidelines, most of this had to be done manually on paper.

This development brought both a welcome sigh of relief and a feeling of dread to drug companies. Keeping all of these records on paper was a terrible headache, so they were delighted to be able to make the transition to computer-based methods. And given that manufacturing companies capture and sort data electronically in all kinds of ways, it was inevitable that regulatory compliance would be handled in this way eventually. However, along with the guidelines for using electronic methods, 21-CFR-11 established some very stringent regulations. Plus, although using computers would ultimately be far superior to using paper, the process of changing methods is costly. In order to report compliance electronically, special software is needed and people must be trained to use the new methods. All of this requires significant investments of time and money.

On top of everything else, this was uncharted waters for the government regulators as well. Some companies claim that the FDA has not been consistent in the way it has interpreted the rules. Gray areas have emerged where it is difficult to say whether compliance is being achieved or not.

In an effort to address similar confusion over the Clean Air Act and the Clean Water Act, the government produced a set of guidelines called Title 5, which include a group of regulations known as the "Cluster Rules." The point was to make it very clear how companies have to operate, which procedures they must follow, what records they must keep, and which permits they must have. Permits are a central element of the regulations; they grant the holder a license to discharge a limited amount of certain pollutants into the air through smokestacks or into a river or a body of water through water treatment plants.

The big question is: Who monitors the emissions? The answer is: The companies themselves. The burden of measuring and proving that emissions don't exceed the limits of the permits falls on each permit owner. Every polluting substance coming out of a plant into the environment must be measured, calculated, and reported. If a company exceeds its limits, in addition to reporting this fact, it must also explain any reactive measures taken, such as cutting back on production in order to reign in its emission levels.

Extremely large sums of money have been spent in recent years by paper companies in response to the Cluster Rules. First, they simply had to make their plants cleaner. By changing equipment or processes, they have worked to reduce emissions so that they can comply with the discharge requirements. But they have also had to install measurement recording systems that give them the ability to prove to federal regulators that they are actually discharging no more of any particular substance than their permit allows. Money that might have been spent on improving production by buying new equipment, increasing automation, or adding a new cost-reducing capability has instead been used to comply with the government's environmental regulations.

Consolidations and Mergers Have Become a Fundamental Tactic

They Reduce Costs, Increase Profits, and Increase Productivity and Efficiency

This trend has been increasing for years and there's no indication that it will change soon. There are many components to this development. Mergers allow companies to:

- Take existing products into new markets
- Consolidate and eliminate overhead from the combined organization
- Use combined efforts synergistically to produce new products
- Expand from being a regional company to being national or global, as opposed to trying to grow gradually over time

To get an idea of how this plays out, imagine being in charge of a large food and beverage company which, after a series of mergers and acquisitions, owns brands that appear in every section of the grocery store. You manufacture multiple brands of cereal, frozen dessert toppings, soft drinks, fruit drinks, powdered drinks, coffee, hot dogs, lunch meats, salad dressings, mayonnaise, frozen pizza, Mexican food, and all kinds of cheese, just for starters. Your challenge is to use the company's size to its advantage. One of the first things to look at is distribution. Before various companies were acquired, they had their own distribution networks. Suddenly, you are managing contracts with many different shipping companies and operating way more warehouses than you really need. By negotiating a better contract with fewer shipping companies and by bringing all of the assorted distribution centers from one region together, you can cut costs dramatically. Part of this is increasing productivity and reducing overhead in payroll and accounting. The consolidation process will be a chore, but you'll be able to manage distribution for the entire company with a fraction of the people used by the various companies independently.

Then turn your attention to production. You may now have more plants than you really need, so you look at them to determine where you might have some excess capacity. Maybe you could use the plant making frozen dessert toppings to produce your new line of specially packaged lunch meat. The plant has extra space, all required utilities, and shipping and receiving capabilities. It also has refrigeration, something you need for the process of producing lunch meat, but not something you find in every food plant. Finally, there are workers available at competitive wages. By taking this step you either are able to shut down a surplus plant or can avoid the high capital expense of building a new one — meaning huge savings regardless.

There are more opportunities available. You have already improved your shipping contracts, but that's just the tip of the iceberg in terms of consolidating your suppliers. After all of the acquisitions, you probably found yourself with hundreds of suppliers all across the country (or around the world, for that matter) providing you with the same items at all sorts of different prices and terms. This can be quite complicated, involving delivery times, delivery rates, penalty rates for missing deliveries, minimum and maximum purchase quantities, lead times, and more. By consolidating your contracts with suppliers, you can gain more leverage for better prices and terms.

Another thing is that having more brands gives you an edge in the competition for shelf space with the mega-retailers. You may have acquired a brand that was extremely popular in the South, but not that well-known elsewhere. Now you have the marketing and distribution infrastructure to promote and sell this product nationally or even internationally, if you choose. Maybe you have an idea for a new product that combines a popular brand of cheese with an equally popular brand of potato chips. Before, these two brands were independent, but now they're under the same roof, so you can turn your product development people loose on the idea. All in all, these possibilities make mergers extremely attractive in many cases.

That's the up side. The down side is that assimilating an acquisition and gaining the prospective value is a tremendous challenge. The newly merged corporation may be fragmented. Different business processes are used in different divisions, and no two companies have the same corporate culture. It takes a concentrated effort to establish standardized processes, and this also requires standardized systems and technologies to support the processes.

The Plant's Relationships with Vendors and Suppliers Have Become More Critical

JIT plays a big role here. Vendors have to accommodate a stepped-up supply chain velocity. But that's not all. Given that consumers are more quality conscious than ever, suppliers have a vital role to play in meeting this challenge. Plus, as plant technology becomes more sophisticated, vendors must follow suit so that information can be exchanged efficiently.

To see a prime example of this, consider the case we mentioned before of car manufacturers using charge-backs on their suppliers for warranty claims that result from problems with supplied parts. This illustrates a shift in the view of warranty management from a customer management issue to a supply chain issue. OEMs are placing more pressure on suppliers to respond in formal and systematic ways to warranty issues coming down from the OEMs and the dealer channel.

There are several reasons for this development, but the primary one is the increase in warranty payouts recently. While there have been a few high-profile warranty cases, the majority of the increase has come from the consumers' and the OEMs' increased sensitivity to any perceived vehicle quality issues. For example, less than 10 years ago, a squealing or pulsating brake would have been ignored by most drivers as a minor inconvenience. Now with cars under long-term warranty commitments, a consumer will immediately demand that the brakes be fixed. Even though surveys show that overall vehicle quality is improving, warranty costs continue to grow. As a result, OEM charge-backs to suppliers for these warranty issues are also growing.

Industry groups are encouraging companies to think of warranty management less as claim administration and more as problem resolution. When you try to resolve a problem, you have to involve everyone — including the suppliers. One of the most important tasks is to make sure the information about any product failures gets to the right people: the quality control departments, the engineering and design departments, and the suppliers. Auto manufacturers have given consumers high expectations by promoting long-term warranty agreements. The only way they can live up to these agreements without bankrupting themselves is to take this more aggressive approach to resolving warranty issues.

The multifaceted benefits of closer relationships with vendors and suppliers have allowed manufacturing companies to seek innovative solutions to all kinds of problems. The food and beverage industry provides some good examples of this. Let's start with milk, the central ingredient of all kinds of food products. The manufacturer's challenge is to produce a product that tastes the same no matter where it's purchased. Consumers want to be able to walk into any grocery store in any part of the country at any time of year and know with complete certainty that the product they're buying will taste exactly how they expect it to taste. But milk comes from cows and there are all different types of cows, eating all different types of feed, living in all different parts of the country, and being affected by the changes of the seasons.

Getting milk that is consistent in terms of fat, protein, solids, nonfat solids, density, viscosity, and flavor, among other things, is no simple matter. You also want to avoid shipping milk any farther than you have to; it's better to ship the finished product instead. So one approach is to build the food processing plant near a group of dairies. You are getting your milk from the same sources consistently, so that eliminates some of the variables. Then you work closely with these suppliers to minimize other variations or at least to take them into account and plan for them. To cut costs, some companies negotiate a price based on a guaranteed minimum volume. Milk will be delivered to the plant on a set schedule, regardless of whether or not each specific delivery is needed at that moment. These "take or pay" arrangements can net a significant savings overall by providing a much better price for whatever is being purchased.

Grain and coffee are other examples. While they may be regarded strictly as commodities in trading markets, in the manufacturing world, they don't function that way. The moisture content of grain can make a big difference when you are turning it into a food product, so you have to think about all of the things that affect moisture content. If the grain is originally loaded into a boxcar many states away, it may be entirely dry by the time it reaches your plant. But if your plant is located in a region where the humidity hovers near 100% all summer long and your supplier keeps some of that grain in silos nearby for very long, it will absorb the moisture from the air. Coffee has a totally different set of equations. It gets shipped here from abroad, so you need to know how long it was on the ship and what type of containers it was shipped in. This is in addition to knowing what time of year it was harvested, how the weather was this year, and so on. With both grain and coffee, the point is that by working more closely with suppliers, food and beverage manufacturers are able to get a better handle on controlling the variations of their ingredients.

Many Companies Are Moving Toward More Use of Contract Manufacturers

There can be significant advantages to having some of your products made by another company. Demand for many products varies seasonally, and in other cases, there can be a spike in demand around special promotions. If your plants are already capacity-constrained, you may be faced with investing a great deal of capital to expand your production capabilities. But given that the excess demand is only temporary, you would then have excess capacity much of the year. The return on your investment of capital doesn't justify the expense in this case. The way to avoid a situation like this is to contract with another company to handle additional production of certain products during periods of excess demand.

Another reason some companies use contract manufacturing is that they want to focus all of their resources on developing new products. The products that are mature and stable can easily be made elsewhere, while the new products that are still evolving require more attention. In other cases, a company might have a flagship product that accounts for the core of the company's business, so it wants to be in close control of making that item. Less significant parts of the product line, however, could be contracted out. One other example is specialty packaging. A company that makes ketchup might contract with another company to handle putting the ketchup into the small, individual-serving packets used in fast-food restaurants. For all of these reasons, some companies are finding contract manufacturing more and more attractive.

THE FUTURE ROLE OF IT

There is one theme in manufacturing that's an integral part of all the others. Information technology has gone from a small blip on the screen to a massive component of every company's infrastructure. IT has a crucial role to play in every change mentioned above. If you want to make an effective response to the pressures brought about by any or all of these changes, you need the right computer software systems.

Many of the productivity gains in recent years have been driven by IT and there is every reason to expect IT to continue in this role. The changes in manufacturing over recent decades are interwoven with the development of information technology, but the IT story is so important that we have devoted an entire chapter to it. So read on.

2

MANUFACTURING IT FROM THE BEGINNING

Fred is the manager of information technology at a major manufacturing company. Late one afternoon, he leans back in his chair, gazes out the window, and reflects upon the changes he has seen, thinking, "A lot has happened in my lifetime. I guess I was probably in grade school when the BOMP first arrived."

THE DEVELOPMENT OF CORPORATE IT

The BOMP (Bill of Material Processor) was certainly one of the first truly useful applications of computers for manufacturing. Fred, in his 50s now, was still just a boy when the BOMP was installed in the early 1960s. The BOMP was basically a computer with a "hard wired" program that modeled the bills of materials for the products a company produced. It performed calculations to determine the quantity of each raw material item or the number of parts that were needed for production. This information provided the purchasing people and the material expediters their marching orders so that production could move ahead as planned without interruptions due to raw material or parts shortages.

Then in the late 1960s and early 1970s the hardware hard code programming of the BOMP began to be replaced by real software. Programming the BOMP was done by manually connecting untold numbers of wires from one specific location to another, producing something akin to the image of the first telephone operators who would sit at a switchboard connecting calls by plugging in the appropriate wires. Software programming quickly made this obsolete.

23

As software capabilities grew, a larger and more functional application called Material Requirements Planning (MRP) appeared. MRP went a step beyond the BOMP by tracking inventory and applying scheduling concerns to orders. The BOMP would tell you what to order, but MRP would tell you how many you have on hand and how many need to be here by what date in order to meet your schedule. By the early 1980s software programming had become much more sophisticated and one result was Material Resource Planning (MRP II). This application provided even more functionality in terms of managing inventory, purchasing, production planning, and production execution. Other programs that offered more specialized functions followed closely behind.

One of the significant changes was that these new software products could now be bought off the shelf. You could walk into a store, or more likely, contact a software vendor, and buy a packaged product. Prior to this, companies that wanted their computers to be able to do what these products did had to develop the programs themselves by having programmers spend endless hours writing the software code required. The ability of commercial off-the-shelf (COTS) products to handle inventory, purchasing, work orders, and production management paved the way for the next evolution, the dominance in the 1990s of MRP II's successor, Enterprise Resource Planning (ERP) systems.

Although Fred wasn't around for the BOMP, he does have a distinct memory of the company's first IBM mainframe, which came in the 1970s and grew and grew through the 1980s. It was a classic: this gigantic computing machine taking up an entire room. Everyone would look through the large glass windows that separated the computing room from the hall and be awed by its immense size. Today that computer room is stark and almost vacant. It's like a big empty gymnasium with a few small server boxes stuck in one corner; 90% of the floor space is empty.

THE FIRST ENGINEERING APPLICATIONS OF COMPUTER TECHNOLOGY

We need to note that Fred's entire career has been at the company's headquarters, which means that he hasn't paid a lot of attention to the operating intricacies of the company's plants. So his reflections about IT history sometimes ignore the direct role computers came to play in the manufacturing processes. This is understandable. After all, in the 1960s and 1970s, there was no connection between the computer work being done in the plant and the software being programmed in the corporate offices, other than the fact the plants had responsibility for doing large amounts of data entry. Engineers are problem solvers and they use whatever tools are available. As they became more and more trained in the use of computers, engineers found countless ways to put them to use in the plant in ways that weren't always obvious to Fred and the staff at corporate.

One of the most important milestones in the evolution of the industrial applications of computers was the invention of the Programmable Logic Controller (PLC) in 1968. The first PLC, which was a small microprocessor-based computer lodged in a box, replaced miles of wire throughout the plant and rows of cabinets containing countless relays. Many mechanical operations involve nothing more than switching something on or off. In any plant there are a million of these operations that occur every second. For example, motors must function intermittently to drive gears, belts, chains, conveyors, pulleys, punches, presses, pumps, fans, dryers, and more. These functions had been handled by all of the hard wiring and relays. The first PLCs worked digitally and had this on/off function down pat. They could turn motors on or off, open or close valves, and respond to a sensor's call to turn something on or off. Additionally, PLCs allowed engineers to set up more complex relationships concerning how equipment reacted to certain events. Before PLCs, the wiring work required made this impractical.

It's not just that PLCs provided an alternative to all of the wires and relays along with some new functions; they also made manufacturing plants dramatically more flexible. When the plant had to start producing a new product, the PLC could be easily reprogrammed to reconfigure the production lines according to the new design specifications. Previously, making this sort of change required calling in a crew of electricians and technicians and took weeks instead of hours. This new ability to change production had far-reaching implications. Innovative solutions to problems that couldn't even be considered before were now being attempted. The manufacturing process changed. Increases in automation reduced the need for labor, factories began producing a wider variety of products, and problems in production could be caught more easily and more quickly. Overall, more products were produced in less time for less money.

But for every million operations covered by the on and off capability of the digital PLC, there are millions more that require a measured action. The valve shouldn't be all the way open or all the way closed. Instead, it needs to be open exactly 48.35% so that the process can achieve a flow rate through the pipe of 318 gallons per minute. Also, the temperature of the liquid must be maintained at 222°. In the early days of automation, most of these operations were instrumented and connected to analog control systems such as loop controllers, which were mechanisms that would allow engineers to specify a specific number or value, not just on or off. Eventually, these functions were handled much more efficiently by distributed control systems (DCS), which replaced loop controllers in a similar fashion to the way PLCs replaced relays. Eventually PLCs became capable of analog control, too, and DCSs grew to be highly networked systems. Together PLCs and DCSs revolutionized the process of automation in factories.

The next layer of computer technology in the plant involved giving operators broader control over all the PLCs and DCSs. This was known as *supervisory control* as opposed to the loop control of a DCS. A good example of loop control (which is also called *regulatory control*) involves taking a temperature reading. In response to this reading, a calculation is made about the required position of a valve, and that information is communicated to the mechanism controlling the valve. Supervisory control takes a broader view of things. In this case, if the loop is determining the correct temperature for a hot water heating system, supervisory control goes beyond the automatic response and takes into account the temperature outside that day. If it's a warm day, supervisory control might tell the loop to aim for a lower temperature.

The supervisory control level can handle multiple loops and it can itself be either an open or a closed loop. An open loop is where human involvement comes into play; a closed loop means that everything is done automatically without any human intervention. A supervisory control loop doesn't necessarily involve human interaction, but it does involve macro data, not just highly specialized data. The case mentioned above is a closed loop, but it is supervisory instead of regulatory because it is not actually controlling the valve, it is controlling a loop that controls the valve. It is supervising the regulatory control systems. Supervisory control implies that either a human or a program is supervising the basic control systems.

Supervisory control actually existed before computers, and it was done through pneumatic devices and analog electronics. The type of thermostat commonly used in homes is a perfect example of closed loop control without a computer. If you took your thermostat and plugged it into a timer that turned it off and on at certain hours each day, you have a supervisory control loop. The clock in the timer overrides the thermostat.

The critical development in plant engineering concerning the use of computer technology in supervisory control came with data acquisition. The ability to retrieve data allowed for more sophisticated use of supervisory control. The combination of these is called supervisory control and data acquisition (SCADA). SCADA systems are enormously useful in the management of the countless PLCs and DCSs in manufacturing plants.

As computers came into greater use within the plant, people besides engineers needed to be able to interact with them. In response to this development, human-machine interface (HMI) programs were created. The one and only purpose of HMI software was to make it easy for people to interact with the SCADA systems. It allowed the people who run the manufacturing processes to use a computer in a simple fashion. They could interact with all of the data and manage supervisory control functions much more easily. In the market today, HMI and SCADA are usually together as one product.

"LIGHTS OUT MANUFACTURING"

Of course, there are always those who will push the envelope. Automation was making the equipment more efficient, more flexible, and more automatic, but some people were working on an entirely different track — employing robots. The distinction between robotics and automation is not always clear, so it might be helpful to look at it this way: Automation involved augmenting and improving existing equipment, while robots were entirely new creations specifically designed to take over mechanical tasks previously done by workers. The automotive industry has had great success using robots to do spot welding and painting, tasks formerly done manually. Robots have also proved themselves indispensable in two other areas. One area is various types of precision work, such as the assembly of certain components in your cell phone where tiny parts must be put into place with only a few microns of tolerance. The other area is the mechanical work required in environments or operations that would be dangerous to a human worker.

Once robots started making inroads into modern factories, a vision came to some engineers to eliminate people from the manufacturing process altogether, or at least getting as close to that as possible. Factories would become huge, black boxes. Just supply raw materials at one end and load up your finished goods onto trucks at the other end. Since there would be no people inside, you wouldn't even need to waste money on using lights, thus the term, "lights out manufacturing."

The appeal was obvious. Engineers love to design things and relished the challenge. Management was thrilled at the possibility of not only a huge reduction in payroll costs, but also the elimination of all kinds of labor problems. The common joke was that the plant would require only a security guard and a dog. The security guard's job was to protect the plant against intruders; the dog's job was to make sure the security guard didn't touch anything. Maybe once a month you would have to send someone in to oil and lube everything, but otherwise it would be just one big, comprehensive piece of equipment. This endeavor wasn't only about automation and robots. It was also about computers. The plan was for a computer system that would determine each week what needed to be produced, what materials would be needed for that production, how to arrange for those materials to be delivered, how to arrange for the products to be shipped, etc.

But it didn't work. In fact, it didn't even come close to working. A lot of money was spent, but most of it was wasted. Not all of it, but most of it. What people did learn was that robots were good welders and good painters, they were good at certain types of precision work, and they were extremely useful in hazardous environments, but the tasks needed to be repetitive and not subject to frequent alteration. The robots were fine for doing the same thing over and over again, but you had better not need to change the tasks right away, because it could take a lot of effort to reprogram and retool them for the changes. The supporters of lights out manufacturing were working from the premise that many plants could be "high volume, low mix," where mix refers to the assortment of different products being produced. What they didn't see was how much product development was changing, as we have already discussed. The accelerated pace of change made low mix a poor bet, indeed. It doesn't matter how much you can reduce your costs, if the products you bring to the market don't sell. A major American automotive company provides a prime example of focusing on cost reduction at the expense of product development. In the 1980s, with Japanese auto imports surging, this company decided to cut costs by pushing for more robots. In the end, what mattered most was product innovation. Their failure to instigate a new effort to improve car design proved to be quite costly.

The bottom line is that robots and computers can't think. Only people can. The idea that "People are so expensive, so let's put in robots and get rid of the payroll expense," was ill-conceived. In fact, companies now see the advantage of having highly trained, highly skilled people doing what robots can't do. Robots can't be creative, they can't think, they are not flexible, they can't figure out how to do things better or how to do things differently, they don't know how to respond to customers' needs or how to respond to changing environments, and they can't respond to difficulties or problems; in short, they are just not up to the challenge of complex and creative tasks. The lesson learned was "Let the robots do what they do best and let people do what they do best."

COMPUTER-INTEGRATED MANUFACTURING

At the same time that manufacturing engineers were discovering the limits of robots, they were also fashioning an important model that envisioned how computers would work across an entire company. This model, which is shown in Figure 2.1, is known as the computer-integrated manufacturing (CIM) model, and because of its shape, it's commonly referred to as the CIM Pyramid. Even though it was supplanted by other models almost a decade ago, if you want to have a firm grasp of the state of manufacturing IT today, you need to understand the history of the CIM Pyramid.

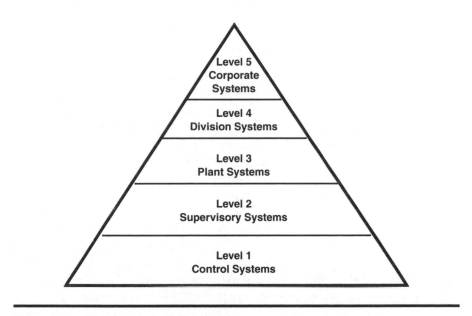

Figure 2.1 CIM Pyramid of the 1980s

First, keep in mind that this was a view of the world created by engineering people. Their domain was Level 1, Control Systems, which included the PLCs and DCSs. Some engineers also added a Level 0 to the CIM Pyramid, which was called Instrumentation and Devices. This was the basic machinery itself: motors, pumps, valves, sensors, switches, photoelectric eyes, fans, and everything else imaginable that did the basic work. Good engineers were in their element in Level 0 and Level 1. Their job was to get all of this equipment working and under the control of the PLC and DCS systems.

Level 1 was clear and concrete throughout the manufacturing business, no question about what it entailed. Level 2, which involved area computers or area management computers, wasn't always so distinctly defined in every industry. Area computers were used to coordinate activities and consolidate information for areas of the plant. In some cases this meant managing a group of different production lines. The basic idea was that area computers were the next step up in the hierarchy and so they provided the coordination and consolidation of the next level down.

This is where the differences between industries started to play a bigger role in terms of devising a uniform model. In steel, for example, each plant would have its own supervisory computer that was designed to assist in that manufacturing area or department of the plant. Minicomputers from companies like DEC, HP, ModComp, and Data General were used by almost everyone for this purpose. But everyone wrote their software for each application from scratch, which meant that the engineers in steel would describe what Level 2 meant to them in one way, while the engineers in another industry would come up with a different story about Level 2 in their plants.

Once you move up the pyramid beyond Level 2, you have entered terra incognito for the engineers. They knew that computers were being used throughout the company and that applications were only going to increase. So they fashioned this hierarchical model that established the basic plant machinery as the foundation. After all, the entire corporation rested on its ability to churn out a specific item of some sort. The engineers knew that they were using programmable control systems to make the machinery work and that they had area computers to coordinate production within sections of the plant. So the next logical step was to use computers to coordinate activities over the entire plant, then over the entire division, and finally over the entire company.

The engineers also knew that as you entered Level 3, you were beginning a transformation from engineering systems to business systems. That meant that the applications at the top would be used to move dollars around, not to open and close valves. This was not their area of expertise, so they didn't always have the clearest vision of how business systems should function in this CIM scheme, but they knew they had a role to play. And any good engineer, when crafting a model, will include everything, even if some of the parts are vague.

There's an important distinction that must be made here. Even though the engineers were in the dark about "division level" systems and corporate systems, corporate IT wasn't in the dark. Corporate IT was immersed in applications that handled finance, payroll, accounting, cash flow, accounts payable, accounts receivable, general ledger, fixed assets management, inventory, purchasing, MRP, order entry, and more. The people handling the corporate computers may not have known the first thing about a PLC, but they were quite knowledgeable about putting their mainframe or minicomputer resources to work on those tasks that were in their domain.

Now, here's the critical point: Neither side — neither corporate IT, nor plant engineers — knew what Level 3 was supposed to be and how it was supposed to work. No one had ever done it. Everyone agreed that it was obviously a critical component of a company's entire IT system, but no one agreed how to define it. You would hear general talk in vague terms about product tracking, overall plant management, process management, plant scheduling, recipe management, inventory management, and other such applications, but when it came to the details, no one could spell it out in detail or explain for every plant how the functions at that level tied together the top and bottom of the pyramid. Very few people even tried to implement plant-level systems and many of the ones that were implemented never worked that well. The idea sounded good, but when you got past the surface, there wasn't a lot of meat there. There was no common definition across a plant, division, or company, much less an industry. One immediate implication of this is that everyone who attempted to implement plant-level systems had to start from scratch. There were no standards whatsoever.

During the 1980s and early 1990s, the CIM Pyramid's role as the explanation of what plant computing should be was gradually taken over by a simpler model from AMR Research, an independent industry and market analysis firm. The AMR 3-Layer Model, which is shown in Figure 2.2, had only three levels stacked on top of each other as interlocking pieces in a column: planning, execution, and control. Planning was all of the CIM Pyramid Levels 4 and 5 systems, and control was Levels 1 and 2. Execution was the still vague Level 3. The benefit of this model and subsequent ones that grew increasingly complex was that more attention was brought to bear on the challenge of developing plant-level systems. A number of different applications were created for a variety of functional needs and many of them have proved to be highly effective. One problem with this model, though, was the inability to make any clear definition of the model fit all manufacturing environments. Another problem was the lack of any standards for integrating all of these applications. No common view of what execution systems should be has emerged. Each application has its own functional capability, its own industry specialization, its own configuration files and definitions, and usually its own database.

In the end, companies needed — but didn't get — unified management of IT. The CIM Pyramid was the engineers' attempt to provide a model for achieving this, but someone needed to be in charge of the entire structure and no one ever stepped into that role. One problem was that the computer people in the plant and the computer people at corporate

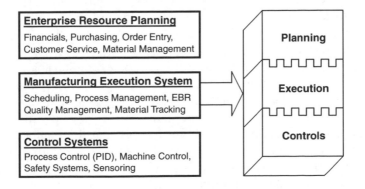

Figure 2.2 AMR 3-Layer Model (Source: AMR 1992. Used with permission.)

headquarters didn't report to the same chiefs. Corporate IT didn't have the power and reach it has today. Information technology was still in its youth. Personal computers (PCs) were just coming out, but they were expensive and people were still not sure how best to use them. When you look at how ubiquitous PCs are today, it's hard to believe how quickly everything has changed. The point here, though, is that today, you have to have companywide IT standards, because everyone is tapping into the same network. But in the 1980s, the idea of developing standards that would apply both to a plant level minicomputer and an IBM® mainframe seemed ludicrous. These were completely separate systems that had no history of interfacing. Plant engineers saw that eventually companies would need to devise one comprehensive approach to information technology, so they created the CIM Pyramid as their model. But no one in corporate IT ever saw it. There was a vast gulf between corporate IT and plant engineering and *the legacy of that gulf is still with us today.*

THE GULF BETWEEN ENGINEERING AND IT

At first the gulf was so big that each side ignored the other and simply continued with their separate strategies for developing information technology. The people in corporate IT didn't regard the plant computing equipment as real computers, so it was natural to ignore them. For many people on corporate IT staffs, if it didn't take up 5000 square feet, it wasn't a computer. Plant projects were funded from different sources, plant engineers reported to a different vice president, and the technology in the plant conformed to different standards, so corporate IT departments saw no common ground.

Gradually, the two sides did start to interact some, but it didn't exactly produce wonderful results. The plant engineers were focused on finding solutions to all of the problems they faced in the plant. They began to acknowledge the fact that they needed support from the corporate IT department and guidance concerning standardization. However, in case after case, they failed to get this support. For example, if a new plant was being built or an existing plant was being expanded, engineers would need to consider which systems to employ to handle their plant needs. Yet efforts to discuss matters of this nature with IT people at corporate headquarters would often go nowhere. It's not that the engineers would be told what they could or couldn't do. The problem was that corporate IT just didn't care. The IT personnel at the corporate level had no interest at all in any of the software applications being used in the plant and as a result they would offer no support. They wouldn't help with the architecture, with the training, or with the standards. And to make matters worse, after the engineers went forward with their plans and had systems in place, IT would find all kinds of faults with what had been done.

As computer technology became more sophisticated, its use by each side expanded, and conflicts arose over vision, strategy, and tactics. Plant-level systems often became an area for contention, instead of the place for joint collaboration. An engineer would say, "I want to create a system that does this, this, and this." Then corporate would say, "Wait a minute. We're already doing all of that on the mainframe. Our equipment is the most sensible place for these operations. In fact, these matters are really our responsibility. You're right that they need to be done, but we can handle it up here."

Corporate IT and plant engineering had different perspectives on applications and this was one of the reasons IT assumed control. The corporate orientation was toward *strategic* issues; it was looking at the big picture. Engineers were task oriented and project funded; they solved very specific problems. It didn't help that many of these engineering problems often sounded too "geek-like." Engineers appeared to be seduced by the fascination of pursuing technology just for technology's sake. Corporate IT's job was to maintain a broad focus. Corporate IT was seen as being busy trying to help the business. It was a classic dichotomy: strategic vs. tactical. Corporate was engaged in strategic planning for the entire scope of the company, while plant engineers were using computers tactically to focus on small areas that pertained only to specific problems in the plant.

This meant that when the plant declared it had found a solution to a specific problem, corporate IT would insist that the solution be structured so that it could have broad applications. The corporate mentality was to create systemwide solutions, so it would reject the specific solutions and embark on an effort to find a broader answer. Plant engineers might have a solution for one small matter, but corporate IT would want to consider how other plants might handle it, how it should be networked, and all of the requirements that should be addressed. Corporate IT would want to take a couple years to figure all of this out. The plant engineer saw this as overkill, but corporate IT saw it as strategic thinking.

From the corporate IT side, there were frustrations as well. When plant engineers put in new systems without considering the overall picture, there could be negative consequences. Engineers might connect a new system to the network without thinking about there not being enough throughput and bandwidth available, issues that corporate IT would have addressed in the design stage. Corporate IT would think about all of the devices involved, all of the traffic involved, total throughput expected, how upgrades and maintenance would be handled, and security. Engineers were notorious for ignoring security issues. They would put systems together without any thought of segregation or firewalls, without any thought of standardization, without any thought of getting spare parts, and without any thought of how everything fits together and affects everything else.

Ultimately it was a clash of cultures, goals, focus, perspectives, priorities, strategies, awareness, understanding, and knowledge. There was a complete lack of common ground. The result was a long series of turf wars. For example, the plant would say that it needed a system to handle scheduling, and corporate would say, "No, we do scheduling up here, and we do it like this." The plant would say, "Sure, that approach to scheduling works fine for your needs, but we have different scheduling needs here." Eventually, corporations put one person over all of the company's information technology, perhaps a vice president of operations or a COO, and this person would have to settle the feuds. Having someone with the authority to do this helped things move along. Until this step was taken, however, the conflicts had no easy resolution.

THE EMERGENCE OF PERSONAL COMPUTERS AND NETWORKS

Another development that brought the two sides into more contact — and more conflict — was the rise of the PC. Engineers were some of the first people to use PCs because corporate IT was slow to change and kept thinking about mainframes, terminals, and big computing. Engineering was using minicomputers, but corporate IT didn't regard them as computers because they weren't tied into the network. Corporate IT still didn't grasp the benefits of distributed computing and as all of the PCs came in, the corporate IT department was initially reluctant to take control of them.

This changed when the IT people at the corporate level began to recognize that PCs were proliferating beyond their control. For one thing, they didn't know what people were buying, and security was a serious concern, because viruses were beginning to appear. It was becoming impossible to protect the company without having control over all of the PCs. In response to this, they established rules about what could and what couldn't be put onto a PC. Another matter was that from their corporate-wide perspective, IT managers could see gross inefficiencies in the way the PCs were being purchased and used. This led them to declare that all PCs must be purchased through the corporate IT department so that wholesale price agreements could be negotiated. Using this approach meant that the PCs would be standardized throughout the enterprise, since they would all be coming from the same computer manufacturer. So in the end, considerations of security and economy prodded corporate IT to establish governance over all PCs. Such matters were outside the realm of the plant engineers. It was a natural fit for corporate IT and this moved the PC firmly into its domain.

A similar phenomenon occurred with networks. Different departments were buying various networks, but network interfaces were not standardized. The result was a proliferation of unconnected networks. It was only a matter of time before someone recognized how much easier certain tasks would be if departments could exchange information electronically. Human resources might want to interact with payroll, for example. But without standardized interfaces, all kinds of problems arose, such as the duplication of addresses, because the addressing schemes were not coordinated across all of the networks. Once more, the solution was governance by a single group within the enterprise. The logical approach was to turn to the people who had the most expertise, so corporate IT took over here as well. Ironically, although corporate IT eventually established oversight of all the computers, their primary computing tool, the mainframe, lost out to the PC. While mainframes can still be found performing vital functions within some corporations, their overall use is highly limited. In contrast, PCs are everywhere.

In the process of handling the emergence of PCs and networks, people in the corporate IT departments became aware that the plants were generating mounds upon mounds of data. Another governance issue arose. Who owned the data? While corporate IT had no particular interest in the use of the plant's data, it did have an interest in making sure the data was handled in certain ways. In other words, no one at the corporate level needed to know such things as the temperature of the batches, but they did want to make sure the data was being collected, stored, and reported in ways that were secure and efficient. For example, if plant engineers were collecting batch data, but not backing it up, the company was being put at risk of losing important information. The solution for governance of data was the same as for governance of PCs and networks. Corporate IT took charge and instituted appropriate standards.

To protect the company's interests and to maximize efficiency, corporate IT finally exerted control over every aspect of company computing. The corporate side won the turf wars, hands down. One reason for this outcome is that information technology became a fundamental driver of business strategies. Engineers were seen as the people who could build physical structures, but the IT specialists were the people who could bring the miracles of computer technology into every aspect of your business. Everyone started understanding the power of acquiring and using vast amounts of data. Books started appearing that touted the importance of information technology in the running of companies. There were no books that explained how to beat the competition by engineering better equipment, but there were books that stressed the competitive advantage of information technology tools. And, with the exception of some dot-com illusions, this vision of the importance of information technology has proven itself to be perfectly true.

THE AFTERMATH OF THE TURF WARS

The impact of corporate IT taking over companywide control of software applications was huge. First and foremost, budgets changed. Suddenly, computer engineering projects in the plant lost their funding, which caused an exodus of the plant's computer engineers to either the IT department or to some other company altogether. In the process, the plant became the applications orphan. IT departments were not particularly concerned with developing better systems for the plant, because that was still seen as thinking tactically instead of strategically. Besides, they had their hands full trying to keep up with the rapidly evolving technology being used to handle corporate functions.

The engineers could see the writing on the wall. Corporate IT wasn't of a mind to engage in a collaborative effort to develop ideas for plant level systems. In light of this fact, engineers put their complete attention on expanding horizontally. It turns out that they accomplished a great deal in this way; we will go into more detail about this in a moment. But the point is that today, in most manufacturing environments where it makes sense, everything is automated. The engineers nailed it in terms of using computer technology to run the machines. The software is mature now. But the whole vertical piece, meaning the communication from the manufacturing shop floor (Level 1 and 2 applications) up to the corporate systems was just abandoned. And it was abandoned by both sides — engineering and IT. The idea of vertical integration was lost. The idea of continuing to develop better systems for the plant was off the radar screen.

THE RISE OF ERP

Even though the idea of vertical integration was lost, corporate IT was aggressively pursuing the goal of comprehensive functionality. To understand the drive for this, let's recall that through the 1980s, corporate IT saw the evolution of *Material Requirements Planning* (MRP) into *Material Resource Planning* (MRP II). The names tell you something about this evolution. MRP focused more narrowly on planning, purchasing, and using materials; MRP II expanded into a broader set of functions that sought to manage production plans and inventories. And even though there were any number of commercial off-the-shelf software programs available, many companies were still writing their own code for a variety of purposes.

They would have a payroll system here, an accounting system there, a general ledger system, and a program to handle payables and receivables, for example.

On top of this, two other trends emerged. One was the sharp increase in mergers and acquisitions. The other, which is in many ways related to mergers, was the increasing globalization of business. Both of these developments put tremendous new stresses on the computer systems in charge of running the business. The mergers or acquisitions left companies with a crazy quilt of applications that didn't match. After merging, you might have a company with five different payroll systems or five different accounting systems. Given the rapid pace of consolidation in some industries, this became a serious challenge and many companies continue to struggle with this issue today.

In response to all of this, software development companies began to envision the big application in the sky, a way of integrating every corporate computer system being used. Obviously, if you have a general ledger, you have payables on one side, receivables on the other side, cash flow management on one side, payroll as part of that, materials management, orders management, taxes — it's all interconnected. In the early 1990s, the application software companies selling MRP II started coming up with a new spin. Their software would deal with *everything* the enterprise had to deal with *and* it would operate on a global basis: orders, suppliers, inventory, accounting, payroll, finance, human resources, *everything*.

While some of the MRP II systems may have covered many of these areas, most couldn't handle international exchange issues or financial consolidation. Even the tax laws in different states could cause problems. Also, MRP II didn't tie everything together financially. ERP, however, did tie it all together. Any and every financial and accounting transaction conducted by anyone in the corporation could be coordinated by using ERP. Every single time a dollar, a yen, a mark, or a peso was paid, received, or moved around in any manner whatsoever, ERP had a way of managing it. As presented by vendors, ERP truly was the magical silver bullet. It was touted as the last piece of software the company would ever need.

ERP boomed beyond belief in the 1990s, and there were both valid and questionable reasons for its unbridled success. The valid reasons were that it went a long way toward solving three fundamental problems:

1. It was an application you could buy, and the company that sold it to you would maintain it for you. You didn't have to write it. To a large degree you could get rid of the massive *and expensive* staff of programmers you had that were busy writing the code for

all of the applications now covered by ERP. It was the ticket that allowed manufacturing companies to get out of the business of writing software.

2. Now, not only could you buy an application without writing code, you could also buy an integrated suite of applications that all worked together. You could buy everything you needed in one package — the entire spectrum was covered. At least, this was how it was marketed. Vendors claimed that ERP was essentially every business function you could ever want, that ERP did it all. If there were some functions not covered, not to worry, some new modules coming out soon would address all of the shortcomings. Although saying that it covered everything was taking matters too far, ERP was indeed far more comprehensive than anything that came before it. In fact, *enterprise resource planning* isn't really the best name because it actually manages every aspect of the business for you. It is much more than resource planning.

3. You can buy an ERP application and install one single system for the entire corporation. It works for the recently acquired division in Singapore; for the newly constructed plant in Africa; for the divisions in North America, South America, Europe, Asia, wherever. No matter where you have offices or factories, this single package of computer software will work there.

The appeal of using ERP to solve these three problems made sales easy for many vendors. But the aura of ERP went much further and this leads us to the questionable reasons for the boom. A mania developed about getting on the ERP bandwagon. It was fashionable, the unquestioned business trend of the day. People took it on faith that the technology would pay off. If everyone was doing it, how could it be wrong? CIOs didn't need to show in concrete terms how ERP would increase profits. They only had to chant this mantra: "The digital economy is here. Get on board, or be left behind as a dinosaur destined for extinction."

It was a powerful mantra, especially coupled with the real advantages ERP had to offer. Money poured forth. CEOs and boards approved budget after budget with millions upon millions — hundreds of millions — of dollars for this new silver bullet. ERP ruled. Its market penetration is now virtually 100% vs. a peak of somewhere between 30% and 40% for MRP II. Since around 1990, ERP has claimed 60% to 70% of the dollars spent on IT. By some estimates, total expenditures for this period run over *$300 billion*. And keep in mind, this money was *not* spent on the IT systems that would help make the plants better at manufacturing.

THE INVISIBLE COMPUTERS

It's not that the IT people forgot about the factories; it's just that they didn't think of plants as having any significant computer functions. The experience one manufacturing company had while working on Y2K issues makes this point vitally clear. After looking over all of the corporate IT systems, someone asked, "What about your manufacturing plants?" The response was, "We don't have any computers out there." The Y2K people then said, "What do you mean you don't have any computers out there?" The corporate IT managers said, "Well, we don't have any computers out there. We don't have any applications out there." The Y2K people said, "Well, look, let's just go out there and check," and it turns out that there were more computers out in the manufacturing plants than in the whole rest of the corporation combined. But they were mostly PCs; it was all distributed applications. Corporate IT doesn't pay much attention to the types of computer systems that function in the plant. IT people have big computers, big applications, and big databases. When they go out to the plants and they don't see any of that, they conclude there are no computers there. The computers and the critical applications in support of manufacturing that are there are sometimes invisible to corporate IT.

This fact has some serious consequences. Corporate IT is aware that the plant has data, but its mentality about collecting data is using data entry clerks, so IT thinks, "If we have to know how many cases the plant made this shift, then we'll just put a terminal in and have someone type it in. How else would we do it?" IT opts for the data-entry-clerk mentality, because it doesn't think about getting the data out of what engineering has already set up. IT is supposed to be responsible for data collection and processing, but it doesn't really consider the idea of integration with the plant systems. Corporate IT doesn't understand what the systems do or how they do it. There is not one big application, nor is there one place to get all of the data. Manufacturing systems are still much more distributed and smaller in scale. So corporate IT often just can't get their arms around the situation.

WHAT ENGINEERING ACHIEVED

The failure to achieve the entire vision of the CIM model shouldn't obscure the fact that engineering organizations have made huge advances in the past twenty years. For starters, even though the CIM Pyramid didn't last, the concept of having models did. The engineers saw the need for total, companywide computer integration and started the whole process of envisioning a solution.

The other thing is that, as we mentioned earlier, engineering can claim huge successes in automating the plant. PLCs and DCSs are everywhere, along with HMI/SCADA systems. There has been a complete transformation. After a brief infatuation, engineers recognized that robots weren't the end-all, be-all they were forecast to be. Replacing human action was not the point. Instead they brought their talents to bear upon the challenge of overall facility automation. They said, "Let's find the right piece of equipment and automate it." At first, this meant taking equipment into the plant and attaching their own controllers to it. Eventually, this evolved into equipment manufacturers selling machinery with PLCs already installed. The end result is that automation is ubiquitous today. It is every bit as much of the infrastructure as plumbing and electricity.

Part of the way engineering achieved all this was by establishing standards. The engineers focused relentlessly on maintenance and reliability and used standardization practices to support this effort. For example, if a circuit board on a PLC fails, someone will be alerted to the problem through an enunciator panel. A spare part can be grabbed immediately and the bad board will be replaced in only 5 minutes. It will not matter which PLC it is because all of the PLCs have been standardized. They all use the same boards, they all use the same pieces of equipment, and they all hook to the network in the same way. The standards apply to everything, such as the screens used by various HMI systems. The way a computer screen indicates a problem with something such as any type of pump is the same from every vendor. In other words, anyone who looks at the diagram on the computer and sees the pump flashing in yellow knows what that means, regardless of the brand of computer software being used. Engineers had a common appreciation of the benefits of standardization and thus were able to avoid battles and divisions about common practices. The architecture of automation in manufacturing plants became totally standard and this was a significant step forward.

Y2K

From our perspective today, the fears generated by the specter of a computer meltdown on January 1, 2000 may seem rather trivial. But they weren't at the time, especially if it was your job to fix everything. The Y2K phenomenon had far-reaching implications, including a significant impact on the world of manufacturing IT.

For starters, it gave companies a good opportunity to rid themselves of many out-of-date legacy systems that had been in their company for years and years. The effort to make sure everything would work on 1/1/2000 forced them to look at everything they had in their company.

The ancient hardware and software uncovered at some companies was mind boggling. People were using long outdated methods that were highly inefficient. Some of the software was totally unsupportable; it couldn't be backed up or upgraded and there was no source for any replacement parts. Or the company that wrote the software was out of business and the application was so old that no one knew how the database was originally designed. In fact, some programs were totally unrecognizable. No one could explain who was using it or what they were trying to do with it.

The end result was that lots of software simply had to be replaced — not fixed and tested for the big date, but thrown out completely. This presented a problem. What do you replace it with? Companies that had never given much thought to establishing corporate-wide standards suddenly were confronted with the issue. In many cases, the decision was made to really clean house, to establish standards across the board and to implement new processes and procedures.

One of the critical issues that arose for companies concerned some specific financial decisions. At first, no one knew how the IRS would treat Y2K expenditures — as capitalization or expense? Enough of a stir was created in the business community that the government finally issued a ruling that companies could write off Y2K expenditures if they were replacing "like functionality with like functionality." That was fine, but it presented some interesting options. The whole software world had been evolving rapidly for years by then. Replacing like functionality with like functionality could mean that you ended up with a lot more than you had before.

For instance, say you had a crude, first-generation word processor and there was nothing you could do to make it Y2K compatible. So you buy a new word processor, but it comes in a package with Microsoft® Office — Excel, Word, Access, PowerPoint®, Outlook®, etc. The tax law said that you could buy this, because you are replacing like functionality with like functionality. You are replacing your word processing software with a package that has much more, but you cannot buy the word processing separately, so you ended up with the entire assortment of programs. The same was true of many other software applications. All of this meant that Y2K prodded many companies to make a huge leap forward with their computer technology.

There's one more aspect of Y2K to consider and that is the fact that it totally consumed IT departments and their budgets for a big chunk of time. This, along with the short-lived dot-com boom, siphoned away valuable resources from other applications. This was particularly true about Y2K. All other useful IT work stopped while everyone scrambled to avert potential disaster.

THE DOT-COM BOOM AND BUST

The dot-com boom has one other quality that also worked against giving attention to IT applications in the plant. This quality was an intense focus outside of the company. The prevailing belief at the time was that everything could be solved by an external customer-facing solution. Ninety-five percent of the dot-coms had something to do with an enabling technology or an enabling solution that was externally facing. People were taking existing business practices and moving them outward, or creating a sales and marketing blitz around some issue usually dealt with internally and turning it outward.

The whole idea was to examine relationships between your company and your customers, between your company and suppliers, and between your company and the world in general. The goal was to get your products into cyberspace so that anyone, anywhere in the world could become one of your customers. About 60% to 75% of the new applications were focused on the interface with the consumer and the others were business-to-business interactions. An example might be a customer relations management (CRM) package or a system for document management, but it was all about external collaboration, everything outside of your world, all of your external facing components. All of these things that came and went were high tech experiments in extranet collaboration.

It is an understatement to say that there was a lot of smoke coming from the dot-com camp. The question was: Is there any real fire there? History will show that there was some innovation produced during this period, but the majority of it was smoke. For example, one "incredible new capability" being touted was business-to-business electronic commerce. A picture was painted of an exclusively electronic global marketplace, where all goods and services would be exchanged. The message was clear: Throw your hat into this ring or prepare for your demise. The problem with this vision was that it wasn't new. An apparatus of this sort already existed and had existed with a broad and deep penetration in some markets for over a decade. Since the early 1980s, any number of companies has engaged in successful e-commerce through electronic data interchange (EDI) technology, but they didn't call it e-commerce because the name hadn't been coined yet.

There can be no doubt that the Internet will be the medium of choice for future business-to-business electronic commerce, but there are all kinds of difficulties with the entire idea of handling vendor relationships this way and these were plain to see all along. It varies from industry to industry, but most manufacturing companies have to balance several factors in addition to price when choosing vendors. They have to consider warranties, quality, terms of delivery, reliability, scheduling, and the ability of a supplier to meet rigid specifications for parts or raw materials. Matters this complex don't lend themselves to negotiations via computer screens.

One unfortunate result of the dot-com boom and bust was that another 3 to 5 years went by and companies were distracted. If you go back to the headlines in the media, it was all about the "new economy." Many of the so-called dinosaurs of the old economy were looking at all of this with skepticism. Even though it turned out that they were right to resist the mania, they still had to struggle with it for a while. They couldn't ignore it, because there was some real innovation that was occurring and there were some real gains being made. Every large company had to spend some time and resources seriously investigating the new economy or risk missing out on changes that had the potential to be critically important. Plus some of their most talented IT people were being siphoned away by the appeal of becoming instant millionaires through initial public offerings of stock in the new dot-com companies being created. You might say that the dot-com boom distracted IT talent with fads in a manner similar to the way plant engineers had often been distracted by technology for technology's sake. All in all, Y2K and the dot-com boom meant that from the late 1990s until recently, not much work was done on deploying new applications for manufacturing.

CONCLUSION

Twenty years ago, corporate IT and plant engineers were toiling away at computer applications on independent paths. Although the engineers began to envision a fully integrated approach to the use of computers in manufacturing companies, they often found themselves at cross purposes with corporate IT, and the vision was never realized.

Eventually, corporate IT convinced companies to spend exorbitantly on ERP and while ERP did do some remarkable things for the enterprise, it didn't help manufacturing itself. The work done by computer engineers in the plant produced tactical solutions that were successful and automation is part of the landscape now as a result of this work, but further development of plant systems has been negligible.

The needs of the plant are clear. The goal is not just achieving integration simply for integration's sake or finding a way to share data. The real challenge is helping manufacturing companies become better at the business of manufacturing by applying information technology intelligently to the plant. The problem is that there is still a gulf between corporate IT and engineering, between ERP systems and plant floor systems, and between corporate data and plant floor data.

So where does all of this leave us? That is the focus of Chapter 3.

3

THE STATE OF MANUFACTURING IT TODAY

In order to get a good sense of where we stand today with manufacturing IT, it's essential to examine the phenomena of ERP in more depth. ERP is now one of the most dominant forces in the arena of corporate-wide information technology, and any advances in manufacturing IT will be made within this context. If you are a plant manager, ERP can sometimes seem like an 800-lb. gorilla sitting between you and all of the software applications you need to make the plant really hum. In the end, you have to find a way to live with this beast, because there's no way to avoid dealing with the presence of ERP systems.

We have already pointed out that ERP claimed well over half of the money spent on IT projects since 1990 and we have given you the basic reasons behind this. What we haven't covered is what ERP meant to the plant and how the history of ERP implementations has changed the way IT budgets are approved. The primary goal of ERP systems was never to focus on the improvement of manufacturing operations, so it only follows that plants have found little benefit from having ERP brought into the company. It goes beyond benign neglect, however, because in many cases, the results have actually been detrimental to the plant. While it's true that many ERP vendors have made great strides in addressing the needs of manufacturing, such changes have only occurred in recent years. This chapter looks at the traditional components of ERP systems and the way these systems affected the plant. The fact that vendors offer optional modules today that go beyond the traditional components of ERP systems underscores the point that such functionality was missing during the first wave of implementations.

ERP has also left its mark on the process of funding IT projects. Through a combination of factors, including ERP's immense cost, its history of lengthy implementations, and the fact that it did little to help manufacturing processes, an entirely new set of guidelines for getting IT projects funded has emerged within most corporations. People bought ERP on faith, but too much money was spent for too little return. The giant ERP projects left many people skeptical about the methods they were using to justify IT expenditures. Now they insist on knowing precisely how a new system will provide a benefit to the business. They want a solid case laid out and this is one result of the tremendous impact ERP has had on manufacturing companies.

THE CAVALRY TO THE RESCUE

ERP is an amazing and wonderful product. If you don't believe us, just ask any ERP salesperson. They rode into town and proclaimed that they could save everyone from everything. It is in fact true that ERP *is* a remarkable product in many ways, but there's ample evidence of serious damage done by this massive software system. Plus, it is also true that some of its promoters have gone overboard with extravagant claims about how comprehensive it is. If you claim to be something you're not, problems are certain to follow. Let's look at this carefully, starting with the promises made by vendors as they presented the ERP "Silver Bullet."

Historically, manufacturing companies had been using a wide assortment of vendors to get all of their IT needs met. ERP promised "comprehensive functionality." This meant that one integrated software package would do everything important that any company needs to do. The sales pitch was, "You don't need 50 different vendors, you only need one — us."

ERP promised to be enterprise-wide, meaning that it covered all business, all entities, and all divisions at all locations around the world. Companies would finally be able to manage the entire enterprise by using one — and only one — comprehensive software package.

Finally, ERP would get companies out of the software business. ERP salespeople also stressed that the software was off-the-shelf and completely ready for implementation. Twenty years ago, most major corporations were still writing their own software. The ERP sales pitch was, "You make cars (or steel or consumer electronics or you name it). That's your area of expertise. We make software and that's our area of expertise. Focus on your area and leave the software design to us."

The truth is, ERP did deliver on *most* of its promises. Its ability to provide integrated financial management and integrated purchasing has been proven beyond any doubt. One company had *61* versions of its general ledger chart of accounts, running in 61 distinct installations of its financial systems, all of which had been assimilated over several years through the various plants and companies it had acquired. The company had 20 people working full time handling the task of just consolidating and reconciling financial information from the 61 sites. Even with all of this work being done to gather the information together, the CEO still couldn't get a good read on how everyone was performing. The most aggravating part of this was the inability to gauge a return on invested capital. Money was being spent in all kinds of ways, but there was no conclusive way to evaluate the outcome of this spending and learn from it.

In a situation like this, ERP is in its element. The corporate-wide ERP system implemented gave them uniform, consolidated financials across the corporation. Every plant rolled up to every division and every division rolled up to corporate in a uniform way. Accounting and measurements of performance were done consistently for the first time. This gave the CEO a clearer picture of financial performance and he could finally start to make assessments of capital investments, based on the history he could now read. This type of information is essential for directing future spending.

A good number of large corporations today are conglomerates and face these same hurdles. Multiple divisions have been acquired and have brought with them different sets of books, different accounting practices, and different computer systems. Their general ledger, their payables, their receivables, their payroll, and more are all on separate systems at various locations, using a vast assortment of computers, some of which are really old. Companies have done ERP for no reason other than the consolidated financials. In this case — in this particular way — ERP delivered the goods.

Many companies have also reaped huge savings from better management of global procurement and sourcing. With ERP, you can go in and quickly view the entire history of any vendor with all parts of a company. This information can provide vital leverage for negotiating prices. For example, the company mentioned above used ERP to integrate 20 different purchasing systems. Prior to this, the lack of coordination across the enterprise kept it from leveraging its volume purchasing power. With some vendors the company had over a dozen different volume purchase contracts in place with different discount levels. The left hand didn't know what the right hand was doing, so the company was missing an opportunity to fully assert its buying clout.

Once ERP integrated purchasing, the company was able to negotiate pricing on a corporate-wide basis with literally hundreds of vendors for everything from office supplies to its primary manufacturing raw materials. For large companies, this affects thousands of items being purchased, so there is a large potential return. ERP also helps because it allows companies to look for trends and patterns that can lead to finding better deals that went completely unnoticed before. It also supports multiple currencies, taxes, transportation costs, and such, so it allows you to look for suppliers worldwide. Here again, ERP made good on its promises. The payback has been enormous.

One part of the payback ERP has delivered comes in the form of reduced payroll expenses. In the process of consolidating financials or purchasing, many jobs become redundant or obsolete, bringing down a company's full-time equivalents (FTEs). One other good example of the way ERP can reduce FTEs involves an aspect of purchasing used by some companies called "3-way match."

The purchasing cycle for anything a company buys starts with a requisition from some source, either from an individual or a department, and it is based on a forecast. The requisition results in a purchase order to a vendor that details exactly what is needed. The vendor fulfills that order and ships it; after the company receives it, a receiving report is created. This report, which records how many were received and possibly how many were returned or rejected, is sent to the accounting department. Then a reconciliation is made between what was quoted from the vendor and what was actually received and kept in order to determine how much should be paid. In light of this information, a check or electronic funds transfer is issued to pay the vendor's invoice.

So the match is between the purchase order, the receiving report, and the vendor's invoice — the 3-way match. There has always been a need to do the reconciliation between the receiving report and the invoice to determine what should be paid, because if you don't, you will end up paying for things that weren't shipped, that were delayed, or that were sent back. At one division of a large automotive corporation, this reconciliation was a manual process that continued for many years. The company's growth caused an increase in paperwork to the point that it eventually took as many as 200 clerical people working all day every day just to handle the load. ERP stepped in and made the bulk of the process work electronically. By automating this process, it eliminated the need for 200 FTEs. Any time a company can reduce nonvalue-added work, it saves money.

ERP IN THE PLANT

Now here is the downside, and it is serious. In most manufacturing environments outside the pure discrete industries like automotive, ERP has been abysmal in its production management functions. Put bluntly, ERP simply doesn't understand the plant as it exists today. Twenty years ago, the bulk of manufacturing in this country was "discrete" manufacturing — the production of items like chairs, PCs, automobiles, and consumer electronics, for example. In the past two decades much of that work has gone to China, Taiwan, Mexico, and Thailand. Our manufacturing is now largely "process" and "hybrid" manufacturing.

Process manufacturers make products in batches that are often liquid, gaseous, or powdered. Even though the materials used to make the product — and the product itself — may be packaged in discrete containers, the manufacturing process itself is built around making the product in batches or in a continuous flow. A hybrid plant would involve both discrete and process elements. If you make the plastic tub used for packaging yogurt, you are a discrete manufacturer. If your plant produces the powdered milk that is part of a yogurt recipe, then you are engaged in process manufacturing. And if you take the powdered milk and mix it with the other ingredients, put it into the tubs, and turn out packaged yogurt ready to ship to grocery stores, you are managing a hybrid plant.

Plants in this country today have more complex challenges than simply making sure all of the parts are available for the assembly line. With a few exceptions this fact has completely slipped under ERP's radar screens. Its systems are designed for an overly simplistic model of what a manufacturing plant is. No wonder ERP stumbles when confronted with the current demands of the factory. The failure of ERP to handle the needs of the people on the plant floor is an important point, so we want to provide several illustrations.

BOM vs. Formula

A good example to start with involves the problem of matching a bill of materials (BOM) to a formula. Most of the early ERP systems were designed for the concept of every manufactured product having a BOM, which was essentially a list of parts and subcomponents, and maybe parts for the subcomponents. The BOM detailed everything that was needed to manufacture the end product. That's all fine and good in discrete manufacturing. If you're building a carburetor, you'd have a list of parts needed to build it and every carburetor coming out of your plant would be built with exactly the parts listed, without exception. While there may be more than one potential supplier for various parts, each supplier has to make those parts to almost identical specifications, so that your products are perfectly consistent in terms of quality.

Cookies, however, are a different matter. Your goal is the same as with the carburetor; you want to produce a product that's uniformly consistent in quality in every respect. The difficulty arises when you discover that the raw materials — the parts — used to make cookies routinely have some variability to them. If you're making a batch of cookies, you put all of your ingredients together and start mixing up the dough. Halfway through this process, you test the dough, and if you discover that this batch is somehow not sweet enough, then you add more sugar.

That's where the problems with ERP come in. If you add more sugar than the formula dictates, then you have violated the BOM for that batch. ERP systems can do amazing things, but they are totally obstinate in some situations. There's no easy way for the system to allow you to alter the BOM, and this has significant implications. You've used more sugar than the record shows, so your inventory is all messed up. Or, if you're given just the materials listed on the BOM, when you need to add more sugar, you don't have it. An analogous scenario never develops with carburetors. You never test a carburetor halfway through production and decide it needs an extra bolt. With most discrete items, the BOM is set and it never changes, but the procedures in process and hybrid manufacturing just don't work that way.

ERP is notorious for this sort of inflexibility. Say you're going to make a type of cereal that requires rice as one of the raw ingredients. An ERP system is designed so that, if you're set up to make 100,000 cases of cereal, it will assume you need, say 50,000 pounds of rice. But what if you've only got 48,000 pounds? Maybe you know you've got the rice coming in right before you need it or maybe you know that the inventory is actually off a little and you actually do have 50,000 pounds — no matter. The ERP system will send up a red flag, because you don't have enough rice according to inventory. It doesn't want you to start work without being assured that you have all of the raw materials you need. It may let you launch the schedule, but only on an exception basis. ERP systems weren't designed to accommodate situations like this; they don't make it easy on the plant floor operators who are trying to meet tight production deadlines.

A similar frustration can occur after you finish making the cereal. Even though your order was for 100,000 cases, maybe you found that the materials used actually allowed you to make 110,000. The ERP system will not accept that, because it claims that you're making something out of nothing. It says that 110,000 cases requires more raw materials than you used, so it rejects your attempt to record the actual number of cases you just produced.

Attempts have been made at many companies to go into the ERP system and correct the records of materials used after a batch was finished. But the people trying to enter this data had to go through several screens to enter data in several fields. The error rate and the time consumed made this approach totally impractical. In the end, most people stopped trying. They reverted to conducting periodic physical inventories and just decided to ignore the ERP system's erroneous calculations. The whole purpose of doing the BOM on the manufacturing side of the ERP system was lost.

Too Many SKUs

This story involves a paper company. An effort was made to implement the order services part of an ERP system, which was really designed for discrete manufacturing, into this hybrid environment. The paper this company makes comes in different grades and is sold in rolls of varying widths, diameters, and core sizes. Some of their customers ordered paper based on weight and paid by weight, but specified a roll of certain dimensions. Other customers simply paid by linear feet. The problem was that the ERP system didn't have a way to handle an order that was specified in total weight or length. Most ERP systems can't model linear products as part of an order. Instead they want a *discrete* end product. They want parts and pieces and in most cases this means a SKU for a finished item.

This presented quite a challenge. There was no way to put in a SKU for each grade of paper and then simply change the dimensions every time a customer ordered a certain width, core size, or weight. So the company's approach was to create an individual SKU, which is known as a *new item master* in the ERP system, for every single different item sold. This may not sound so bad, until you realize that given all of the variables, the company ended up with literally thousands upon thousands of new SKUs. Plus creating new item masters in the ERP system was an involved process.

Still, the entire process may have had a chance of succeeding if not for one other problem. With so many different items available, it became exceedingly difficult to go into the catalog and find the exact item a customer was requesting. Customer service representatives sometimes simply gave up. Instead of finding the item, they just made a new item master for whatever product their customer specified. The more this practice was used, the more useless the ERP order system became. The company eventually gave up and bought an entirely different order management system that was designed specifically for the paper industry.

Although the company continued using ERP financials and purchasing and all other parts of the system that worked well in its environment, it had to abandon the effort to use the ERP order management. The design of ERP systems that are made to work in the discrete environment just couldn't accommodate the analog nature of the products and the variability of the ways the products were sold to its customers. The company wasted about 2 years and hundreds of thousands of dollars trying to fit a square peg into a round hole. It was a drag on the company, it had a negative impact on customer service, and overall it was a detriment to the company. It should have been obvious that the company was going down the wrong path from the start, but the sales pitch from the ERP folks was persuasive, and it was at the height of ERP-mania. Somehow, it seemed like the right thing to do at the time.

Scheduling Difficulties

For many manufacturers, scheduling production gets really tricky in almost no time. The number of variables involved is daunting. To get a feeling for this, consider all of the planning elements present in a typical plant. You could start by looking at the availability of personnel. This means reviewing shifts, vacations, holidays, and so on. Then look at your equipment availability in light of other production needs, maintenance schedules, and cleaning schedules. Add to this the fact that you have several different production lines and that you can make several different products on each line. But it turns out that, while every product can be made on more than one line, no single line can handle every product. This means that you can switch products around to some degree, but not in any direction you choose at any given time. The whole thing starts to sound like a logic puzzle that even the most avid fan could not solve.

Getting a detailed schedule that accounts for all of these variables was too much for the traditional components of ERP systems. In short, they just couldn't handle this type of scheduling. ERP didn't understand different lines, it couldn't integrate maintenance and cleaning schedules, it couldn't handle the granularity, it couldn't handle personnel scheduling, and it couldn't handle shifts, especially weird shifts that overlap with personnel doubling up for an hour or two. You need finite capacity and constraint-based scheduling, and ERP did not provide it.

Then there are other critical aspects of scheduling besides all of these variables. For one thing, schedules frequently have to be changed as production proceeds. If your system spits out a schedule that can't be altered in response to developments occurring during production, then the schedule you have may end up being meaningless. You could have an equipment malfunction that slows you down, or you could have everything go remarkably smoothly and finish way ahead of schedule. You may have excess spoilage and need to make it up. You may get asked to bump what you're running so that some other product can be rushed through for a special order.

All of these real-time manufacturing events that happen on the shop floor need to be part of a feedback loop with the scheduling system to enable it to adapt to the reality of what is actually happening. But don't expect to find this sort of functionality in an ERP system. It isn't there. In all fairness, there aren't many software products that handle the complexities of scheduling sufficiently well. The point here is that many companies spent millions upon millions of dollars for ERP systems and were promised that scheduling was part of the package. There are many cases where the plant personnel just turned off the ERP scheduling and went back to whatever scheduling method they were using before, after going through massive headaches in a futile attempt to make it work.

Quality — Not a Black and White Issue

Another holdout from the era of discrete manufacturing is the way that ERP naïvely views quality in black and white terms when, in fact, there is a lot of gray there. If your software doesn't acknowledge that quality is a matter of degree, it can't offer you any help in managing quality on the shop floor in process or hybrid environments. ERP's quality management programs are generally set up to regard a product as one of two things: It is either good for shipping or it is not. If it is not, it must be scrapped or reworked. In reality, there are any number of manufacturing environments where quality is much more of a gray area. It may be that a product doesn't meet your first customer's specifications, but it does meet a second customer's specifications for the same product. ERP doesn't have room for the concept of there being different specifications for what is essentially the same product.

A good example in the paper industry is that you can produce a roll of paper that you intend to sell as first grade, but that actually ends up failing your quality tests. However, even though it exceeded a certain level of tolerances for some of the analog parameters, such as caliper of thickness, basis weight, or moisture, it still falls within the parameters of your second grade products. So, although your production plan was to make a grade of paper that certain customers will buy, you find yourself with a different grade of paper that other customers will buy. Your schedule may be messed up as a result, but you still have a valuable product that doesn't need to be scrapped. The problem is that if you produced it specifically for one customer, the ERP system typically wants to see it as a good roll or a bad roll. By and large, ERP systems have no way of dealing with this. They don't understand that products can be downgraded. You can lose a lot of money in a hurry if your quality management system is telling you to scrap products that could be sold. One paper company simply went back to checking rolls manually. The quality management function of its ERP system was useless for this purpose, so the company just shut it off.

Lack of Support for Quality

Even in the cases where the ERP system provides a way for you to enter quality information concerning products, there is no support for getting that information in the first place. It's as if ERP just assumes that you have some magical way of assessing quality. It will let you record that a product passed all of the quality checks, but it could care less how you actually ascertained that the product was acceptable for shipping.

Quality control can involve loads of different testing mechanisms depending upon the product being tested. Some of the typical types at food plants are sensory testing, microbiological testing, analytical testing, and packaging testing. The processes themselves are quite complicated, involving different types of instruments, different types of procedures and methods, different series of specifications, and different requirements. You may also want to do statistical analysis on the data, engage in regression testing, or apply different kinds of statistical models to the data. In some cases, you might apply different kinds of rules, such as Westinghouse Rules or Nelson Rules, that say "based on the way the data is mapping, we should take the following actions." There are different curves and algorithms on the data to determine specifically which actions to take. ERP is lost in this world.

Here's a simple example. Some testing procedures start by assigning a percentage grade to products. If a product scores above 90%, then it's okay and ready to ship. But if it's between 80% and 90%, then you have to do five other tests to determine what is really going on. ERP doesn't want to bother. It's either good or bad.

Another problem is the need to test production equipment, in addition to testing products. An example of this is an environmental test or a *swab test*. In order to determine if there are any biological contaminants or foreign material present, you swab the equipment and examine the swab. You may also want to test cleaning solutions or check for residue in the wash water.

All of these things are integral to quality and need to be supported by the software system you use to manage quality, but ERP systems don't include that functionality. They just assume that one way or another you will determine that a given product has passed or failed on quality and how you do that is no concern of theirs. They don't provide the support needed for specifications, tests, methods, procedures, statistical analysis, rules, or business processes. ERP systems simply don't have what it takes to support quality in manufacturing systems. As a result, problems on the manufacturing floor can develop, as illustrated in Table 3.1.

THE REASONS BEHIND ERP'S SHORTCOMINGS

Now the next question: Why did ERP fail in these ways? Lots of reasons. For starters, there was a foundational flaw. The mentality that guided the design was based on an accounting perspective, not a manufacturing

Table 3.1   Typical Problems on the Manufacturing Floor

- *"What? This system doesn't support fractions?"*
- *"What do you mean that our production units must belong to a unique lot in order to track our quality data?"*
- *"I have to key in 12 fields in 3 different windows before you can record production?"*
- *"This system can't talk to our automated packaging line?"*
- *"I'm an operator, not a data entry clerk ... sure I make some errors."*

perspective. ERP systems were designed to be ledger driven. They use ledger-driven time cycles — year, month, day, shift — instead of real-time manufacturing cycles — when a production run or a batch started, when it ended, when production shifted from one step to the next step, and so on. The granularity of information produced is to a degree that suits accounting practices, not manufacturing practices. Any plant manager will tell you that accountants are clueless about the timing needs and information granularity needs of the real manufacturing environment.

The ERP mentality also was based on outmoded and narrow manufacturing and business process models that had very little flexibility or multimode capability. Many of the examples already given illustrate this. ERP doesn't understand that change occurs on the plant floor all the time. Production is moved from one line to another. The way products are routed through the factory isn't static; it's dynamic and always subject to alteration.

The functional scope of ERP was too limited, with no attention given to measuring performance in the process. ERP doesn't comprehend that raw materials aren't always used precisely according to the list on a bill of materials. It doesn't measure equipment downtime or record the reasons, so it can't support efforts to analyze problems with machinery. ERP isn't interested in what causes waste to occur, so it can't help you reduce waste or avoid committing the same error twice. The people who designed ERP never considered how valuable it would be to have a production record that tells you which machine was used, who operated the equipment, what the machine speed was, what the temperature was, and what the pressure was, among other things. The proper collection and use of this type of data can result in untold savings for a company.

And if ERP's designers didn't consider the advantages of having this type of production record, you can be sure it never crossed their minds to collect and provide real-time data. The end product was all that concerned the people behind ERP. Plus, the transaction-centric architecture and work processes were designed and built for white collar workers sitting at office desks, not blue collar workers struggling to use the system to produce products within the plant.

THE LEGACY OF THE GULF BETWEEN CORPORATE IT AND PLANT ENGINEERING

Describing ERP's failures in the plant is a tricky matter. It could be argued that ERP didn't actually fail at supporting plant operations. To fail at something, you have to attempt it and ERP never really made much of an effort to address plant functions in the first place. Remember, there has been a pervasive corporate IT mentality that the only computers in the plant are the ones using the corporate ERP application. If there is no clear idea about computers in the plant, there can be no clear idea about helping those computers work more efficiently. The people masterminding the design of ERP knew that they had to handle financial transactions and they did their homework in this area. They hired financial experts and accountants and they exhaustively tracked down every little detail about every conceivable transaction a company would encounter in any office or plant located anywhere in the world.

Looking at an example of how ERP works will help illustrate this point. One thing to note is that it can take a huge effort to get an ERP system set up. Before anything else, analysis of the company's existing business systems must be done to determine which functions the ERP system will replace. Then a detailed map must be completed that will indicate how each of these defined business processes will be satisfied by the ERP system. Then the system has to be configured. If you want to buy grain from Russia Wheat Company, you have to get it into your database. You have to put in who it is, where it is located, what currency you will use in transactions with it, what units of measurement will be used (tons, pounds, etc.), what banks you will be using, what shipping methods will be employed, and what taxes are involved. And this is just the short list. Once everything is in, you just record the transaction, and it uses all of the information you have set up.

When you buy this grain from Russia, let's say that you have to pay a tariff and an export duty, that you have to ship the grain through a port in Vladivostok, that it has got to go on a carrier to Japan where it's going to be held several days for a quality inspection, that more tariffs are charged there, that it's then shipped to the U.S. on a different shipping line, that domestic taxes are due, and so on. ERP can handle as complicated a scenario as you want. You just have to configure it all ahead of time.

In the past, all of these transactions were done manually or on local computer systems. Imagine buying wheat from 18 different countries in 12 different currencies. Before ERP, you might have separate sets of books in different currencies or computer systems located in other countries that did the purchasing in that country. So if you bought the wheat in Russia and shipped it through Germany and France before shipping it on to the U.S., you would have transactions in the Russian computer, the German computer, the French computer, and the U.S. computer. You can see what a huge ordeal just to buy one shipment of grain would be. Then at the end of the month, the quarter, or at year's end, consolidation of all of these records was performed manually. This amounted to tons of work. ERP really is the cavalry that comes to your rescue in this situation. It can do all of this easily because the financial people, the accountants, everyone who had been struggling with these sorts of headaches was consulted during the design phase.

But no one from the ERP companies ever bothered to go into the plant and say, "What do you need? What type of systems are you using now? What applications are you using and how do they work? How will it affect the plant if we design a new system in this way?" That is further complicated by the fact that they would have gotten very different answers in every different type of manufacturing environment. The needs of a manufacturing operation in the paper industry are vastly different from the needs of a food processing plant. Corporate IT never developed a distinct sense of the value of applying IT to the plant. This is the legacy of the gulf between corporate IT and plant engineering. The plant is off the radar screen. With the CFOs caught up in the Herculean task of ERP implementation, attention hasn't been given to plant systems. The top financial people haven't been thinking that there's money to be made by applying IT intelligently to the plant, so in their minds, ERP is doing everything they'd want it to do. For them, it *is* comprehensive. It *is* the silver bullet.

AMR RESEARCH REPORT, FEBRUARY 2000

We are making a lot of claims about ERP's failure to support plant operations, but you don't have to take it from us alone. Instead, get it straight from the people who know the story better than anyone — the plant managers themselves. In 2000, AMR Research went to 20 manufacturing sites and interviewed plant managers and their staff to gather information about the impact of ERP implementations on the plant. The results are illustrated in Figure 3.1. *Over half of the people interviewed — 53% — said that ERP's impact on the plant was negative.* Another 29% reported mixed results, with only 18% claiming a positive impact.

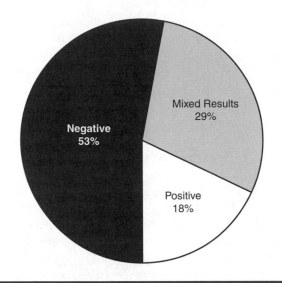

Figure 3.1 ERP's Impact on the Plant (Source: AMR Research Report, Between ERP and a Hard Place: The Plant Manager, February 2000. Used with permission.)

One of the most important elements of the report was the list of specific areas that were missing after ERP implementations, which is shown in Figure 3.2. Three quarters of the respondents said that ERP lacked sufficient manufacturing analysis, 70% mentioned quality management as a gap, 60% included plant scheduling on the list, and 50% also pointed to production sequencing and shop-floor control as missing from ERP implementations. And the AMR Research report focused on 20 *discrete* manufacturing plants.

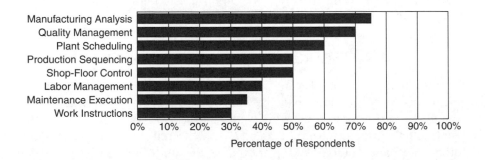

Figure 3.2 What's Missing after ERP Implementations? (Source: AMR Research Report, Between ERP and a Hard Place: The Plant Manager, February 2000. Used with permission.)

We mentioned earlier that this is the sector where ERP systems generally have their *best fit* functionally. Suffice it to say that this isn't the kind of report card you really want when you're playing in your strongest field.

UNFULFILLED PROMISES

As you can see, this was important research that deserves to be examined more closely. First, let's look at some of the claims made by ERP vendors compared with what they actually delivered. For some time in many plants, the plant managers plus the people working in production, inventory, quality control, engineering, and so on have all turned to Microsoft®'s Excel spreadsheets to monitor, report on, and analyze plant operations. Using Excel has proven to be time-consuming, labor intensive, and error prone, because data has to be collected from many different sources and then manually reentered. The survey tells of one plant manager who estimated that his production clerks spent four days every week managing this process of getting the data into the Excel spreadsheets. Think of how much time and effort could be saved if all of these systems producing the data were integrated.

And that's exactly what ERP promised. Plant managers were shown samples of weekly reports that were supposed to demonstrate how ERP would make data collection and analysis a breeze. In fact, this was one of the biggest selling points used by corporate IT when presenting ERP to the plant. Unfortunately, things didn't go so smoothly in reality. Instead of making life easier for plant managers, on too many occasions, ERP threw a wrench in the works.

Loss of Legacy Systems

One important thing to understand is that when ERP was switched on, quite a few of the plant's legacy systems were switched off. Many plants had developed systems that helped consolidate data. These systems were not particularly adept at analyzing the data, but they helped reduce the amount of time required to collect it. The net result of installing ERP was to make a lot of the data more difficult to hunt down and collect, not less difficult as promised. ERP didn't really provide the analysis functions needed, so most plants still rely on Excel. (The fact that Excel is the most popular manufacturing software application around is due in part to the shortcomings of ERP.) In many cases there has been the added burden of rebuilding data collection and consolidation systems, which were lost once ERP took over.

This has happened over and over again. In one paper mill, once the new ERP system started, the company's ability to track rolls stopped. Paper companies need to be able to keep track of each and every roll they sell, and they do this by assigning a unique tracking number to each one. Individual rolls are cut from larger reels. The ERP system allowed the company to assign a number to each reel, but that left it without any way to distinguish individual rolls coming out of one reel. If a customer called to report a quality problem with a roll, the company could tell which reel it was from, but it couldn't tell whether it was from the first set of rolls, the second set of rolls, or the third set of rolls that came out of that reel.

There's a lot of paper on a reel, and it's quite possible for the paper on some parts of that reel to have quality problems that the paper on others parts of the reel doesn't have. So, if one roll is found to have a problem, it doesn't necessarily mean that the entire reel is bad. What you want to be able to do is find the specific rolls that are most closely associated with the bad roll. But, if you don't have the tracking ability to do this, you might have to recall every roll that came from the same reel. The problem didn't last long. The company lost its ability both to track the genealogy of the rolls and to associate the quality data with the tracking numbers, and this loss quickly proved to be far too costly. The legacy system had worked fine, so the company went back to it.

At an automotive parts company, the ERP system knocked out a legacy system in charge of scheduling. This company is a "first-tier supplier," which means that it makes parts for the assembly plants that produce the finished cars. Given that the assembly plant required just-in-time delivery, the parts company had to be able to plan production on a really tight schedule. This meant that the assembly plant was giving the parts company a 4-hour schedule and also the sequence for what was going to be made next at the plant's lines. Certain specified parts needed to be delivered to the plant every 2 hours. In a case like this, it's critical that the schedules for the plant and the supplier be in sync.

The problem was that the parts company's new ERP system didn't have sufficient resolution. It could do no better than a once-a-day schedule, so the company lost the ability that it had had with its legacy system to create schedules that were tightly synchronized with the assembly plant's schedules. The net result was that the company ignored the ERP's scheduling completely, because it couldn't get down to minutes, which is what it needed. The ERP system kept spitting out a schedule every day, but it was of no use. Instead the company went to an Excel spreadsheet and used paper schedules faxed in from the assembly plant.

To make matters worse, the ERP master production scheduling system was inaccurate and this affected the company's ability to reorder parts from its suppliers. So, on top of not being able to use the scheduling, it had to use human oversight to override purchasing requirements coming from the ERP system. While we acknowledge that most ERP companies have addressed this functional lapse, so that today most ERP systems can handle the resolution needed, this is still an example of the limits of some ERP systems and the problems that can arise when legacy systems are removed during ERP implementations.

Scheduling Queues

Here's another example of problems with ERP's scheduling shortfalls and it involves an automotive parts supplier as well. The problem revolved around the need to reschedule production in response to any number of problems that can occur. Specifically, its production schedule was set out as work queues for each production line. A typical plan would give the sequence of what needed to be built, along with the quantity required. Sometimes because it was acutely necessary, and other times because it was just common sense, a supervisor would rearrange the work queues in the schedule. In other words, work on one order or one particular part would be put aside so that work on another order or part could be handled first instead. This could be the result of a sudden rush order or a problem with getting the needed supplies in time. Perhaps a die or mold broke that makes a particular part. In that case, the line would stop what it was doing, pull that die or mold out, and begin making something else.

This sort of flexibility is crucial to maintaining good levels of productivity, but flexibility is not one of ERP's strong suits. The ERP system created the work queues for each production line, but that was all it could do. Resequencing the queues wasn't an option. The supplier could do this in the legacy system, but once the ERP system came in, that function went out. The ERP system wouldn't accept schedule changes from the floor. If the supplier was supposed to make 500 widgets, but after making only 200, it needed to shift to gadgets, and then make the 300 additional widgets later, the ERP system couldn't adapt. Unable to accommodate small changes, it insisted that an entirely new master schedule be designed.

Determined not to lose efficiency just because the computer system couldn't keep up, the supplier eventually started ignoring the ERP scheduling for these purposes. Its solution was to download the master schedule once a day, then take an Excel spreadsheet and make its own production schedule. If someone had to change a work queue, the supplier went back and adjusted things in the Excel spreadsheet. If a run was interrupted, this had to be manually accounted for on the spreadsheet. The legacy scheduling system had handled all of this without problem, but was lost when the ERP system came in. Instead the supplier used America's number one manufacturing application package, Microsoft® Excel, and built what it needed to limp along. Meanwhile, the ERP system continued telling the supplier what to make, even though it was oblivious to all of the changes occurring as each day progressed, and thus completely in the dark about what was really possible or what made the most sense from the operating environment of the shop floor.

These stories exemplify one of our themes — too many times, at too many companies, corporate IT has been so focused on its own projects that it has lost sight of supporting the plant in ways that help it become better at manufacturing. ERP implementation has meant the elimination of scores of legacy systems, but in many cases, no plans were made to replace some of the functions that were lost when these systems were sent to the software graveyard. No research was done to ensure that the new systems would actually function according to the vendor's promises. Too often, plant managers have had to scramble to restore lost functionality. Sometimes they end up worse off than before ERP.

"BRING ON THE DATA ENTRY CLERKS"

The appeal of integrated data collection systems is obvious, but some plant managers became suspicious of the idea even before all of the problems materialized. Their skepticism was aroused when they heard corporate IT explain how ERP would eliminate expediters. They had been led down this path before and knew that none of the similar claims from the past had ever panned out. A plant uses expediters to manage shop orders. Plant managers depend on these people to know all of the details of each order's status. One of the cruel ironies of an ERP implementation is that expeditors find their jobs to be more difficult, not easier. ERP systems require constant data entry to satisfy reporting requirements. Expediters have found that they have less time on the shop floor, because they are so busy entering data.

The same holds true for supervisors and it's even worse. ERP data entry procedures, even for simple tasks, can involve numerous screen changes and an untold number of keystrokes. This is fine if your job is to sit in front of a computer all day, and you're paid for your ability to enter data quickly and correctly. But that isn't what plant personnel were hired to do. So, when this chore is forced upon them, two things happen. One is they get less other work done; the other is they make mistakes. Supervisors found that ERP meant spending additional time correcting data entry errors made by plant operators. Their solution? Hire more people or somehow get more resources for expediting and supervising.

"Five Minutes to Enter the Data"

The ERP implementation at one food-processing plant provides a textbook case. The original idea that came with the new ERP system was for all data to be entered at the end of each shift. With assurances from the vendor that "it won't take you five minutes to enter all of your data," the plant supervisors dove in. Five hours after their shift ended, these guys were still entering their data. If you worked the swing shift and were supposed to get off at midnight, you were still there at 5:00 in the morning entering data.

Guess what — the supervisors weren't happy about this. But there was no alternative method for getting the data in, because the ERP system can't handle data coming in any other way — it has to be entered manually. So they decided to relax the rules a little bit and allow people to enter the data the next day. This didn't work either, because people were having conflicts between entering data and being shift supervisors. Plus the data was a day old and part of the purpose of collecting it was to have the ability to analyze it and use it immediately. Also, at first the data was just a day old, but gradually data entry got put off for days, so that the data was often a week old.

Eventually, the supervisors revolted. Some of the key plant people quit and those who stayed drew a line in the sand and made it known that they were going to spend their time managing people and managing production — the jobs they were hired to do. They simply refused to comply with the data entry demands and made it clear by saying, "If you don't like it, fire me!" The company still really wanted the data, so it hired data entry clerks, but this was expensive and it raised some thorny union issues. The company did find a way to get the data entered, but it's a shame that it spent so much on ERP in the first place and then had to spend so much more money adjusting its practices to make it work.

A Problem of Design

The crucial issue is why it takes so long to enter data. The problem is one of design. The screens tend to be laid out in forms that were created to conform to the data needs of the system, as opposed to being laid out in a way that corresponds to the way operators and production people actually do their work. As it is, entering much of the data required by ERP systems forces you to go back and forth from field to field and from screen to screen. A lot of time is wasted navigating the system, time that would be better spent focused on the manufacturing process. Designing the screens to follow the flow of production would facilitate this effort.

These data entry problems pop up all over the place. An automotive company that used an ERP plant maintenance system wanted to be able to enter some simple information about machine malfunctions. The point was to be able to generate work orders for the maintenance crew. It wasn't impossible, but the data entry process was so cumbersome and complex that the company looked for an alternative solution. It was using radio frequency (RF) equipment throughout the plant, which meant hand-helds everywhere and terminals on the fork trucks and at the stations. Since the ERP system didn't run on any of the handhelds, the company wrote a simple interface application that runs on its RF equipment. In a very simple, easy-to-use way, this application collects a little bit of data, such as which piece of equipment is involved, how and why it broke down, and when it broke down, and then transmits it as a transaction up to the ERP system. The solution will work, but why should the company have to do this? It is only necessary since ERP's screens are so complex.

The amount of time it takes to enter the data is not the only problem. The complexity of the screens has resulted in data records that are riddled with errors. This is exactly what happened after an ERP system was implemented at one paper mill. We have talked about the fact that rolls of paper are cut from a larger reel. This happens at a piece of equipment called a winder. In this case, the winder operator was required to record each "turn-up," which is the paper industry word for the completion of production. This data was needed for the ERP system's product tracking function.

It turns out that the procedure for entering this data took you through 3 different screens where you entered a total of 12 different items. Maybe this wouldn't be so bad if it only had to be done once at the end of the shift, but in reality, the operator of the winder had to stop and go over to his computer terminal about every 15 minutes and deal with the cumbersome data entry process. After finishing, he would rush back and do his job for 15 more minutes before stopping once again to enter the data. Aside from making the winder operator unproductive, this resulted in a huge amount of data entry errors. It doesn't take a tremendous amount of insight to see that this approach made absolutely no sense. Essentially, the company was trying to turn someone who was trained to cut rolls of paper from a reel into a data entry clerk. After about 4 months, it discovered that the inventory system was completely messed up and that its finished goods system had massive errors. Its ability to ship products was severely hampered. The operators had done their best to keep up, but in the end, it was asking too much of them. The solution? Turn off the ERP function and go back to the old system.

Outsmarting the System

Another tale that provides an almost comically sad example of a similar problem comes from a plant that makes plastic resin chips out of synthetic polymer. These chips are used by other companies for injection molding and they are shipped in special, very large cartons. The production process is set up so that one of these cartons must be put in place first to accept a liner and then to accept a large load of chips. Given the size of these boxes and the thickness of the cardboard used, a carton-making machine was necessary to assemble them. This machine took the precut cardboard form, folded it into a box, and stapled the bottom shut.

After implementing its ERP system, the company decided that it wanted the person loading this carton maker to record every lot of cartons put into it. The established procedure was to stop after unsnapping each new pallet of flat cartons, walk over to a terminal, and handle the transaction. In this case, the ERP system required the operator to enter about six fields over two screens. This would record the tracking number for the pallet and that he had just put this load of cartons into the machine. While it isn't clear that this was really one of the best uses of an ERP system, this is what the company attempted to do.

It was a bad decision on the company's part. The man in charge of the carton-making machine wasn't about to bother with navigating the data entry screens; he managed to figure out how to beat the system by going through the screens at the end of the day, entering fictitious data. He didn't need to quit or draw a line in the sand, because he simply outsmarted the system and went on about his business. It didn't take long for the carton inventory system to become totally inaccurate. The company started to see that there were errors, but couldn't figure out where the errors were coming from. Without a clear idea of the inventory levels, the company didn't know how many cartons it needed. Soon the company was experiencing carton shortages and it would actually run out during a run and have no place to put the chips. On two occasions, the production line had to be shut down just for the want of a box.

The company's big mistake was taking someone who had no desire to learn about data entry and asking him to interrupt his work routine in order to handle some complex data entry tasks. He failed, so the system failed, and inventory records were wrecked. The company didn't know how many of these very expensive cartons had been used, how many were in stock, and how many had been scrapped for one reason or another. Once again, we see the futility of trying to turn a shop floor production worker, who has a lot of things to do, into a data entry clerk, instead of using another method to reach the same data collection goal.

A story like this is not presented so much as an illustration of the flaws of the ERP systems. In this case, it is more of a failure of the people trying to implement the system. There is a distinct failure to understand the shop floor or the manufacturing environment. The ERP systems may not have been designed to do these jobs, but the real culprits here were the people who led the implementation or designed the implementation. They set up the ERP system to fail by asking it to do something it really wasn't designed to do. Then they made matters worse by requiring plant personnel to support the needs of the ERP system in ways that were totally out of sync with what happened on the plant floor. Usually the people who did this came from white collar environments. While they may have been quite adept at putting in financial systems, they really didn't understand manufacturing that well and as a result, they left a lot of failures in their wake.

It should come as no surprise that a decline in worker productivity was mentioned across the board by the plant managers interviewed in the AMR study. In all fairness, it should be acknowledged that, given the massive scope of ERP systems, getting up to speed is no simple matter. This means that even if the system functions perfectly in the long run, a stiff learning curve at the outset will cause a temporary drop in productivity. Nevertheless, most managers were not optimistic about the future. There are just too many added tasks required of plant personnel. All in all, ERP means more work for the plant and that means lower productivity.

There is one more point concerning data collection that must be stressed. Without the data, an ERP system is incapable of providing the benefits that it has the potential to provide. Too many companies have settled for less from their ERP systems than they expected, simply because they haven't bothered to understand how ERP systems *should* be applied at the plant level. Most ERP functions need to be enabled by adequate data collection.

Even the most sophisticated and ingenious ERP software in the world has its Achilles' heel: getting the mounds and mounds of data into the system. The solution for many companies is to design and implement separate systems that enable data collection in the plant to feed critical ERP functions. Without the plant-level data, the ERP system can't deliver the functions it is capable of providing, and it also can't adequately perform the larger corporate management functions that are its bread and butter. The result is that companies then find themselves getting a smaller return on a massive capital investment.

Listen carefully to the ERP vendors. You're likely to hear extensive and detailed descriptions of the system's analytical and organizational capabilities, but only generalized and vague claims about how well the system fits into the plant and makes day-to-day life easier for manufacturing operations. The ERP system has legitimate and important data needs, but taking plant operators and trying to turn them into data entry clerks, or hiring an army of data entry people at the plant is not the best plan for meeting these needs. There are better ways to make the ERP investment successful, while helping the plant improve performance and productivity at the same time.

THE NEED FOR — AND LACK OF — IT SUPPORT

Could some of these plants have done a better job of implementing ERP? Yes and no. Actually, the question is unfair. We should ask if the *company*, not the *plant* could have done a better job. The answer there definitely is "yes." The plant could have done a better job, if it was given the IT support it needed. The overwhelming demands of implementing ERP systems put tremendous stress on corporate IT departments. With IT resources stretched thin, guess who suffers. After all, the plant was never the reason for buying ERP to begin with. Plant managers state that corporate IT pulled resources out of the plant, while at the same time creating conditions that required additional IT support. As plant managers scrambled to find third-party systems to replace the fully functioning legacy systems that were shut down, they needed more assistance from IT professionals — but they didn't get it. One result was system implementations that didn't match previous IT standards. So, even if the systems were doing the job, it eventually became apparent that IT couldn't support them. One plant reported the aggravation of spending $100,000 to internally develop a data collection system only to discover that it would cost another $100,000 to integrate it into the ERP system. The plant ended up throwing it out instead.

FILLING IN THE GAPS

Given all of these problems, how did plant managers adapt? Above all else, they hired more people. We saw this already in our discussion of the data entry demands of ERP. In their effort to keep the plant running as smoothly as possible, plant managers have increased their head count. The new additions are mainly there to enter data, thus allowing production operators to tend to their normal duties without excessive interruptions. And while these data entry personnel are busily plowing through the ERP screens to provide the information required there, they are also using Excel to provide the analysis needed by the plant. In fact, Excel is one of the main tools used to fill in the functional gaps created by ERP implementations. In the survey, 80% of the respondents mentioned people as one way they filled in the gaps and 60% mentioned Excel (see Figure 3.3).

Other systems that were used to make up for lost functionality include data collection systems (40% used these) and manufacturing execution systems (30% used these). One additional approach used by a fifth of the

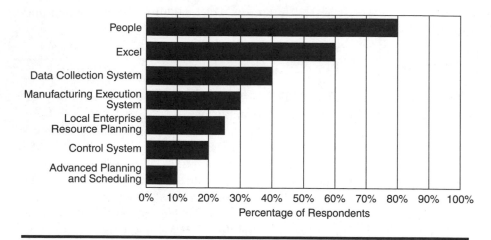

Figure 3.3   How the ERP Gap Is Filled (Source: AMR Research Report, Between ERP and a Hard Place: The Plant Manager, February 2000. Used with permission.)

respondents was to reconfigure control systems to communicate with the ERP systems. Plants with highly automated processes had the best success with this tactic. Of course, all of this costs money. Most of the plant managers were looking at project costs that ranged between $500,000 and $1 million. So, the overall picture is this: After a company spends millions upon millions of dollars to implement an ERP project, the plant has to hire more people and spend additional big bucks to accommodate the problems this implementation has caused.

A good example of this happened at a plant that makes yogurt. One critical element of the manufacture of yogurt is the use of some highly perishable raw ingredients. This means that yogurt has a short shelf life, usually about 20 days. All of this makes the entire process more complicated. All of the company's raw materials, especially the fruit that it is putting into the yogurt is very fresh, so it has to be refrigerated. The company has found that, in order to maximize the shelf life and get the full 20 days, it is best to refrigerate different ingredients at different temperatures. Some ingredients it takes all the way to freezing, with some of these put into a hard freeze and others a light freeze. Then some are near freezing (very cold, but not frozen) and others will be lightly refrigerated. And everything is kept at various levels of humidity — some wet, some dry, and some in the middle. In order to accommodate this variety of refrigeration requirements, the company has multiple storage locations where the ingredients are kept. This presents the obvious challenge of maintaining an inventory for each location. When the company is ready to produce a batch of a particular yogurt, it brings all of the ingredients needed together just before the run and puts them in a special location.

The result is a scheduling, purchasing, and inventory nightmare. The company starts with a month's plan and then devises a week's plan for the ingredients needed. The problem is that the ERP system doesn't have a good way to keep track of all of these storage locations. There may be a way to do it, but it's so convoluted and cumbersome that, for all practical purposes, it doesn't exist. So, instead of having all of those locations put into the ERP system, the company uses an Excel spreadsheet. The spreadsheet allows the company to look at various options in terms of planning, purchasing, and movement in ways that the ERP system cannot support. Right next to the spreadsheet is the ERP terminal, so when the company needs to enter some information into it, it's right there. Then the ERP system is used exclusively for after-the-fact transactions. The company tells the system what it did, what was made, what materials were used, even though it didn't help plan anything. This use of Excel next to an ERP system is quite common. It's one of the ways to fill the gaps left by ERP implementations.

WAS ERP WORTH THE PRICE?

The AMR Research report paints a vivid picture of how ERP affects plants within manufacturing companies. The problems in the plant must be weighed against the benefits that ERP brings to the company overall. And as we have already stated, those benefits can be substantial. What we have not already stated is that it's an open debate as to whether the benefits can be regarded as sufficient. The big question is: Did ERP deliver a reasonable return on the investments made into it?

This is a hotly debated topic. The benefits of ERP may be impressive, but its price tag is enormous. The initial cost of an ERP system can run into the hundreds of millions of dollars. Add to this the scope creep that is inevitable with any project this massive and the annual licensing fees of around 20% of the initial cost and the figure looms even larger. But wait, that's not all. Scope creep is one thing and smart business people expect and account for it to a reasonable degree. What wasn't fully anticipated was the excessive time and energy that implementations have required and the damaging disruption and culture shock caused as a result. It may be impossible to put dollar figures on these problems, but one thing is perfectly clear: *ERP has cost a bundle.*

TECHNOLOGY MANIA

There are ramifications to all of this, particularly in the way IT projects get funded today. We spoke in Chapter 2 about some of the "questionable reasons" that ERP had become so popular. It was the business trend of the day. In fact, it's fair to say that a mania developed around ERP. Companies didn't always demand a hard return-on-investment (ROI) scenario. They were venturing into new technologies and it wasn't always easy to stipulate in concrete terms exactly where the payback would be. If you saw another successful company jumping on the ERP bandwagon, you had to consider doing it yourself, particularly if this other company was one of your competitors. Make the wrong decision about this new technology and in a few years you could be showing up in a Harvard Business School case study as an example of the demise of a large corporation.

It's not that these were necessarily unsound decisions. If you see a well-respected company using new technology, it only makes sense to learn more. And the context for the mania over ERP was a more general mania about technology in general — "technology's going to the save the world." There's a history to this. For two decades, numerous studies documented the productivity gains made from implementing technology. From a broader perspective, it goes back much further than the last 20 years. Since the industrial revolution in the 19th century, adopting new technology has proven to be not only an effective way to move forward, but also an essential element of business survival.

BUYING ON FAITH

None of this is to say that companies simply forgot about ROI. They didn't. The point is that they let other elements substitute for a hard, detailed, concrete ROI. For example, they invested on faith that the payback would come. A CFO at one company was tearing his hair out trying to keep all of his books straight. You can imagine him saying, "Here I am at a $3 billion company and I can't tell you how much any of my products cost. It takes me three months to do a month-ending statement on my books. I have books left over from the way accounting was done when the founder was still a kid in college in 1906. If I'm just going to do one thing before I die, I'm going to get a computer system in here that sorts this mess out and gives me an integrated set of books." He doesn't know what the payback will be, but he can't imagine that it will not be worth the cost. He is determined to bring his accounting practices out of the stone age and into the computer age.

His idea is valid. When you're working in 15 different countries, have 15 different computer systems, 15 different data centers, plus a staff of up to 10 people maintaining each data center, and you put it all on one technology and consolidate it, you're going to reduce your costs. It takes a little while for it to pay off, since you may be spending millions of dollars up front, but the savings are there.

Here's another example. A CEO of a Fortune 500 manufacturing company was told that acquiring an ERP system that would integrate, standardize, and consolidate all financial systems across the company would cost more than $25 million. Without hesitating, he said, "Do it now." He oversaw an annual capital budget of more than $1 billion, but due to the fragmentation of the information and financial systems already in place, he could never get a definitive picture of which operations, plants, or divisions were producing a good return on the capital being spent on each. He reasoned that having accurate and timely financial information that was comprehensive for the entire company would allow him to recoup the $25 million in a short time.

Of course, there always will be situations where getting a firm figure for projected savings is highly difficult, if not impossible. It is a catch-22 of sorts. If your bookkeeping is a mess of disconnected systems, then how do you calculate anything? In both of these examples, there may have been some good ROI numbers to back up part of the ERP idea, but there were also intangibles. How much cost savings vs. how many millions of dollars up front is the question. That's where faith comes in.

That's also where the vendor's promises come in. One element that played a role in ERP's rise was the power of marketing. ERP salespeople promised the moon and made it sound irresistible. The marketing pitch was particularly effective when delivered by one of the "must have" vendors. This echoes the commonly understood notion that part of IBM's success as a hardware vendor in the 1970s and 1980s was that IBM was able to claim the role as the safe bet. Nobody ever got fired for buying from IBM. If a computer system failed and you were the person responsible for having chosen the computer vendor, you didn't want anyone to be able to say, "Why didn't you get IBM?" The same is true for the dominant ERP software vendors. Also, given that the technology is new in so many respects, many companies aren't well equipped to scrutinize it carefully. If the vendor says that ERP will reduce costs this much, add value in these ways, and be installed and running within this time frame, how can anyone substantially dispute it? Never having been through an ERP implementation before, companies often chose in part to take the vendors' claims on faith.

IT BUDGETS — PAST AND PRESENT

One of the ways companies managed IT expenditures prior to the "mega IT project" era that started in the late 1980s and early 1990s was to set up an annual IT budget for the corporation. Then every year, IT departments would spend their budget and that was it. Corporations knew information technology was essential for improving the business, but there wasn't any set way to establish a budget. For the most part, budgets came to be established simply by historical trends. They generally stayed about the same each year, maybe increasing by a small percentage annually. One of the peculiarities of big corporations is that if they do not spend their budget each year, it gets reduced the next year. So departments end up having all of these sudden expenditures toward the end of each year, just to make sure all of their budget money gets spent.

The point is that a budget system like this does two things. One is that it reduces the need for hard justifications and the other is that it doesn't allow for big swings in costs from year to year. Instead, IT departments simply spend, in one way or another, precisely what they are allowed to spend each year. If you saw the need for a substantial project that would require a big budget one year and a small budget the next, you were out of luck. This wouldn't fit into the annual budget system. Many large companies couldn't handle the roller coaster effect that came with large, budget-busting projects. So the big projects didn't get approved, but projects that fell within the budget were not scrutinized carefully to make sure they had a clear ROI.

Today, many companies approach IT expenditures by having two IT budgets. One is sometimes referred to as the "lights on" budget, which funds the maintenance of the bare essentials. It is the baseline. You have to spend this money every year to keep your servers running, to keep your e-mail up, and to handle other standard tasks — to keep your lights on, in other words. If you refuse to pay your electric bill, you lose your electricity. If you fail to maintain your IT systems, they will fail to work properly.

The lights on budget — a straight operating expense — is a given part of the annual budget and may not change much from year to year. The justification for spending this money is clearly understood and need not be reestablished each year. The lights on budget is kept to the barest minimum, even though some people are always trying to expand it as much as possible. If you have an item that you need, you try to argue that it is a lights on item, because you know that that budget will be approved.

The other budget is the project budget, and this funds anything added to the existing systems. Everything new, even replacing a server, getting some new PCs, or upgrading a software program, is all in the project budget. In contrast to the lights on budget, everything must have a hard justification, because the project budget faces intense corporate scrutiny. If the payback can't be clearly spelled out, the funds will not be approved. Previously, this distinction between two different types of funding for IT wasn't made. Consequently, no pattern of establishing a definite payback developed.

THE NEW ORDER — HARD JUSTIFICATION

Today, post–ERP-mania, hard justifications are insisted upon before any IT project gets the nod. If your proposal for an IT project can't show an ROI clearly and concretely, then don't waste your time making a presentation. You have to demonstrate that you can do one of two things: reduce costs or add capabilities. The most direct way to establish a clear payback is to show how operating costs can be reduced. The other justification for funding is by adding or enhancing a capability that will help the business grow or be more profitable. The one exception to this rule of either cutting costs or adding capabilities involves regulatory compliance. If you can show that the IT project will significantly improve the company's compliance with government regulations, then funding will be justified in most cases. In addition to showing a solid ROI, your project must be aligned with the company's business goals and metrics.

Most companies have become firm about demonstrating the payback. They aren't going to do anything without a solid ROI. They're just not going to do anything, period, unless it can be shown that they are going to get a concrete benefit or reduce a cost. They're just going to stand pat and beyond that, they're going to try to shrink their IT expenditures. Faith, fashion, and vendor's promises all substituted for concrete ROI in the past, but those days are over.

Hard justification means being able to reduce costs, add value, increase capability, increase revenue, increase customer satisfaction, increase brand loyalty, increase repeat business, or increase efficiency. Reducing costs could be avoiding costs; it could be doing things better, faster, or cheaper. It doesn't necessarily mean reducing people. It could mean reducing waste, getting better prices on raw materials, reducing inventory, or any other of a number of possibilities.

Adding value or capability could mean producing or shipping the product two days quicker or getting orders processed in one day instead of two. In the end, the improvement must be something that you can leverage. It has to show up on the bottom line. You want to get a leg up on your competition. So if you can demonstrate any of these, your project will get funded.

One other contributing factor to this change in funding approval is that computers have gradually become demystified. Before PCs became commonplace, everyone thought computers were beyond their understanding. Computer technology was approved in corporate budgets, even though the people approving the funds didn't always understand what they should be getting for their money. Now, executives look at the IT budget in the same way they look at any other project. They want to understand it and to scrutinize it before they approve it.

CONCLUSION

What does all of this mean for the company's IT managers? For one thing, every major expenditure must be clearly and precisely justified. If you want to spend money on a new IT system, then that system had better reduce the company's operating costs or provide valuable capabilities for the enterprise. People from corporate finance are now sitting on the project teams, so the proposal must meet their scrutiny from the start. You will not get very far telling these folks just to spend the money on faith; they want some hard numbers. On top of that, projects usually start small and have to prove themselves before they can go forward in a big way.

On the positive side, though, is the fact that there is a huge potential for achieving a payback on IT dollars. By using other tools to fill in the gaps left by ERP, a tremendous return on investment is possible. The trick is either to reduce costs or to add valuable new capabilities. In most cases, the right tools actually do at least some of both at the same time. In Chapter 4, we pinpoint the areas where payback can be achieved.

4

WAYS TO CUT COSTS AND ADD CAPABILITIES

Reducing costs and adding valuable capabilities — those improvements are the heart of what this book is all about. In this chapter, we'll examine these in great detail. Our aim is to pinpoint the areas where paybacks can be achieved. The fact is, there is gold in the plant that hasn't been mined. Before we talk about the tools needed to get the gold out of the ground, let's focus on finding it in the first place.

THE VALUE OF FOCUSING ON THE SUPPLY CHAIN

There seems to be an endless stream of books being published today about the *supply chain*, but this isn't one of them. Our focus is on manufacturing itself, an often neglected, yet totally essential, part of the supply chain. Our goal is to point out that manufacturing companies can make substantial gains by improving the way their plants function. At the same time, we want to acknowledge the value of also focusing on the parts of the supply chain that exist outside of the plant.

The very phrase is omnipresent. You can't open a book on business today without getting an eyeful about the importance of the supply chain. Now higher management positions at many corporations have titles such as vice president of supply chain planning or vice president of global sourcing. There is a good reason for this. By focusing on the entire process of starting with raw materials and ending with bringing products to the market, companies have learned to collaborate in remarkable new ways, and this collaborative effort has produced serious dividends. IT systems such as ERP and supply chain planning have been a big part of this. These systems can facilitate the coordination necessary to reap the rewards.

The rewards have come not only from thinking about the *external* supply chain, but also about the *internal* supply chain. The mentality of collaborative efforts has affected the corporate culture of many companies. Not so long ago, it was common for companies to be highly Balkanized. The operations group always kept its focus strictly on internal affairs. The purchasing group thought only about purchasing. The sales and marketing group thought only about sales and marketing; likewise with people handling outbound logistics and distribution. None of these people were talking to each other.

Supply chain thinking has brought all these groups together to actually communicate about how they can make the company work more efficiently. People aren't thinking in silos anymore. Instead they're realizing that everything is interrelated. They're also seeing that the pace of change is increasing and that to stay on top of the game, you have to form an integrated way of looking at everything your company does.

Worldwide Sourcing

One of the ways that companies have applied supply chain theory involves the consolidation of procurement along with the expansion of the pool of possible suppliers. This is called "worldwide sourcing." Over the last 10 to 20 years, many companies have grown for a number of reasons, chief among them being that the economy has grown and that mergers have been rampant. As a result, more and more corporations are functioning on a global basis.

One consequence is that a large corporation may suddenly find itself buying the same product from many different vendors. This is the age old problem of the right hand not knowing what the left hand is doing; only we are talking about a beast with perhaps several dozen hands. If you have 10 plants that need widgets, the Michigan plant is buying them from True Widgets, Inc., the California plant is buying them from Reliable Widget Supply, the Mexico plant is buying them from Widgets International, Ltd., and so on, then you would be well-advised to consolidate your purchasing.

ERP is great for this. It knows about every single widget any part of the corporation buys from any vendor in the world. There's no difficulty in finding out how many widgets you buy every year or every month, how much you pay for them, where they come from, how quickly they're shipped, and more. This puts you in the position to negotiate with vendors for a better price, a better product, and better service. Significant savings have been made from this sort of procurement standardization.

This tactic applies not only to materials actually used in production, such as the individual parts that make up a widget, but also all types of commodity items such as paper towels, work gloves, cleaning supplies, etc. It doesn't just work for discrete items, such as widgets; it also applies to purchasing bulk products — like corn syrup and milk — and services — like shipping.

Shipping is an interesting example because of how much it has changed recently. There has been a revolution in the shipping industry in the past 20 years. The speed at which goods can be moved around the globe is phenomenal. We may have begun to take it for granted, but it hasn't been this way for that long. The smart companies have taken advantage of these changes, and as a result they can keep tighter just-in-time schedules for the delivery of parts, provide better service to customers, and shorten their overall production cycles. In the same way that large merged corporations sometimes find themselves buying the same product from many different sources, they can also find that they have many different shipping procedures at different locations and divisions. Many of these large enterprises have been able to reduce costs through a corporate-wide standardization of their shipping procedures.

The consolidation of purchasing is one side of the coin; the expansion of available suppliers is the other side. There have been and will continue to be advantages to working with suppliers that are located nearby, but sometimes distant suppliers can offer price, quality, or even service advantages that are too good to pass up. The point is that everything is becoming more global, which makes it simpler to consider a much broader range of companies as potential suppliers.

MANUFACTURING'S PLACE IN THE SUPPLY CHAIN

Some people tend to forget that the plant has an important role to play in the supply chain, but it's a fact that cannot be denied. Illustrated in Figure 4.1, this fact becomes painfully clear when you realize that manufacturing often is the *largest single value-added component* of the total sales volume of a product. To fully appreciate how this works, it would help if we could take you to the plant that makes one of the breakfast cereals that the kids in your house love to eat.

The main ingredient of this cereal might be oats, wheat, corn, or rice, but let's say it's wheat. We would take you over where the rail cars bring in the raw wheat. This is the wheat that's been harvested, but not yet milled; it isn't a pretty sight. When you consider that cereal companies start with that and end up with the product your kids gobble up by the bowl, you begin to get a good idea of how value is added to a product.

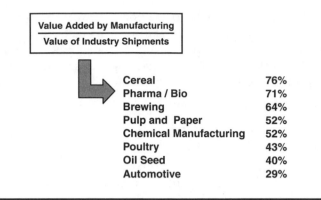

Value Added by Manufacturing	
Value of Industry Shipments	
Cereal	76%
Pharma / Bio	71%
Brewing	64%
Pulp and Paper	52%
Chemical Manufacturing	52%
Poultry	43%
Oil Seed	40%
Automotive	29%

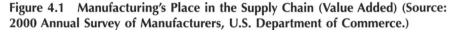

Figure 4.1 Manufacturing's Place in the Supply Chain (Value Added) (Source: 2000 Annual Survey of Manufacturers, U.S. Department of Commerce.)

Cereal has value to consumers because it means they get to eat something they like without having to bother with growing the grain, harvesting it, milling it, and cooking it with other ingredients that they'd have to also buy or grow. That's a lot of work that gets saved every time you buy a box of your favorite breakfast cereal.

Making the cereal that goes into the boxes is only part of it. The boxes themselves form part of the value in that people want to buy different amounts of cereal, so the store's shelves are full of boxes of all sizes. Some boxes have inner packaging that is resealable, which keeps the product fresher after it's opened. Value is different things to different people and value is added in ways other than manufacturing. Convenience and consistency are values that are becoming more and more important. People want to be able to get the same type of cereal anywhere in the country, and they want to be able to get it at any time of day. So shipping, inventory, store location, and store hours play a role here.

Value is added in all kinds of ways, but many people overlook the massive role manufacturing plays in this process. In some cases, such as cereal, manufacturing adds over three-quarters of the entire value of the product. That's astounding! Even half of the entire value of the product means that there is tremendous potential there for cost reductions. The point is this: Say that manufacturing added only about 5% of the value. In this case, even if you increased efficiency by 50% (which is way beyond most realistic expectations), you would be increasing profits only by 2.5%. But when you consider the cereal-making process, where manufacturing is responsible for about 75% of the value, it's an entirely different story. In this case, an increase in efficiency of only 10% would mean increasing profits by 7.5%. Having so much of the value added in manufacturing means that cutting costs or increasing productivity can result in big savings overall. Cereal may be at the top end of the spectrum, but the percentages listed in Figure 4.1 give ample evidence that there are other industries where manufacturing is a really large portion of the total sales value.

MANUFACTURING'S ROLE GETS OVERLOOKED

Despite the fact that in many industries manufacturing represents a big component of the overall value of a product, people tend to forget about the plant. While ERP and supply chain systems have captured everyone's attention, IT applications for manufacturing plants have been largely neglected and ignored. There are a number of reasons for this. For many people, the natural response to the idea of the supply chain is to look outward. They immediately think of externally facing relationships, suppliers on the one hand and customers on the other hand.

It's also the case that other ways to improve the overall functioning of the supply chain have taken precedence. The examples mentioned before of the consolidation of suppliers and improved shipping could be thought of as "low-hanging fruit." When you're sent to pick the apples from the tree, you start by grabbing the ones you can reach easily. It's just human nature.

Another reason manufacturing gets overlooked is that making things can be extremely complex. It's not so easy to get your grip on the situation. Manufacturing is like a black box. You put the raw materials in at one end and the finished product comes out the other end. People think, "I'm not exactly sure what's going on in there, so I had better not mess with it." Also, plants are spread out away from corporate headquarters. Frequently, they're in rural areas, so it's a case of out of sight, out of mind. In the end, for all sorts of reasons, no one has paid much attention to the real needs of manufacturing and to the things that can help the plants improve their performance. Instead, management has been consumed with the low hanging fruit that can be harvested with corporate systems.

Make no mistake about it — the focus on ways to improve the entire supply chain has proven to be highly effective for many companies. But supply chain management can be made even more effective by focusing more attention on finding ways to help the plant. In many cases, this has too often been ignored. The solution is not narrowing the focus to the plant alone and forgetting about the rest of the supply chain. That would only be tunnel vision of a different nature. Rather, the step that needs to be taken is to fully integrate the plant into the vision of a complete supply chain.

This means that there's a trend that needs to be altered. In the 1990s, ERP was king and the plant was ignored. As 2000 approached, Y2K claimed everyone's attention and the plant was ignored. As we begin this century, supply chain systems are the rage and the plant is still being ignored. Giving more attention to the IT needs of manufacturing plants need not happen at the expense of neglecting other valuable business ideas. The point is simple: Include the "make" part of the equation when looking at the entire picture.

ERP has done wonders for back office functions, such as financials and purchasing, and it has played a huge role in bringing greater coordination to the entire supply chain. The problem is that it has shortchanged the plant in some ways. ERP hasn't helped with improving product quality, reducing manufacturing waste, or providing the detailed view of production. All of these factors help the local teams improve plant performance. What's worse, there have been too many cases where it has reached into the plant and done more harm than good, as the AMR survey emphatically demonstrated. The solution to this problem is the intelligent use of manufacturing systems. It may take some effort to reach it, but this tree has more fruit just sitting there waiting to be picked.

HOW MANUFACTURING SYSTEMS CAN ACHIEVE REAL PAYBACK

There are all kinds of ways to improve manufacturing through the intelligent use of manufacturing IT, but it all comes down to two things. *Either you're reducing costs or adding capabilities.* In many cases, you're doing both at the same time. For example, a system that supports regulatory compliance may reduce paperwork chores enough to allow you to reduce your staff, thus cutting costs; while at the same time providing the valuable new capability of helping you avoid fines for noncompliance. Even though many efforts to improve manufacturing may reduce costs *and* provide new capabilities, making the distinction between these two areas can help us get a handle on all of the opportunities that exist.

REDUCING WASTE AND LOSS

Waste is a by-product of every system. There's no way around it; every plant has it. But, there are ways to reduce it, and reducing waste is an excellent way to reduce overall operating costs. First, let's look at where the waste exists. It generally falls into these three categories:

1. Labor (and full-time equivalents)

2. Materials (direct or indirect)
3. Asset utilization (line or machine time)

Manufacturing waste streams are an aggravating problem. You know it's there, but you're not always sure exactly where it is or what is causing it, which means you can't be sure how to stop it. To help visualize this point, imagine that you have a big tank of some valuable commodity sitting in the middle of one of your plants. Plus, you know for certain that there are three persistent leaks out of this tank. Labor waste, material waste, and capacity waste are persistent waste streams that exist in every plant. Intelligent use of manufacturing systems will not necessarily eliminate them completely, but it can help you take a huge step forward in the effort to slow them down.

HOW TO ATTACK THE WASTE STREAMS

You can't fix something you can't see or don't know the cause of, so one of the first priorities has to be measuring and monitoring waste and attempting to capture the root causes. Plants of every sort, every shape, and every size lack the tools needed to do root cause analysis of waste streams. It's true that many plants produce mounds upon mounds of data, but what data really matters? For some time, people have been striving to determine which indicators are key, which show you the real root cause of problems, and which give the most fundamental measurements about your manufacturing processes. The effort to sift through all of this information and to make sense of it has resulted in the development of key performance indicators (KPIs). One of the most essential qualities of KPIs is that the raw data has been put into context so that it becomes information and knowledge. These indicators are the most important pieces of information that provide visibility into how the plant's processes are running. They are similar to the gauges on your automobile. The oil pressure gauge, the tachometer, and the speedometer all help you know that your engine is running well. You don't need to examine every little bit of information, but you do need to keep your eye on the most important data coming in.

Then there's the next challenge. Not only do you need to be able to identify and monitor your KPIs, you also need to be able to get this information in real time, not a month or even just a week later. There is certainly some benefit to historical analysis. You can spot long-term trends and you can see that certain aberrations, which may seem significant right when they occur, are only minor issues in the big picture. But there are all kinds of situations where having information instantly can prevent you from having serious headaches — and it can save you tons of money.

Imagine if you only received your car's oil pressure information once every week. You wouldn't know in a timely fashion that you were running low on oil, which could seriously damage your engine, resulting in additional headaches and costs.

Examples abound that can show how this actually works in manufacturing plants. Here are just a few.

Importance of Real-Time Data

Drug Manufacturing

In some niches of the pharmaceutical industry, a plant may make approximately 25 batches of a drug each year. For example, the biotechnology employed to produce certain drugs involves the use of bacteria. Over the course of several weeks, the bacteria are fed specific substances, so that their excretions can be harvested to produce the drug being manufactured. The process itself may not be extremely costly, but each batch could easily be worth something in the range of $25 million to $200 million. That means that there's a lot at stake with every single batch and you don't want to get to the end of a month-long batch process and discover that the entire product is flawed. You want to know everything you can as fast as you can. You will pay a lot of money to have the knowledge capability you need. If a batch takes 20 days, and some KPIs come in on the 3rd day showing you that the batch is flawed, you will just scrap the whole batch and start over. If your data collection system doesn't give you real-time feedback and it takes you 2 weeks to learn about something wrong that happened on the 3rd day, you have wasted a lot of time (and money) for nothing.

Food Manufacturing

Think about frozen dessert topping, which is sold by weight and always comes in the same size tubs. When you make this product, you have to be careful about the density. If it's too dense, the required portion will fill up less of the tub, leading customers to think that they didn't get all that they are paying for. And if it's not as dense as it should be, the required portion will not even fit in the tub. In the plant, different people are in charge of mixing the product and getting it into the tubs. The people doing the mixing have had "high volume, low cost" drilled into their minds and as a result might not be keeping a careful eye on the density. Perhaps the procedure is that 10 batches of the product usually get made before the 1st of those 10 is being put into tubs, and if you don't have real-time data collection and analysis, you could have 10 bad batches before you discover the problem. If you did have real-time collection and analysis, you would know the density was off in the very first batch. This type of information is critical for attacking the waste streams. Once you have this capability and use it for any length of time, you wonder how you ever lived without it.

Reducing Waste and Loss in Terms of Materials

Making Cheese

You may have seen advertisements on television for some types of cheese that say every slice contains so many ounces of milk. This is because the cheese-making process requires that much milk to produce that much cheese. So, if you're in the business of making cheese, you have to buy a lot of milk. There are other ingredients in cheese that may be more expensive than milk, pound for pound, but the sheer volume of milk needed makes it the most expensive component of cheese. Milk is also the ingredient that presents the most problems in terms of spoilage, because so much is used and it undergoes so many complicated processes. All in all, a lot of the money that goes into making cheese is tied up in milk.

One of the simple ways to track the amount of milk used is called a *yield* or a *mass balance*. The idea is simple: You have to balance the amount coming into the plant with the amount used by the plant. For example, at a cheese plant, you start with raw milk and you end up with cheese. It's critical that you measure the materials carefully as they go in and as they come out. Then, to get a reading on the yield, you perform analytical tests. If the yield is less than the standard, the analysis should provide some clues to the source of the problem. By keeping a close eye on yields and jumping onto problems as soon as they're spotted, it's possible to prevent the waste of lots of expensive raw materials. Over time, this practice strengthens the basic production practices, so that yields consistently meet the minimum standards.

The next step is to look at ways to raise the minimum standard. Here again, using the analysis available can point to ways of improving yields. The point to be made here is that, given the large quantities involved — 20 to 30 tanker truckloads of milk each day — even a small percentage increase in the yield of each batch can mean massive savings on materials costs over the course of a year.

The devil is in the details, however. Once the cheese leaves the vats, it goes to a dry mat conveyor, which takes most of the moisture out. Then it goes into barrels, where more moisture is removed, before being put into cold storage for aging. Since it's almost impossible to do a perfectly accurate mass balance for the total milk coming into the plant against the total cheese going out, the best idea is to focus on each step individually. This allows you to see precisely what happens in each stage. Even though the entire process of making cheese is somewhat involved, each individual part of the process is rather simple. As you examine each step, you can spot the specific areas where the loss is the most significant and make those steps your highest priorities for increasing yields.

Making Cereal

Almost all cereals are made from grains, such as rice, wheat, or corn, which are either puffed, flaked, or toasted. Then in most cases, some sort of coating is applied, such as a sugar or vitamin coating. All together, the process of making cereal involves several steps. First the raw grain goes into a cooker, then to a dryer, then perhaps a flaking roll, where it's smushed into flakes or a puffer/toaster. After that, it may get coated and then sent through another dryer. Finally, the packaging occurs, starting with a bag, which goes into a box. That box is put into a larger box, which is stacked on pallets ready for shipping.

Each step presents the possibility of loss or waste. For example, maybe some of the grain gets stuck in the cooker and doesn't come out when you dump it into the dryer, but you don't notice until you start cleaning the cooker. At that point, you just have to throw it out. Similar problems could happen in the dryer or the toaster. If the rolls in the flaker aren't adjusted properly, some of the grain will not get smushed the way it should and will have to be thrown out. Plus there's the problem of sifting through all of it and sorting out the good flakes from the bad ones. Or the coating process is uneven and more is ruined.

The same yield analysis approach used in the cheese plant helps here in the cereal plant. The plant has a yield target, so if it's missing the target, it can search for the source of the problem and fix it. The computer systems gather the data and help analyze it for root causes.

Processing Coffee

Coffee processing may not be as complicated as making cheese or cereal, but it does involve a few steps: roasting, grinding, blending, and packaging. In your efforts to maximize yields, you want to focus on the blending step. Each blend has a recipe that calls for beans of different quality levels, which in turn have different costs. If one blend is made up of 80% of one type of less expensive coffee bean and 20% of a more expensive coffee bean, you need to measure carefully, so that you don't use more of the expensive beans than necessary.

This may sound simple, but consider how the plant works. If you have a large order for several thousand pounds of coffee, the plant will be busy with roasters, grinders, and blenders all going at once. So you have a lot of things to watch. You don't want to roast or grind more coffee than you need, nor blend more than you need. The appropriate computer software will keep track of what you need, what is in progress in each roaster, each grinder, and each blender, and what is completed at each step, so that you make exactly what has been ordered. This can dramatically reduce waste, because it's no simple matter to manage all of this otherwise.

Reducing Waste and Loss in Terms of Labor

A Soft Drink Plant

Professional football came to a city where a soft drink plant is located and the plant was full of football fans. This shouldn't have presented any problems, given that the games were played on Sunday and the plant scheduled its production to be handled only on weekdays. The plan was to run around-the-clock Monday through Friday and close over the weekends. It wasn't working out that way, though. The plant couldn't get everything produced by the end of the day on Friday, so it started working Saturdays and Sundays to make up the difference. While many of the employees liked getting the overtime pay, there was a large contingent who didn't want to come in on Sundays. They wanted to be at the game, if it was a home game, or be at home watching the game on TV, if the team played away.

So the plant undertook a major effort to find the source of the problem that kept it from getting everything produced within the regular workweek. It discovered that one of the biggest culprits was downtime, both planned and unplanned. Of course, downtime jumps out as an obvious candidate for causing the problem of reduced production. The challenge was to see specifically which pieces of equipment went down, when they went down, and why they went down. This involved collecting data and doing root cause analysis.

What the plant found was that there were certain stages in production that functioned as bottlenecks in the entire process. If the equipment at a bottleneck went down, that slowed the entire plant's production output. There were other places where equipment downtime was occurring, but it was largely insignificant, because that equipment had excess capacity.

The next step was to focus on the critical machines and see what could be done to improve the situation. It turned out that the downtime on this equipment followed an 80/20 rule, meaning that 80% of the downtime was being caused by things that occurred only 20% of the time. In other words, the plant narrowed its focus to the one-fifth of the downtime problems for this equipment that had proven to be most critical.

This type of information is invaluable. Anyone could decide to improve downtime problems, but when they are spread over an entire factory, where do you start? The use of computer software here allowed the plant to pinpoint, first, the most important pieces of equipment, then the most critical problems affecting that equipment. The efficiency of its efforts increased exponentially. This saved the company money outright, but that isn't all it did. Working 7 days just to get its regular orders met meant the company had no excess capacity. So, if additional orders came in, it was straining the system to meet them, if it could even do it at all.

Another aspect is the impact on the workers. While it's true that some workers preferred having the overtime work, because it meant sizeable increases in their paychecks, the increases in productivity also translated into more money. Bonuses that were tied to productivity increased, so the workers were getting additional money without spending any additional time at the plant. Plus everyone who wanted to made it to the game on Sundays.

There's planned downtime and unplanned downtime. Unplanned is whenever equipment can't be run due to a malfunction or some other unexpected reason. Planned downtime, in contrast, occurs for intended reasons, such as worker breaks, shift changes, scheduled maintenance or cleaning, and set-up changes. An example of a set-up change, which is also called a changeover, is when you need to stop processing one grade of product and start working on a different grade.

One thing this company discovered was that changeovers were taking longer than planned. The plant had allotted 15 minutes for certain product changeovers and although there were times when it could do it that quickly, there were more times that it took 30 minutes or even an hour. Once you start taking this much extra time for changeovers several times a week, it starts adding up. So the company examined the situation. It turned out that tools, components, and other items often weren't readily available. It was a simple matter of not being diligently organized. So the company made a comprehensive list of everything that would be needed and made absolutely certain that everything on that list was exactly where it should be to facilitate efficient changeovers. The result was a significant reduction in changeover time.

It turns out that the analysis also uncovered the fact that frequently there were unplanned changeovers. So the company looked further to see what was causing this and saw that a variety of things were happening. For one thing, sometimes the plant would be in the middle of producing a certain product when it would run out of a raw material. The company was using offsite warehouses to store some materials, and on occasion, a delivery would be late, causing the shortage. So the plant had to stop work on that product and set up for a different one. Then it would continue work on that interim product until the raw materials arrived. Once the materials were available, the plant would shut down again and changeover and return to the original product.

Another problem concerns packaging. If the plant was supposed to be putting the soft drink in individual cans, but suddenly ran out, it would stop and changeover to bottles. Still another issue is the sequencing of production. In order to reduce the need for cleaning the equipment, products should be processed in a specific sequence, doing the cleanest process first and the dirtiest last. But if these unplanned changeovers mess up the sequence, additional cleaning time would be required. Even if these changeovers take only 15 minutes and the extra cleanings take only 30 minutes, they add up and before you know it, you're working on Sunday.

The right computer system helps you schedule production in the most efficient manner in the first place, with respect to minimizing changeovers and cleanings. Then it helps you plan the delivery of raw materials and helps you ensure that you have everything you need to complete all of your runs. In this case, this meant making a more detailed schedule for their offsite warehouse and transportation company. The additional detail was critical because the plant had limited loading dock space. Without careful planning, there would be a logjam of delivery trucks backed up in the lot. All of this work allowed them to make longer runs, and significantly reduce the number of changeovers needed.

A Paper Mill

Paper machines are large, expensive, and complex. They take a bunch of pulp at one end and produce a wide continuous sheet of paper at the other end that's constantly being rolled up and taken away. Given that these machines involve so much capital expense and that they run at such a high speed, paper companies put a high priority on avoiding downtime.

Paper mills routinely make paper of various grades on the same equipment and the machines continue to run while the grade changeovers occur. The main distinctions between grades are the thickness (or the caliper) of the paper and the weight of the paper, which is called the "basis weight." In order to produce a different grade of paper, they have to make adjustments that control the caliper and the basis weight. Since the machines are running constantly while the adjustments are being made, they end up with some paper that isn't exactly one grade or the other. Sometimes they can find a buyer for this paper, but it's generally considered to be waste. So, in order to reduce material waste and to reduce the amount of time that waste paper is being produced, they try to make these changeovers as quickly as possible.

Automation has allowed companies to make some big advances in this area. One of the main methods used is to start by creating historical profiles of the best grade changeovers that they have done in the past. They create this record by collecting data from many sources. This data is carefully analyzed, cross-referenced, and put into context, with particular emphasis not only on discovering waste and loss, but also on discerning the root causes of any waste or loss. Then they try to replicate the precise techniques, the settings (things like machine speed and dryer temperature), and the order of events that have worked so well before. One thing to remember is that any paper mill may have several different grades of paper it regularly produces. One implication of this is that a changeover from Grade E to Grade B isn't necessarily the same process as a changeover from Grade C to Grade A. So there can be several different types of changeovers that they study to see how each one can be done best. In effect, they are establishing a description of best practices for making changeovers.

INFORMED DECISION MAKING

Collecting and analyzing the key data in real time are parts of a larger effort called informed decision making. Managers get paid to make decisions, but good decisions require good information. One general example of how this applies involves the fact that many manufacturing plants produce products of different grades of many products, such as orange juice, cheese, paper, motor oil, and paint. This may not always be apparent to consumers, because the different grades are commonly sold as separate brands. People often realize that they're buying a lower grade when they purchase a less expensive brand, but for the most part, they would just as soon not think about it in those terms. So everyone is happier without the words "Lower Grade" printed on the package.

In the plant, having different grades of the same basic product presents both problems and opportunities, plus plenty of decisions to be made as a result. One common opportunity starts this way: While you're in the middle of producing a high grade product, you discover that there are problems. The opportunity is that you can salvage the work you've done by downgrading the product and selling it to a different customer. But here is where the decisions can get tricky. You're in the middle of the batch or production run, so you want to finish it, but you're suddenly behind schedule in getting the higher grade product produced, since this batch has been downgraded.

Your first decision is: Do I make the grade changeover immediately or keep running until I've finished this batch and then make the changeover? In order to make a good decision here, there are all kinds of information that would be helpful. You would want to know how other lines are scheduled and if the schedules can be shifted around in any way. You would want to know if you have all of the raw materials needed to immediately start another high-grade batch, because it would be really frustrating to get the line changed over and discover that you should have gone ahead and finished the batch you were working on.

This is really only the beginning of the complexity involved in many plants on a daily or even hourly basis. Having the right information at your fingertips can be a tremendous advantage, and the right software package can provide this for you. Decisions around grade changes are just one example of the benefits that come with good support for informed decision making.

Cutting Paper with Real-Time Quality Data

One challenge faced by many paper companies is that different customers have different tolerances for their quality specifications concerning such characteristics as caliper, basis weight, opacity, moisture, and more. If papermaking were an exact science, this would never be a problem. The reality is that paper has inconsistencies. As paper initially comes off of the big machines, it's wound onto reels, which may be hundreds of inches wide. You can think about all of the paper on a reel in two ways. First the paper starts at the core and comes out to the outer edge, and that is called "machine direction." You can also see that the paper extends from one side of the reel to the other, and that is called "cross direction." The reels have to be cut into rolls before the paper is delivered to customers, but the roll that comes from the left end of the reel might not have the same quality characteristics as the second roll cut from the reel, which means that the quality is not consistent across the reel. It may also be the case that the quality is not consistent from the beginning to the end of each roll.

The task of the paper companies is to monitor the quality, so that they make certain each customer gets the paper they require in terms of quality. Some customers have more tolerance for variations in caliper than other customers. In other cases, the customers have differing restrictions on how much the opacity varies. This means that a roll of paper that would be rejected by one customer would be accepted by another. In practice, the problem is that too many rolls have to be scrapped, downgraded, or put into inventory, because they can't be sold immediately.

The real problem has been that they couldn't predetermine the quality until after they cut the rolls from the reel, and the rolls are cut specifically to size to meet specific customer orders. So, if they cut a roll from the left end of a reel to the size needed by customer A, but then find out that the roll doesn't meet the quality requirements of that customer, they may have to scrap that roll. Customer B might be willing to take paper of that quality, but they want the roll cut to a different size.

The availability of real-time quality measurement has changed this situation dramatically. This software capability allows paper companies to monitor the quality of the paper before the rolls are cut from the reel. This information means that they have a map, so to speak, of the reel in terms of quality, and they use this map to see which parts of the reel should be used for which customers. If they know that the left end of the reel has some significant variations in terms of caliper that aren't present in the middle of the reel, they can determine which part of the reel should be used for each customer.

Reducing Overpack through Statistical Process Control

Any package of food or a container of a beverage indicates how much the package or container should hold. If you buy a canned soft drink that says 12 oz., you expect there to be 12 oz. in that can. The FDA has specific regulations that establish the parameters for passing inspection concerning the volume or weight of food and beverage products. For example, it may be acceptable for the net weight in some packages to be slightly under what the label says, but there can only be a certain percentage of those shipped to the customer. For example, 1 box per 100 boxes may be allowable to be shipped underweight.

The difficulty is that measuring something like cereal is not an exact science. There will always be some variance in the weight of the cereal put into different boxes. So the practice at many companies had always been to go a little over weight, just to be certain no boxes were under weight. If the box says 10 oz., then they would shoot for 10.1, 10.2, or 10.3 oz. This extra amount is known as *overpack* or *giveaway*. Obviously, this is an area ripe for improvement. If you can reduce the extra product you're putting into your boxes, you'll save big bucks.

This is where statistical process control (SPC) comes in concerning weight control. Some cereal manufacturers took samples of their product and weighed the samples on a scale that would show weight to a finer degree than they normally measured. For example, it would show 100ths, instead of only 10ths. Using this information, the SPC system could spot trends and set target limits, warning limits, and control limits. Next the system established rules that stipulate how many data points above or below these limits are allowed before an adjustment should be made to the control point. The aim is to monitor the process that puts the product into the bag and adjust it as needed to ensure you always get enough, but never too much, overpack.

There are two ways that this works: open loop and closed loop. With open loop, an operator gets the results from the system, makes a decision based on those results, and perhaps makes an adjustment manually. In a closed loop, the operator is taken out of the process. The system takes the results and uses an algorithm to make the adjustment automatically.

Some products are particularly difficult to weigh. One example is frozen dessert topping, because it's relatively light. In this case, it's very difficult to keep the overpack low. After a close study, the company making this product determined that the amount of the product it was giving away had definitely gotten out of hand. It started by trying to refine the effectiveness of its existing equipment. Then it put in a closed-loop SPC weight control system that included a high-speed weighing device in the production line. Each tub was weighed and this real-time information was immediately analyzed so that trends were spotted quickly. Then, through the closed-loop mechanism, a command would be sent to the filler nozzles to make ever-so-slight adjustments to get the amount being packed back within acceptable limits.

Here again, even a small percentage improvement can have a tremendous impact on savings. Let's say that each tub is supposed to have 10 oz., but you have routinely averaged 10.1 oz. simply to avoid shipping under weight products. If you bring that average down even to 10.05, you have in effect saved 1 tub for every 200 you produce. Multiply that by the tens of thousands you produce each week by the weeks in the year and the savings are immense. And it does not have to stop by getting the overpack down to 10.05 oz. You can continue to inch your way lower still. This company found this use of SPC weight control so valuable that it decided to apply the technology to its production lines for every product in the entire plant. The main cost of using this software tool comes with the first application. Expanding it to other lines is much less expensive.

Controlling Moisture Content through SPC

Moisture is a critical element in the making of croutons. The wrong moisture content can have several negative consequences. Croutons that are too wet will not take a coating the way they should. More moisture means a higher density, so the same volume of product weighs more, and this messes up the volume-to-weight ratio used for packaging. Finally, too much moisture can even affect the taste and, as we have already noted, consumers expect products to taste the same every time, no matter what. If something tastes a little strange, there's a good chance some buyers will avoid that product in the future.

Controlling moisture is no simple matter, because there are various factors that must be managed. For starters, remember that raw grain, which is the basic ingredient of croutons, can vary widely in its moisture content. So depending on how wet it is originally, you have to adjust other ingredients and processes. For really dry grain, you may adjust the coatings to add more moisture. Then depending on the moisture content after cooking, you will have to adjust the ways the dryers are set, such as the heat of the dryer and the speed of the conveyor belt that takes the product through it. The same goes for other steps in the process.

In order to determine moisture content, samples are taken at certain time intervals and tested. Then this information is put into the system and adjustments are made in response to the data. The basic method is not substantially different from what was done before. The significant difference is the level of detail and the sophistication of the computer analysis. By testing at more stages in the process and testing more frequently, the company got a firmer grip on how moisture content varied. The computer program could alert the company to trends and provide specific, highly detailed instructions for adjusting the equipment to compensate for the variances.

Using KPIs to Support Informed Decision Making

In the food and beverage industry, KPIs are concentrated on productivity, cost, inventory, delivery, yield, labor, safety, customer satisfaction, and employee morale. Here are examples of key points for some of these categories:

- Productivity focuses on cases per hour, tons per hour, cases per person-hour, etc.
- Cost is broken down per batch, per ton, per case, etc.
- Inventory looks at the length of time products stay in inventory.
- Delivery concerns on-time percentages.
- Yield involves measuring percentages of material coming in per product going out.
- Safety includes matters such as lost-time incidents.

By careful examination of KPI data, you can spot trends, uncover waste issues, pinpoint productivity gains and losses, detect small problems before they become larger, compare data week-to-week, month-to-month, and quarter-to-quarter, and in many other ways gain valuable information for managing the business effectively.

One company that found KPIs to be indispensable had the problem of collecting all of this information manually and then manually generating a report. Generally, it took a week to complete one report, so it was always looking at KPIs that were a week old. The labor involved was daunting. The company would have some people who collected the data. Then other people were employed to analyze the data. But the company wanted the information badly, so it was willing to commit the resources necessary to do it. In addition to the difficulty of collecting and analyzing the data and having it be a week old, the company didn't have any good way to save the data and make it continually accessible for additional analysis.

All of this motivated the company to seek an electronic method of managing the entire KPI process. The first thing this does is allow the company to collect all of its data into one central data warehouse. The collection methods include:

- Hooking up the PLCs in the control systems directly to the KPI system
- Having some data entered manually
- Employing bar-code, wireless, and handheld technologies
- Using forklift-mounted terminals

Once all of the data is in, it has to be analyzed through a series of calculations to produce the key performance indicators.

The result of the analysis is contained in reports. In the past, the reports produced were limited to the basic standard set of parameters. This report would be used by anyone and everyone. With the use of computer technology, a variety of reports can be provided. Different people in the company have different needs and the system can be instructed to accommodate those needs. For example, one person might want data that pertained only to certain days, not for the entire month; for only certain products, not every product produced; or for only certain lines on certain days when certain products were run. The potential for isolating data and combining data is endless. The data can be easily transformed into various kinds of easy-to-read graphics, such as pie charts, bar charts, and graphs. Plus, there are levels of depth to analysis and some methods are much more complex than others. The right computer software will allow you to perform extensive statistical analysis in highly sophisticated ways.

One additional feature of the KPI system concerns the concept of *visibility*. By using displays that mimic the dashboards of cars or the cockpits of airplanes, the computer system gives you immediate readings on the most critical KPIs of your choice. When you drive a car, with just a quick glance to the dashboard, you can know the speed you are traveling, the level of fuel in the gas tank, the temperature of the engine coolant, the amount of charge in the electrical system, and how many miles you have driven. The dashboard for your manufacturing plant can tell you at a glance the number of cases produced, the length of time spent running each product, the status of each line in terms of whether it is running and what it is running, the yield percentages, the number of shipments made, and more.

REDUCING WASTE THROUGH SUPPLIER INTEGRATION

One of the critical elements in the supply chain is the relationship between a manufacturer and a supplier. In Chapter 1, we talked about JIT and how it revolutionized the way manufacturing companies manage inventory. We should look more closely at how this works, because the effectiveness of having vendors deliver supplies just in time for a manufacturer to use them hinges on close collaboration between the supplier and the manufacturer. Computer systems are an essential part of this, for they allow companies to become much more closely linked to suppliers.

JIT, which is part of the larger concept known as *lean manufacturing*, actually produces savings that go beyond reducing inventory costs. Given that the manufacturing process adds much of the value to any product, having that product sit in inventory means not only carrying unnecessary inventory costs, but also failing to get a timely return on the labor and machine capacity costs. Through sharing information such as inventory and production scheduling, plants can produce more closely the amount of their products that are needed at any given time. Demand drives production, as opposed to the goal of keeping an inventory well stocked. The close collaboration between manufacturers and suppliers through computer-enabled sharing of vital information allows everyone in the supply chain to function more efficiently.

Suppliers work with manufacturers closely in other ways besides the timing of deliveries. Manufacturers share data concerning quality requirements and make agreements for the supplier to test their products to ensure they meet the requirements. Given that formulas, and thus quality specifications, can change at any time, it becomes critical to maintain current information between the manufacturer and the supplier.

Looking at an example will allow us to highlight some of the important points about collaboration. Suppose you sell vitamins and minerals to a cereal company. If you look at the nutrition label on any box of cereal, you'll see a long list of vitamins and minerals listed there. The cereal company buys these in formulas from vendors, but unlike the cereals themselves, vitamins have a short shelf life. And unlike the main ingredient, which is generally some type of grain, vitamin and mineral formulas are expensive. So you have this expensive product that has a short shelf life, which means it would cost you a lot of money to simply make tons of it and keep a huge inventory. In that case, how are you supposed to deliver your product at the drop of a hat when the cereal company's purchasing department gives you a call? What if you could get on your computer, hook up to its system and see exactly how much of your product the plant has in stock at any time? If you see that it's getting low, you can plan to make some more, even before the cereal company calls to order it.

But that isn't all. Many smart managers are taking it a step further and letting their suppliers see production schedules. If you knew not only the plant inventory, but also when the plant was planning to make more cereal, this would help you be even more efficient in your own production scheduling. Then, what if the manufacturer was willing to share its recipe? If you know the cereal maker's needs, you can suggest a cheaper, more efficient way to meet those needs, such as a less expensive vitamin formula or a way to use the same formula for more than one cereal. This gets into sharing product specifications. You may tell the manufacturer that your research and development (R&D) labs have come up with this wonderful new formula, but that it will require a change in the nonfat dry milk formula currently being used, because this new vitamin formula doesn't work with that specific nonfat dry milk. Maybe you can even suggest better dry milk as well. This is true supplier collaboration. This sort of supply chain collaboration and visibility has resulted in huge savings in all kinds of ways, one of them being reduced inventory costs. Our focus may have broadened in this discussion from the specific point of attacking waste streams, but reducing waste is one benefit of supplier integration and collaboration, and none of this can be done without the right IT systems.

Achieving success with collaboration requires a big shift in the traditional industry mentality, which has always been to play your cards close to your chest. Extensive partnerships of this sort require a level of trust and cooperation that isn't that common. A willingness to allow people from outside the company to have access to vital company information is new. The standard mentality is the same one anyone would have who was shopping around at car dealers for a new car. You wouldn't want to give any dealer any information about what other dealers are offering you. You are dealing with a true commodity and you want to force the various car dealers to compete by lowering the price. But the smart manufacturers have realized that the materials they purchase aren't always commodities, strictly speaking, and that there are big advantages to working closely with vendors. Our experience is that the risk is well worth the payoff. Stealing formulas or making inappropriate use of proprietary information is rare. The worst that may happen is that a vendor sometimes makes mistakes managing the inventory.

REDUCING WASTE THROUGH MANAGEMENT OF QUALITY

If you're still relying on inspection as your sole quality control technique, you're in the dark ages. There's a long list of problems with this approach. For one thing, inspection occurs after everything is done. You may be able to find some of your mistakes this way, but it's way too late to prevent them. And you can't even find all of them. You may be able to prevent some bad products from getting to the market, but you can't inspect every single item. Quality control is another area where real-time data collection and analysis is critical.

Let's say that you get a customer complaint about one of your cereals. The consumer is the ultimate quality inspector. The complaint could be anything — the cereal tastes burnt or like charcoal, it's stale, it's brownish or dark, or the almonds are overcooked — you name it. How do you deal with this? Without sophisticated computer-based quality control methods, you would first have to somehow find out where the cereal was made and when it was made — which plant and on whose shift. Then you could talk to the cooker in charge of that batch and ask how it went. The cooker would have to look at his log book and might tell you that everything went fine. Maybe the batch got overheated at first, but that was a minor aberration in the cooker's view, so it didn't get noted.

Then you ask the plant manager where the wheat came from, because you know that wheat from one source near the plant has a high moisture content, while wheat from another source many states away is shipped on rail cars for days and arrives drier than 20-year-old bones. The plant needs to know this sort of detail, so that cooking methods can be adjusted accordingly. You also might want to check when the cooking bin was last cleaned, given that the danger of residue from a cleanser could affect the cooking process. Maybe during your talks with people at the plant someone says, "You know, I think that batch came through just when we started using the new film to make the plastic bag holding the cereal inside the box." New film? No one checked with you about using new film. The purchasing department found a way to save some money on film, but didn't check with production about how different films interact with the cereal. When asked about this, purchasing says, "We knew this film used a slightly different chemical preservative, but we didn't figure that would matter."

If you had the quality systems you need, you could track down the problem in no time. You wouldn't have to ask the cooker about the cooking temperatures, because they would all be recorded. You would have data on moisture content, wheat source, cooking bin cleaning schedules, etc. If you got a number of customer complaints and you tracked all of them, you might see that every batch came from Cooking Bin 12. And getting this information could be done quickly on the computer terminal in your office. In the end, the really important point here is that you would probably never get the complaint in the first place, because a bad product would be discovered before it ever got out of the plant and into the consumer's hands.

In the past, companies didn't even attempt to find out the cause of many problems. If a customer complained, the company would apologize and send out a coupon for a free box of cereal. What was the point of spending a lot of time to determine the cause of something that happened weeks ago? It was a waste of resources. Between the time when the problem occurred and when the complaint came in, so much could have happened that it would be impossible to find out what happened anyway. The equipment may have been cleaned again or had maintenance work done on it. If no more complaints were coming in, why bother?

Will ERP give you this detailed data and lead you to these root causes? In a word, no. This gets back to the ledger-driven nature of ERP and the nature of the data that ERP systems collect because of that design philosophy. ERP can tell you which day you bought the wheat, how much wheat you bought, who sold it to you, how much it cost, and how much you consumed. It will give you dates, not minutes and seconds. It will give you dollars, not temperatures and pressures. It will tell you where the wheat was stored, but not extensive data about how it was processed. To get at root causes, you need data about what happened *and also enough data to provide a context to what happened*. To achieve this, you need good manufacturing IT systems. With the appropriate systems, you can use all of these tools to substantially reduce waste and operating costs.

PROVIDING NEW CAPABILITIES

Reducing costs is only half the story. Manufacturing IT today provides tremendous opportunities for bringing new capabilities to your company. If you can deliver goods in 1 day instead of 2, if you can offer your product in a variety of sizes while your competitors only offer one size, if you can increase your reliability so that your delivery times or quality guarantees are more secure, or if you can enhance your company's ability to meet regulatory compliance, you will have provided a valuable new capability to your company. As it turns out, you may also cut costs in the process, but our focus now is on how various applications can add value.

The Use of Overall Equipment Effectiveness

The idea behind overall equipment effectiveness (OEE) is that you are trying to manage your capital equipment so that you maximize its productivity. As a metric, OEE is defined to include three components: availability, performance, and quality (see Table 4.1). *Availability* measures whether or not equipment is running when it is scheduled to be running. *Performance* measures the capacity of the equipment; this can be illustrated by thinking about a car. The car may be running, but if it can't go faster than 10 mph, then it's not performing well and may be almost or entirely useless. *Quality* measures the quality of the products produced by the equipment. OEE is expressed as a percentage, combining the percentage of the equipment's availability, the percentage of its performance, and the percentage of the quality of the products it produces on its first pass.

Major food and beverage manufacturers find OEE valuable because it helps them increase capacity without increasing costs by giving them information about the source of problems around availability, performance, and quality. It works as a money saver because it helps them increase capacity by doing more than simply examining these three components. As the company continues to grow and increase its market share in many different areas, it's common for a plant manager to report reaching the limit of the plant's capacity. The implication is that the plant needs a new line, some new equipment, and some additional personnel. "I've got to have a new packaging line to go on the end of my processing line. I need two new packaging machines." The cost for these changes starts in the millions of dollars and goes into the tens of millions.

It could turn out, however, that the plant's capacity hasn't reached its limits. The OEE metrics can help establish this fact. Simply by having this critical knowledge provided by OEE, one company has saved millions of dollars in capital expenditures. For example, think about having 10 lines that are making tea and deciding that you need another line. But first, you look at your OEE numbers and discover that the percentages aren't

Table 4.1 Overall Equipment Effectiveness

OEE = Availability x Performance Rate x Quality Rate
(Expressed as a percentage)

so good. If you increase the capacity of each line by 10%, you will have the same capacity gained by adding another line. The savings can be enormous.

Improving Customer Service

For years, a paper company that made two basics types of paper and sold it in large rolls had wrapped and sold the paper in the same basic way. At one point, however, customers starting asking for it to be packaged differently. For one thing, customers who had previously been willing to cut the rolls down themselves started asking for the option of buying the rolls already cut. For example, they might request that one large roll be cut down into five smaller rolls and that all five rolls be packaged together as one large roll. Another customer might want only four small rolls, but want them packaged individually. Add to this other packaging variations, such as the straps needed on each roll, the side cardboard, the outside wrapping material, and the labeling. The possible combinations of all these options quickly became enormous. It wasn't just that different customers wanted rolls in different ways, some customers even wanted a wide assortment of roll sizes and packaging options within one order. So the company was facing the challenge of cutting and wrapping rolls in ways that it had never bothered with before.

The solution was to build a packaging line that could handle all of these demands in steps along a conveyor. Then the company created a computer system that would take the customers' orders and track the rolls through each step of packaging so that each order was shipped as requested. All of the steps, including printing the labels, were hooked into the computer system. It was highly successful. Customers were impressed by the company's ability to send them whatever complicated mix of items they requested.

Reducing Set-Up Times

The amount of time spent setting up a line should be kept to a minimum. That goes without saying. Doing all of the things that help minimize set-up or changeover time is not always as simple as it sounds, however. Scheduling is one part of this. To do a changeover efficiently, you need to know in advance when you will be doing it. This means knowing when the product you are currently running will be finished. Next, you need to know what you'll be running next, so that you can have everything at hand needed to set up for that product.

One company approached this by putting in some relatively simple computer systems that were designed to provide this information. An operator could tap into this system to find out the current status of the production run, when it will be finished, which product will need to be run next, and everything needed for the changeover to occur efficiently.

Imagine that you're the operator in charge of making yogurt. If you look at the computer and see that you're about to change from vanilla to strawberry in 2 hours, you know that you'll need to get the strawberries out and have them handy. You may also know that this changeover means using a different nozzle, so you get that out and have it ready. The details go on and on. Having this information readily available helps everyone work more efficiently.

Scheduling Package Changes

Think about the fact that some cereals are constantly changing the person or cartoon character staring out at you from the front of the box. Another thing many cereals do is add coupons, games, toys, or prizes to the boxes. And even though the person pictured on the box changes, the cereal is the same. Some boxes have this prize, others have a different prize, but the promotion is all with the same cereal. So this presents a particular packaging challenge for the plant.

This is where a computer system can help out. First, you can use the system to set up the basic schedule for making a specific cereal. You can have this schedule show the details of how many boxes get this toy, how many get that toy, how many have this box design, how many have these coupons, and so on. By hooking this system up to your production equipment, you can track everything as it happens. Operators can monitor production and manage things very efficiently.

Optimizing the Use of Raw Materials

As a food item in your home, dry dog food is rather plain and simple. Manufacturing it, however, isn't so simple. There are a variety of ingredients that make up the recipe and the end product has to have certain amounts of protein, vitamins, minerals, fats, and so on. These components of dog food can be altered by adding certain ingredients during production. At one company, in order to ensure that each batch of dog food has the required levels of each component, it routinely puts in more than is really needed of some ingredients. In the same way that boxes can have too much overpack in order to ensure no box is under weight, batches of dog food can have too much of certain ingredients in order to ensure no package of dog food has less protein, vitamins, and minerals than it should. Although these methods were effective for producing a good product, the company decided that it should be able to reduce the excess components while still making the same quality of dog food.

The first step was to set up tests for all of its raw ingredients, so that the company knew exactly what each one would contribute to the overall quantities in each component category, such as protein or minerals. In all, the company was testing for about 25 components. Next, it established a starting point, made a batch according to the recipe, and tested the batch to see how it came out. This process provided a baseline from which to make adjustments.

The trick at this point was to use the mathematical process of optimizing equations. In this case, the company wanted to minimize the cost while keeping all of the components at the required levels. The problem is complicated by the fact that different ingredients can vary widely in cost, so adding a miniscule amount of one ingredient can cost more than adding a significant amount of a different ingredient. The result was a good example of real-time formulation optimization.

This company found that it could save thousands of dollars per shift, per line, per plant throughout the company. That's how much money was being wasted by adding too much of various ingredients to over-achieve their targets for the required components. Even though the computation involved can be quite complicated, the system is easy for operators to use.

Improving Production Performance and Quality

There's a flavored drink plant that focused on high-volume, low-cost production. The plant ran a limited variety of products, but it ran them continuously 5 days a week, 50 weeks a year. The goal was for this plant to be the main worldwide source for these products. Any excess demand would be met by having employees work on weekends or with another plant entirely. Given that the plant was intended to be a low-cost facility, the budget didn't allow for money to be spent on overtime pay. Another part of meeting the low-cost goal was to keep wastes down, while maximizing yields, quality, and productivity. So it was continuously looking for ways to cut costs further. Anytime the plant managers could tighten the belt one more notch, they would.

One of the things they discovered was that each time they started up after a changeover, there was a fair amount of waste with the first batch. The analysis process helped the company discern what was working and what wasn't. There are a series of tasks that must be completed with each changeover, but these tasks vary according to the specific products involved, both the product that just finished being run and the product that is about to be run. It turned out that changing over from Product A to Product B took a good bit longer than changing over from Product A to Product C. And this is actually the simplest representation of a rather complex set of variables. The computer system also helped show ways to increase yield, reduce waste, and increase productivity.

The system works by doing several things. First, it assists with the changeovers by listing everything that should happen with each type of product. It also tracks all of the data concerning the set-ups: what products are involved, which equipment is being used, how much waste was lost, and how long they take. Then the system can process the data to track trends and provide historical analysis. Everything can be tied together — the schedule of maintenance, the set-up trends, equipment performance, dips or gains in productivity, rises or falls in yield percentages, downtime, quality, packaging, and delivery. All of this information is given in real time and can be provided easily in all kinds of reports.

SUPPORTING REGULATORY COMPLIANCE

When you pick up the morning paper and see that a drug company has agreed to pay *$500 million* to the government for repeatedly failing to fix manufacturing problems at its drug plants, you begin to understand that regulatory compliance is a very serious matter. For good reasons, there are extremely strict rules about the manufacture of drugs. Procedures must be followed to the letter and documentation has to be bulletproof. If you are in charge of a batch and something goes wrong, you should know how to correct the problem. There's a lot of money involved, so you do what is needed to correct the mistake and the product is fine. But wait! What if your method of correcting the problem isn't allowed under the established procedures? It doesn't matter that the product is good; if you failed to follow the correct procedures, then you're liable for accusations of noncompliance. One of the problems one company faced was the remote chance that some drugs were lacking a key ingredient. As far as the FDA is concerned, remote isn't good enough.

How do you prevent these problems? There are several applications that apply to batch management and execution. Once installed, these will not let you deviate from the rules, or they will let you deviate only within certain established parameters. To get an idea of how this works, consider this procedure for starting your car: Go to the garage, open the garage door, open the car door, get in the car, close the car door, put your seat belt on, put the key in the ignition, and turn the key while simultaneously depressing the accelerator pedal. The point is that these systems walk you through the order of events and force you to sign off on each step. The program wants to know if something has been done, who did it, when it was done, if it worked correctly, if there were any errors, and so on. Complying with regulations requires that you have extensive and conclusive records. Every step you take needs to be documented and recorded, so that you can demonstrate that you are indeed following all of the procedures.

If you don't have to deal with the FDA, you may have to be prepared for inspections by the USDA, the EPA, or at the very least, OSHA. Handling these matters can be overwhelming. We know of one paper company that estimated that complying with regulations without the aid of computer software would have meant adding an average of 20 people per paper mill. Having the right manufacturing system to support regulatory compliance can mean a huge savings on staff along with a successful compliance record.

Electronic Compliance with the Cluster Rules

The Cluster Rules are a group of regulations that took all of the Clean Air Act and Clean Water Act legislation and produced a group of specific restrictions in terms of such matters as discharge limits. The paper companies are required to constantly monitor and report their compliance against their limits or licenses concerning effluent streams into the air or the water.

The way this works is that companies obtain licenses or permits that allow them to discharge certain amounts of specific pollutants over a certain period of time. Then they're required to constantly monitor and report their emissions in order to verify that they're remaining within their limits. In the case that they exceed a limit, they have to explain what type of remedial action they will take to rectify the situation.

One important advantage of having a real-time quality environmental-compliance management system is that it tracks all of your emissions against your licenses, so you can constantly gauge where your emissions stand in relation to what you're allowed. This system will give you a warning whenever it detects a trend toward exceeding the limits. This means that if you're past the halfway mark in your emissions, but short of your halfway mark for a time period, you will know it, and you will know that you need to find a way to cut back to avoid a noncompliance event.

Another benefit is that these systems make reporting a snap. As opposed to manually collecting the data and filling out reams of compliance forms for both state and federal regulatory agencies, the computer system produces the needed documentation at the touch of a button. This feature alone has dramatically reduced the labor involved in handling regulatory compliance for most paper mills. The ability to measure and report emissions in real time combined with the ability to provide documentation make this software highly valuable to paper companies.

Creating and Maintaining Regulatory Documentation for OSHA 1910.119

This federal regulation specifies how companies must handle hazardous materials used in their plants. There are several parts to this. First, companies have to maintain data sheets describing every hazardous material that is used. These sheets, which identify the dangers of the materials, must be available to every employee. Companies also have to document all of the processes in which the materials are used, including diagrams of piping and instrumentation.

Manually maintaining all of this documentation is a huge chore. Handling it with computer software, however, is much more manageable. The use of CAD (computer-aided design) systems and databases designed to accommodate regulatory compliance has streamlined this entire process. With these tools, it's both easier to create the documents and to maintain them.

CONCLUSION

Manufacturing is the neglected piece of the supply chain, but it doesn't need to stay that way. There are all kinds of ways for today's manufacturing companies to achieve real payback for investing in manufacturing IT systems. The payback may be cutting costs or adding value. In many cases, it is both.

What exactly are these systems? We have mapped out where the veins of gold run, so now it's time to describe the tools needed to mine that gold. Our next chapter offers a detailed examination of the IT systems that can be used to improve the manufacturing process.

5

THE PORTFOLIO

THE INTEGRATION CHASM

In the last chapter we laid out where the gold lies and in this chapter we will talk about the tools needed to mine it. An ERP salesperson will tell you that ERP has these tools, but we obviously don't agree. However, ERP is an established system and it does reach into the plant in various ways, so any attempt to install new manufacturing systems must be done within this context. ERP has modules that start on the path to addressing warehouse management, production planning, materials management, and product quality information (see Table 5.1). In order for the ERP system to work effectively, it has to have some plant information. It has to know about material movement and consumption. It has to monitor actual production, which means it has to know recipes and production orders. It also must have a quality Certificate of Analysis (COA) and material disposition data in addition to information on asset history and work order generation. The problem is that ERP modules fall short, because they're not designed from a manufacturing point of view and, as a result, they commonly don't get fully implemented and integrated into the plant's operations. Once ERP is installed, there's frequently a chasm between ERP and the plant's real requirements.

BUILDING A BRIDGE BETWEEN ERP AND THE PLANT

The solution is to bridge this information gap, and the way to build the bridge is to get the best manufacturing systems fully integrated into the company's existing IT structure. You don't just have to take our word on this. Gartner, the research and advisory firm, has stated that the return on an ERP investment can be increased by as much as 50% through integration with real-time plant information. Given that ERP investments run into

Table 5.1 Points that Plant-Centric ERP Models Address

Some plant-centric ERP models can begin to address:
- Warehouse management
- Production planning
- Materials management
- Quality

But there is an integration chasm to cross ...

many millions of dollars, increasing the ROI by 50% — or even 25% — could mean millions of dollars in added benefits. The Gartner report listed these methods for unlocking the potential of integrating the plant with the ERP system:

- Data collection with radio frequency and bar code devices
- Communication with both process control and SCADA systems
- Communication with lab, process, and quality systems
- Simple user interfaces for the plant floor
- Real-time manufacturing performance measurement
- Plant-level collection, analysis, and reporting of data

There are manufacturing systems that will do all of this and do it well. Install and integrate the systems you need and you'll have built a bridge over the chasm, as illustrated in Figure 5.1.

THE PORTFOLIO

There are five major areas where manufacturing systems can play a pivotal role. We call these five groupings of IT functions the Portfolio. The systems that make up the Portfolio are the key to bringing a significant ROI to

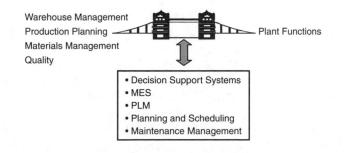

Figure 5.1 Bridging the Gap

manufacturing IT today. While these five areas are not mutually exclusive and distinct in every way, they largely correspond to concentrations of functional requirements that are generally accepted within manufacturing. The five groupings are:

- Manufacturing Execution Systems (MES)
- Product Lifecycle Management (PLM)
- Decision Support Systems (DSS)
- Advanced Planning and Scheduling (APS) Systems
- Computerized Maintenance Management Systems (CMMS)

Two points should be stressed. The first one is that these five classifications cover the *major* areas of manufacturing IT, not *all* of the areas. Every plant is different, so there may be other systems needed to round out the Portfolio in some cases, but our work has shown us that these are the most common ways to fill in the gaps left by ERP.

The second point is that the Portfolio is a portfolio of *functions*, not *vendors*. You may choose to work with several vendors or with just one vendor. There are valid reasons for both approaches. Many people in the IT community use what's known as *the portfolio process* to identify a selection of vendors and to set standards concerning these vendors and their products. This process is well established and has been especially beneficial to large companies. The focus of this chapter, however, is *not* on the process of choosing vendors. Regardless of whether you end up using one or several vendors, you still have to address the same functional issues. Our goal is to address the functional solutions that will help your company improve.

The idea of the Portfolio started years ago when most manufacturing companies saw their IT staff start to shrink. It was then that support of IT systems became a major issue for these companies. In the 1980s, a large company with 20 to 30 plants had a different version of software in each plant, even though the basic purpose of the software was the same. Plant 1 had Product X, Plant 2 had written its own software, Plant 3 was bought from another company and was still using the system that company made or bought, and so on. There was a hodgepodge of systems spread throughout the company's plants. Nothing was standardized. This may not have been the most efficient way to go about handling plant systems, but there were reasons that it evolved this way, and as long as the plants had sufficient IT personnel, these systems could be supported.

But, as we explained in Chapter 2, one of the big changes over the last 20 years has been that IT resources have been pulled out of the plant. As this happened, plant managers began to realize that they could no longer continue business as usual. They just didn't have the staff needed to deploy and support so many different pieces of software. If you have 20 plants with 20 different systems that are all in charge of monitoring quality, why not come up with one system that is used in all 20 plants? With 20 different systems, you need 20 different people who know each system; but with one system, one person can be in charge of them all. This brought about the push for developing a common suite of applications, which came to be known as the Portfolio. They wanted standard software that was going to handle specific functions in every plant where the need existed. If they needed quality control, then they knew which package to use, no matter where the plant was located. They couldn't have IT people at every plant, so they had to form a central group to be in charge of implementation and to provide ongoing support.

Not every company has made this evolution. Computer technology has advanced so fast in so many areas that just keeping abreast of the changes is no small feat. In the 1980s, if a team of computer engineers talked about setting up a comprehensive custom manufacturing information system for the plant, they were looking at a monumental task. This effort could require something like 10,000 hours of work writing lines and lines of code and take a couple of years to complete. It could cost several million dollars and there could be an enormous risk associated with delivering the right functionality on time and within budget. Eventually efforts to reduce the labor-intensive nature of providing systems for the plant resulted in the software "toolkits" of the 1990s. The vendors of these toolkits may have promoted them as COTS software, but no one who used them was fooled. The toolkits sometimes had enough of the systems in place so that the labor of getting them up and running was reduced, but it was probably only reduced by half at the most. It would still take approximately 5,000 hours of work, at least, to produce a functioning system for the plant. Today, there are fully functional and configurable COTS software applications on the market that will address almost all of the functions we list in the Portfolio. The need to write a custom code application is now rare.

Sadly, many manufacturing company executives, and also their IT specialists, remain in the dark about the range and scope of the specific COTS products for manufacturing that exist. ERP has succeeded as a universal solution because the dollar transaction challenges it addresses are more universal than the challenges faced by the plants. Whether your plants are producing cars or drugs or cheese, you still have many of the same issues around financial, inventory, and purchasing transactions. But the IT needs of a plant that makes cars are substantially different from the IT needs of a plant that produces cheese. Every ERP vendor is offering more or less the same product. It's all there in one nice, neat package. It all works together and it's all tightly integrated. In contrast, manufacturers face a big headache putting together all of the plant systems. There are only limited and emerging industry standards. While it's true that ERP is not strictly ruled by industry standards either, it has become somewhat standardized from the influence of the American Production and Inventory Control Society (APICS) and the business principles taught by that organization. Standardization may come to the rest of manufacturing IT, but that development still lies in the future. The challenge today, as illustrated in Figure 5.2, is finding the right pieces of the puzzle to fit the needs of your plant.

Manufacturing Execution Systems

Manufacturing execution systems (MES) handle a variety of functions, all of which are connected to the flow of work in the manufacturing process. MES stands at the heart of the entire Portfolio (see Figure 5.3), since it deals with everything directly pertaining to the basic elements of running a plant. To this end, a good MES will collect data concerning all of the fundamental aspects of the manufacturing process, including machines, materials, people, costs, and results. It will also provide context to this data so that the information collected can be critically analyzed. This context is essential, because the value of raw data is marginal at best.

Of all five pieces of the Portfolio, MES has the broadest range of applications and thus it's the least distinct. The very name, manufacturing

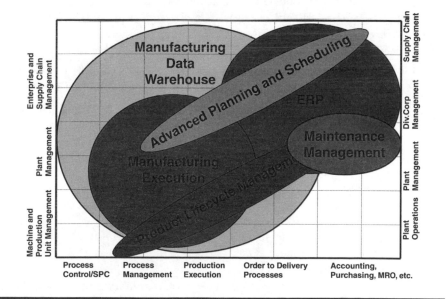

Figure 5.2   AMR Illustration (Source: AMR Research. Modified with permission.)

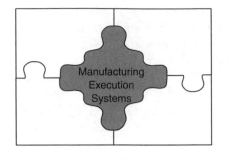

Figure 5.3 The Plant Portfolio — MES

execution systems, can mean different things to different people. "Execution" is used both in broad and narrow terms, depending on the context and the speaker. The matter is further complicated by the fact that many MES functions overlap with the functions of the other four pieces. And given how much the actual work of manufacturing can vary from industry to industry, there is a great variation in the ways MES can be approached.

In the end, regardless of how the term is used, the real point is the functions that need to be addressed. Software packages that handle these functions will come and go and the labels assigned to these packages come and go with them. The functions, however, remain and have to be dealt with one way or another. So, don't be overly concerned with debates over terms such as "execution." We think that manufacturing execution systems is a good label, but our goal is to help you get the software you need for your company, no matter what it's called.

Given that MES can be defined in different ways, the next step is to provide a good picture of this valuable software tool. We'll start with listing some basic qualities and then we'll look at the history of MES and see how it developed. Next, we'll examine the ways MES can be structured to fit into various industries.

MES in a Nutshell

MES is a computer software system that will help manufacturing companies manage the following tasks:

- The flow of work in the manufacturing process
- The collection and analysis of data generated by and during the manufacturing process
- The creation of a genealogy record of manufacturing — materials, machines, people, costs, results

- The management of critical events and decision points in the manufacturing process, including quality states and unexpected changes

In order to manage these tasks, MES performs the following functions:

- It manages work orders or production orders.
- It maintains material use and material status information.
- It monitors and analyzes quality information.
- It collects data and puts it into context so that the data can be used both for real-time decision-making and for historical analysis.
- It manages work flow, work queues, and provides general schedule visibility.

To get a bare bones idea of how this plays out, consider the following scenario. The sales department tells the ERP system or some other system that a customer needs a certain product, in a certain quantity, and by a certain date. The manufacturing plant then gets a work order, a production order, a recipe, or the like from the ERP system and then MES takes over. It creates a plan for which resources need to be used, how production will be routed through the factory, what machines will be used, which shifts will be affected, and when the product will be ready for shipping. After the work order is released and production starts, MES tracks and reports the process in real time. If there's a quality problem, it can be spotted quickly. If production needs to be interrupted, MES can change the work queue accordingly. All through production, MES records the materials used, the equipment performance, the quality status, and the shipping status. Once the job is cleared for shipment and is gone, MES has completed this round of production.

The History of MES

Although it may be impossible to create one definitive model for MES, a look at some of the attempts can be informative. The first thing to understand is that the terminology itself isn't consistent. If we look back at the CIM Pyramid (see Figure 5.4), we see that the vaguely defined Level 3 was called Plant Systems. This is the start of an idea of manufacturing execution systems. This pyramid model was replaced by a model that has only three parts, the AMR 3-Layer Model (see Figure 5.5). In this case, the term execution is used for the systems that function between the control computers in the plant and the corporate planning computers at headquarters.

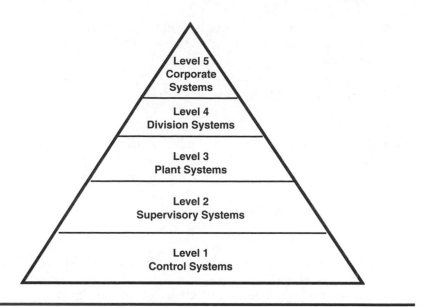

Figure 5.4   CIM Pyramid of the 1980s

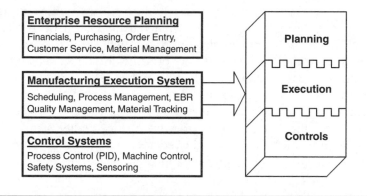

Figure 5.5   AMR 3-Layer Model (Source: AMR 1992. Used with permission.)

The problem still remained: What exactly was execution? A subsequent model, the MESA Functional Model (see Figure 5.6), took a big step toward defining what manufacturing execution actually involved. Created by the Manufacturing Execution Systems Association, this model acted as a laundry list of functions needed in manufacturing plants. In order to be successful in the factory, a computer software system needed to have some combination of the elements listed in this model.

As a list of functions that should be considered in putting together an execution system, the MESA model worked well. You may not need every function listed, but you should consider each of them as you evaluate

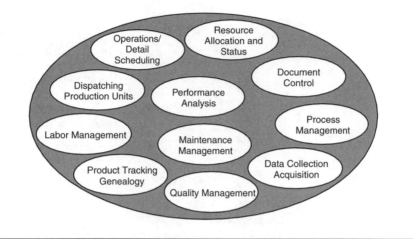

Figure 5.6   MESA Functional Model (Source: MESA. Used with permission.)

your company's requirements. On the other hand, the image can encourage "silo thinking," where the web of connections is ignored. For example, the model lists Dispatching Production Units, Operations/Detail Scheduling, Resource Allocation and Status, and Process Management as separate functions, yet they cannot be handled separately in practice.

In an attempt to get a more accurate representation of the complexity of the manufacturing process, AMR came out with the REPAC Model (see Figure 5.7), which gives some idea of how work originates and flows in a plant. The idea of "Ready" is thinking about what you're going to do, how you're going to do it, where you're going to do it, and what you're going to use to make it. The point is to consider all of the materials, labor, time, tools, and equipment that will be needed.

Then "Execute" is the management of the production process. This is always complicated by the fact that nothing ever seems to go according to plans. Even at Step 1, changes may be necessary, so the execution of a plan has to include the ability to make adjustments to the plan. "Process" refers to the actual work of manufacturing the product. "Analyze" is critical because that is when you come back and figure out what you did, how well you did it, and how you can do it better.

With "Coordinate" there's a micro level and macro level. At the micro level you're using real-time feedback to coordinate everything necessary to get this production run completed. At the macro level you're using historical analysis to make adjustments that increase overall productivity and performance. Micro is the last 5 minutes; macro is the last 12 months. Micro is "I just made 93, but I need 100, so I need to make 7 more." Macro is "Shift 2 always makes 100, but Shift 3 never makes more than 93, so we need to give our attention to this problem."

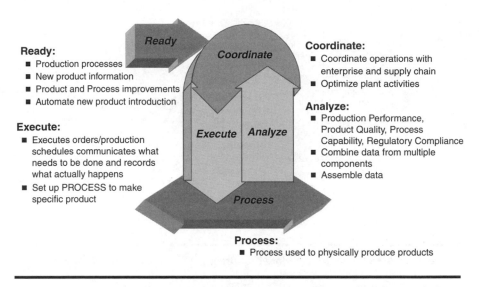

Ready:
- Production processes
- New product information
- Product and Process improvements
- Automate new product introduction

Execute:
- Executes orders/production schedules communicates what needs to be done and records what actually happens
- Set up PROCESS to make specific product

Coordinate:
- Coordinate operations with enterprise and supply chain
- Optimize plant activities

Analyze:
- Production Performance, Product Quality, Process Capability, Regulatory Compliance
- Combine data from multiple components
- Assemble data

Process:
- Process used to physically produce products

Figure 5.7 AMR REPAC Model (Source: AMR Research. Used with permission.)

Even though no one has managed to create a generally accepted, standardized functional model, these attempts prompted people to think in more detail about which IT programs were needed in the plant. As a result, there are now mature COTS applications that address many of these functions. The lack of standardization for functionality remains, however, because of the breadth and differentiation of requirements from industry to industry at this functional level. Each COTS application still has its own configuration process and its own database. In spite of the difficulty, efforts are being made to find common views for ways to integrate the various MES products with corporate systems. A good example of this is the effort of the ISA standards committees to establish common functional definitions and interfaces based on business processes as seen in S88 and S95.

The purpose of reviewing these models is to give you some idea of the evolution of MES and of the difficulty of reaching a common consensus on what MES is. Say "MES" to five different people in manufacturing IT today and it's a safe bet that each of them will have a different idea of what it means. By continuing to add a greater number of specialized modules for use in manufacturing, ERP vendors are trying to stake their claim to the role as MES providers. The engineers in charge of controls in the plant sometimes push from the other side, expanding their HMI/SCADA systems to address more operating functions. They call this MES. The software industry has matured to such a degree that there are all sorts of MES vendors today, many of which claim to have the "one, true MES." Despite the presence of a wide assortment of MES commercial off-the-shelf products, some people insist that the only fully functional MES is one created with custom code.

You may think that the best bet for finding an authoritative definition of MES would lie with the Manufacturing Execution Systems Association. The problem here is that MESA now stands for Manufacturing Enterprise Solutions Association. The name change corresponds to the fact that their new aim is to encompass a range of applications that goes beyond execution. For many people, MES is now the entire range of applications that are covered by all five parts of the Portfolio, not just the functions centered around managing work orders. Organizationally within corporations, there are now MES groups or departments and directors of MES strategy. In these cases, the scope of their responsibilities is everything involved in manufacturing IT, not just execution.

It goes without saying that this can be very confusing to anyone trying to decide what computer systems to buy for the company's plants. Our goal with this book is to dispel some of that confusion. By taking all of the IT functions needed in the manufacturing environment and breaking them down into the five parts of the Portfolio, we hope that a clearer picture emerges. For our purposes, the term MES is used for the execution tasks we listed in our nutshell definition. Now, in order to get a firmer grip on how MES fits into your business, let's look at how MES varies from industry to industry.

Three Characteristics of MES

If you conduct an exhaustive search of all of the MES packages available today, you'll be looking at around 20 different vendors, each with a different product. One way to sort them out is to examine them according to three characteristics (see Figure 5.8):

1. Vertical industry capability
2. Functions
3. Implementation design

Vertical industry capability means that you can't expect any single MES package to work equally well in all vertical industries. A failure to recognize this fact from the start can be the recipe for big troubles later on. Although vendors realize that their products fit particular niches, if a customer is just a little outside of the niche, some vendors will still try to make it fit. Every MES grew up in a particular industry and several are clearly the industry leaders in their vertical markets. But they vary a great deal in what they can do. It's strictly a matter of fit. The best MES in the world in one vertical market could be an abject failure in another vertical

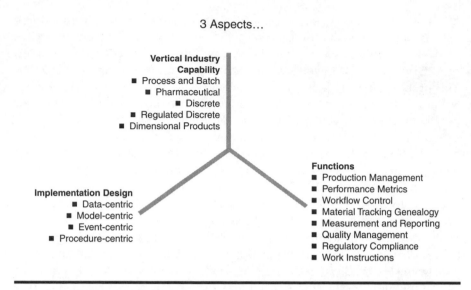

Figure 5.8 MES in Terms of COTS

market; there's not one single MES package that will cut across all vertical markets. Some MES packages do have overlap for more than one vertical market, but none stretch over all industries.

In general, you can characterize a MES by its fit with one of the following industry categories:

■ *Continuous process and batch process* (packaged food products such as cheese, margarine, beverages, specialty chemicals) — Although there are some differences between what's required for continuous processing vs. what's required for batch processing, these two types of manufacturing have similar functional require-ments.

■ *Pharmaceuticals and life sciences* (over-the-counter drugs, prescrip-tion drugs, injectable drugs) — The most critical functions for these industries concern regulatory control.

■ *Discrete manufacturing* (durable goods such as cars, electronics, fans, chairs, etc.) — There are more similarities than differences concerning the functional requirements of a broad range of different discrete industries.

■ *Regulated discrete* (aerospace, parts for the manned space program) — Here critical functions are more centered on regulatory require-ments and record-keeping than on the process itself. This group is separate from pharmaceuticals because, even though the focus in both is on regulatory control, the production processes in each do matter and they differ tremendously.

- *Dimensional products* (paper, film, fiber sheet, woven products, certain metals, roll products) — These products have a critical dimensional aspect that's a central element of the manufacturing process.

Within these five categories, there are subcategories that further narrow the functionality required. The reason that no vendor can create a "one size fits all MES" is that the requirements are different, depending on the manufacturing sector, the type of product, and the type of manufacturing process that needs to be supported. Ignoring this fact dooms you to failure.

Consider the fact that making cookie dough and making some drugs can involve strikingly similar manufacturing processes, but the MES needed for each is drastically different. The drug maker is intensely focused on regulatory compliance and doesn't care much about efficiency, downtime, or productivity. The focus instead is on creating a detailed batch record that the FDA will accept as an assurance that the quality control is flawless. The cookie dough maker, on the other hand, is focused on getting the product made cost effectively. His margin is really low, while the drug maker's margin is gigantic. A cookie dough MES is made to respond to different functional requirements than the drug MES. Or take a MES designed for a turbine manufacturer and put it into a paper mill and it's a disaster, because it can't deal with the dimensional aspect at all.

An Example of a Good MES in the Wrong Environment

This company makes wine and is vertically integrated, which means that it not only makes the wine, but also makes the bottles and bottles the wine itself. The company wanted to use a MES to help manage the manufacturing process in its bottling facilities. The process entailed bottles coming in, being filled with wine, being corked, and then being put into cartons or cases that would be packed up and shipped out. The company's goals with the MES were to track downtime, uptime, production, lots, changeovers, and SKUs. The company needed to track the SKUs because the same wine went into different bottles that had to be shipped to various regions and states around the country. The complication of putting the same wine into different bottles was necessary because labels may differ from state to state and the company has some brands that are marketed regionally.

The company went to a vendor that was based in the region and whose MES had a good track record in the electronics industry. The problem was that this MES was suited to a situation where there are multiple components being routed through several work stations and assembled to make the finished product. The orientation of the system is the bill of materials and the assembly. In a wine bottling plant, however, there is not much of a bill of materials. There is just the bottle, the label, the wine, and the cork. Since there aren't multiple components, there's no routing from one workstation to the next. There's one single production path through the plant. The entire focus is to fill the bottles as efficiently as possible. So this MES didn't meet the company's needs at all. It couldn't be configured so that it collected the data needed without requiring a lot of cumbersome work. It turns out that the original vendors sold the wine company a bill of goods, promising that this MES would work great in a high-speed bottling plant, when there was no good reason to think that it could handle a manufacturing environment substantially different from the electronics industry. One important lesson to glean from this is that you can learn a good deal about the design of any specific MES by looking at some of its existing installations.

Functions simply refers to the software capabilities provided. Any commercial off-the-shelf MES will have some set of the following functions:

- Production management
- Performance metrics
- Workflow control
- Material tracking and genealogy
- Measurement and reporting
- Quality management
- Regulatory compliance
- Work instructions

Implementation design concerns the fact that the structure of each MES is affected by the goals it's attempting to achieve. In other words, there are guiding principles to the design. The functional capabilities are structured in such a way to produce the overall results needed for each situation. There are four classifications for implementation design:

1. Data-centric
2. Model-centric
3. Event-centric
4. Procedure-centric

Data-Centric

Data-centric systems build everything by starting with the data and going from there. They take process data, real-time quality data, user inputs, plus other similar data and build a system by putting context around it all to create useful information. The guiding principle of the design is the need to have all of the data readily available with the appropriate context. This allows the data to be used in all kinds of ways to construct information that in turn is used to build functionality. Vertical industries that find this approach attractive include quality-focused process manufacturers, food and beverage, pulp and paper, and consumer products. The plants in all of these types of companies generate tons of data, so it comes as no surprise that they find data-centric systems a good fit.

To get a good sense of how this works, think about making cookie dough. The process data would include temperature, pressure, flows, batch time, rotation, speed of rotors, batch profile, and things such as when steam was used, how long it was used, and how hot it was. Real-time quality data would include viscosity, sugar content, moisture, fat content, and density. You might take a sample halfway though the batch and have the lab test it immediately for all of these qualities, thus giving you real-time quality data. User inputs are involved when an operator adds extra sugar, vitamins, yeast, chocolate chips, or coloring agent. If the test coming back from the lab reveals that the sugar is low, he would put more sugar in manually, first scanning the sugar and then typing in the amount.

The data is collected and organized to provide meaningful context. Say that there is a quality problem — maybe some of the cookies came out not tasting sweet enough. You have the temperature, pressure, sugar content, when the sugar was put in, for every minute of every day, but you need data only for a certain situation. Right now, you're not interested in the temperature curve for the last 6 months; you need it for only the last batch. You want to know the test data for when the batch started and when the batch ended. You want to know if the equipment went down while the batch was running, how long it was down, if the equipment was clean, when it was last cleaned (just before the batch or 6 weeks ago), what materials were used, which lot numbers were on these materials, which tools were used (the big propeller or the small propeller), who was operating the equipment, and more.

Having ready access to this data can make all the difference in the world when it comes to solving quality problems like this. However, not every MES will tell you which propeller was used. Some companies don't need that capability, but others do. Defining exactly what you need to know is a formidable task and we talk more about that in the final section of the book. The first point to be made here is that you have to know what your needs are before you choose a MES. Otherwise, you will be in danger of getting a system that cannot do what you need it to do. You could end up with a process control system that knows the motor speed, temperature, and pressure, but cannot tell you anything else.

The second point to be made is that context is everything. A piece of data alone is almost worthless. You may have collected data and can see that the batch temperature was 78°, but you need to put that with other data such as the precise time the batch was at 78°, how long the temperature stayed 78°, what temperatures have been recorded for other batches, whether the ingredients were altered for this batch, if there were other irregularities during the process, and so on. If you can't put some context around 78°, then that one bit of data gets you nowhere.

Providing context means being able to gather data from multiple sources and organize it according to your needs. You may have a lab system that knows you did a test on a sample of cookie dough concerning the sugar, fat, vitamins, and other qualities at 7:00 P.M. on Friday. Then you also have an MRP system that issued the materials, telling you to use this lot of this, that lot of that. Context is putting all of your data together and saying, "Ah ha! Batch 10206 is the culprit for the customer complaints we've received. Now we need to find out everything we can about this particular batch and what exactly went wrong."

A good data-centric MES will give you the ability to collect the data and to put it into context. It will take mountains of data and turn it into information. This information is then used in turn to build the applications that perform functions. All too often this hierarchy is reversed; instead of letting the data requirements guide the functions, the functions are established first. Then the already established functions determine the scope of data collected. In contrast, the data-centric implementation design puts data requirements at its core and works out from there.

Model-Centric

The model-centric MES operates on the idea that by building a computer-based model of the plant, you can see every option for the flow of work through the plant. Everything in the system grows out of this model. All of the transactions, all of the events, and all of the data that is collected are driven by a dynamic model of the manufacturing process; this model manages and drives the workflow of the plant.

The point here is that in certain industries, there are multiple routings that a production order can take through the plant. It could start on Line 1 and go to Lines 3, 4, or 5, then go to Lines 6, 7, or 8, then go to Work Centers 14, 15, or 17. It is evaluated at the work center and depending on what else is required, it could go to either Work Centers 18 or 19. Finally, it could be packaged on Lines A, B, F, or G of the 14 packaging lines. In all, there can be a remarkable range of options for getting work through the plant.

With a model-centric MES, you can dynamically route production orders through the plant so that you make the best use of capacity. It's the nature of manufacturing at some plants that production schedules are changing constantly. Sometimes work takes longer than scheduled; while at other times, it's done ahead of schedule. Maybe a machine breaks down or there's a quality problem somewhere. Given that the best plans are always vulnerable to unforeseen events, the ability to alter production routings can be a boon. The model-centric MES gives you the flexibility to alter routes, so that you work around all of these events and make the best use of capacity, eliminating waste, reducing work-in-process (WIP), and debottlenecking as much as possible.

In order to do its job, the model used by the MES must be constraint-based and capability-based. It must constantly examine the current status and progress of work through the plant as measured by work orders and units of production. On top of this, it has to know how those capacities and capabilities relate to each specific product being made. And it has to give you the information in real time so that you can make decisions about switching this to there and that to here.

Tires are a good example. The first step is making the rubber. It's made in two machines that produce all of the rubber for all of the tires. This is the main bottleneck, because everything else depends upon it. Then there's a component building section where there may be two or three machines. If one machine is backed up with work, some of the work may be sent to other machines. Consider that MES will know that Machine D can produce 80 tires an hour, while Machine G can produce only 20 an hour. When you have 20 finishing machines, how do you queue everything up? A good model-centric MES will tell you the most efficient way to do this.

This type of MES isn't the right fit for every plant. Car manufacturers don't need this type of model because there's only one basic production route through the plant. The bottling plant mentioned before is another good example. It has no use for models, because once again, there's only one way that work flows through the plant. Companies that benefit from the use of a model-centric MES include manufacturers of electronics and semiconductors as well as discrete manufacturers who have processes that can be consistently modeled.

Event-Centric

Every manufacturing process is a series of events. The design of event-centric systems is based on the idea that events should be the reason for collecting data. An event can be starting or stopping a batch, a production order, or a production run. It can be having a downtime, taking a reading every 30 minutes, changing from one SKU to another SKU, or changing from one carton size to another carton size.

Events drive the action of the MES. The only thing stored in the MES are events and anything that concerns those events, such as the piece of equipment, the work order number, the batch number, the SKU, and so on. Data isn't gathered from all sources on a continuous nonstop basis; rather, the system is designed to wait until an event occurs before data collection is initiated. An event happens and data is collected surrounding that event. The event may automatically trigger data collection, or it may be necessary for the person managing the batch to enter it, but in either case, the event is the central focus.

While a data-centric MES gives you all kinds of information and you can see when a batch stopped, an event-centric MES tells you outright that a batch stopped and it gives you all of the data surrounding that event. Events are predefined so that the MES can instantly tell you when the batch stopped, why it stopped, how long it took, and everything else you might want to know. Most companies that choose to use an event-centric MES can actually use a data-centric MES as well. The reason that some prefer the event-centric focus is that they have mountains of electronic data and thus they can really benefit from the event-centric functions. Many food and beverage and consumer goods manufacturers find the event-centric approach an appropriate match for their plants. It's also used by some hybrid and discrete manufacturers.

Procedure-Centric

In some industries, such as aerospace and pharmaceuticals, it's critical that plant managers have firm control over the work flow. They need mechanisms to ensure that established procedures are consistently and comprehensively followed and then documented as the manufacturing process is executed. The purpose isn't efficiency, but documentation, control, and support for regulatory compliance. Data and events only exist as they are tied to procedure steps. To meet this need, a procedure-centric MES has the following components:

- Documented work process
- Work flow control
- Record keeping

Remember that one batch at a pharmaceutical plant can be worth many millions of dollars. If you fail to adequately document how procedures were followed, you may have to throw out an entire batch, whether the product is good or not. Documenting every step of each procedure is top priority. It follows from this that the execution systems will be designed around work flow engines or document management systems or both.

Everything is recorded so that you can prove that all procedures were followed. You also have to verify that all equipment operators are certified. A great deal of attention must be given to activities that serve no purpose other than regulatory compliance. The degree of record keeping is extreme. For example, if a seat on an airplane breaks, you need to be able to know who made the metal for the struts 2 decades ago. Everything on an airplane has records that go back 30 years. If a bottle of cold medicine is bad, you have to have complete records on how that batch was made.

One thing that distinguishes a procedure-centric MES is the amount of human interaction. With a data-centric MES, you can manage the entire system after the fact, meaning that a human being never intervenes while all of the data is collected and analyzed. An event-centric MES is not that different, except that it may require some data to be entered manually. In a procedure-centric MES, however, there's constant human interaction. None of the work of the manufacturing process can be done without compliance with the procedure. Every move an operator takes must be documented and the operator must be careful not to do anything outside of the procedure.

Who MES Works For and Why

Manufacturing Execution Systems are being used successfully by a wide variety of companies involved in process, hybrid, and discrete manufacturing. Here are some examples of how various companies benefit from using MES.

Process and Hybrid

- *Pulp and paper companies* — These companies use MES for controlling and managing quality. It helps them be certain that all products meet the required specifications, so that they know only good products are going out their door. They also use MES for production management; this keeps them informed about what they're making, when they're making it, and how it fits into their customers' orders. Another way they use MES is to manage capacity, which helps them get the most out of their paper machines. And given the high capital costs of paper mills, it only makes sense that MES would be used for capital utilization analysis. MES provides pulp and paper companies with the information they need to evaluate the success of capital expenditures. This helps them make well-informed decisions about their next budget.

- *Food and beverage companies* — By providing extensive data about production performance plus the analysis of this data, MES helps food and beverage companies engage in continuous process improvement. These companies also benefit from the way MES uses feedback loops between analysis and execution to control quality and consistency. Another aspect of MES popular in this industry is OEE, which helps companies analyze equipment in terms of performance and efficiency, quality, and uptime vs. downtime. The result is greater productivity and efficiency plus increased reliability, predictability, and repeatability. One of the reasons all of these functions are so important to the food and beverage industry is that raw materials can be such a high cost component of the end products. Milk serves as a good example of a raw ingredient that is a central component in many food products. Given how expensive it is, a small change in a production process that involves milk can have a big impact on the overall cost of the item being manufactured. The industry is also highly automated, so labor costs generally don't dominate, and capacity is not nearly as critical a factor as it is in the pulp and paper industry. Shifts may run less frequently, but when they do run them, they need to have high reliability. For example, if they want to make 50,000 cases and it's going to take them 3 hours and 22 minutes to make those cases, then they want to know that it's going to work exactly that way. They want it to be predictable and repeatable. It's not always critical that they be able to do it any quicker, but they do need to be consistent, so that products are shipped in a timely fashion and customers' orders are filled just as requested.

- *Pharmaceutical and biotechnology companies* — MES provides these companies with the software mechanisms needed to address regulatory compliance. These industries are watched closely by the FDA, and it's absolutely essential that they be able to show proof of compliance. To this end, MES will collect all of the data that demonstrates precisely and conclusively how a product was manufactured and that all rules were diligently followed. Because the financial risk of fines can be so great, pharmaceutical companies will spend millions of dollars to develop finely-tuned flow charts to map and record production. The FDA examines these and monitors them for any deviations from the strict federal requirements. All of this means that these companies need a software system that can ensure all production processes are perfectly consistent and repeatable. For this need, they turn to a procedure-centric MES package.

Discrete

- *Automotive companies* — The use of MES in automotive companies and automotive suppliers includes focusing on labor, rework, quality, and continuous process improvement. They also use OEE to monitor and increase manufacturing performance. One good example of an important MES application is warranty and recall management. Here the MES has to monitor quality and maintain a detailed genealogy. If you supply a part to a car manufacturer and there's a customer complaint that concerns your part, you have to be able to prove you made it exactly to the specifications required. If you can't, then the car manufacturer will charge you for any warranty claims. If you can document that you've done everything according to their specs, you can refute the claim. This is a significant issue. If the switch on an electronic door of a car has gone bad, the maker of the car may have to manage a recall. The issue is compounded by the fact that car warranties extend for more than 5 years in many cases, which is longer than ever before. The longer the warranties, the more chances for payouts. People take their cars in for every little thing if it's still under warranty. If you're responsible for the problem, you don't just pay for the switch replacement, you pay for the total cost of the recall. The right MES can be indispensable in these situations.
- *Electronics companies* — MES is used by electronics companies to manage BOM and routing, work orders, work instructions, capacity, costs, genealogy, scrap, and yields. By facilitating flexibility in manufacturing, MES helps companies meet demands for customization. MES is also the key to managing the development of new products, because tracking and tracing is used to find product failures and respond to customer complaints. Companies need to know if problems occurred during production or if there was a problem with components. Many times components can vary enough between two suppliers that it can be the difference between success and failure, so it's critical to be able to trace that information back to its source.
- *Machining companies* — These companies use MES for managing work orders, engineering drawings, set up and changeover, labor costs, machine time, work queues, quality, routings, production accuracy, and yield. One example of how MES works in this environment is that it monitors *erosion*. Erosion involves any aspect of a production process where quality or performance gradually slips or erodes during the production run, such as a device that cuts something. Cutting occurs in countless manufacturing situations, and the material being cut can be paper, cardboard, plastic, metal, or any combination of

these. In many of these situations, the piece of equipment doing the cutting becomes dull with repeated use. Eventually the production line must be stopped so that a blade can be changed. One way to handle this is simply to plan to change it frequently enough to ensure it never gets too dull. But this might mean wasting time changing the blade when you could actually get more use out of it. Another approach is to wait until you can see that the product isn't being cut sufficiently well, but this could cause you to spoil some of your products. The use of computer software in this situation allows you to monitor the quality of the cutting tool and change it only as often as it absolutely needs to be changed, but never later than it needs to be changed. Over time, this type of capability can significantly reduce costs.

■ *Aerospace companies* — This industry uses MES to manage regulatory compliance, work instructions, genealogy, work orders, labor costs, rework, work queues, and quality. If a product will be used where human life is at risk, the federal government imposes strict rules governing the manufacturing process. Companies have to verify that everything is being done correctly, and they have to maintain extensive records about everything produced. It's incumbent on the manufacturer to make sure that they have established quality standards and procedures for every part of the manufacturing process. Companies also have to make sure they do everything they say they are going to do. If they say that they're going to inspect a floor beam for an aircraft at some particular point, then they have to be able to document that they did indeed inspect it at that point. It could be voluntary on their part, but if they say they are going to do it, they must have accountability and tracability, and MES gives them this.

Choosing the Right MES for Your Company

So, is MES right for your company and, if so, which type should you choose? That depends on a number of factors. Food and beverage companies need extensive data concerning raw materials, pharmaceutical companies need tight management of data that documents procedures, and a bottled water manufacturer might not need much data at all. Pharmaceutical companies are highly concerned about regulatory compliance, but not so focused on managing labor costs. Automotive companies need to watch labor costs very closely, but they don't have to collect data about variances in raw materials the way food and beverage companies do. It's essential that you understand the specific needs of your company.

How do you want MES to drive manufacturing operations and influence behaviors in your company? How can MES help your efforts to improve productivity, increase capital effectiveness, and reduce waste? For example, the particular waste stream issues of a plant could affect which MES is best suited for that plant. On top of all this, you should consider how the MES application will integrate with other pieces of your IT architecture.

Given that this integration question can be a huge challenge, we examine it in greater detail in Chapter 8, but we want to explore it a little more right now. A list of typical ERP functions would include financials, purchasing, human resources, maintenance management, and costing. The list for MES could include production management, data collection, interface with control, downtime measurement, OEE, and statistical process control with statistical quality control (SPC/SQC). But the point is that both lists could include the following functions: product quality, scheduling, production orders, product tracking, WIP inventory, and product specifications and master data. This overlap, illustrated in Figure 5.9, in what ERP offers and what MES can handle, can be a major stumbling block on the path to establishing an effective IT solution for the plant. It is by no means an insurmountable problem. The real danger is simply ignoring that the overlaps exist. If you are aware of the issue, you can use it as a guide as you develop an effective plan for the integration of MES with your ERP environment.

For example, if your company has decided that the ERP system is going to control production work orders, you're only going to create problems if you try to duplicate that function in your MES. In this case, a MES that is weak on work orders could be a good fit, because it would not depend on controlling work orders to make its systems work or to get some of the other functions in place. On the other hand, if ERP's

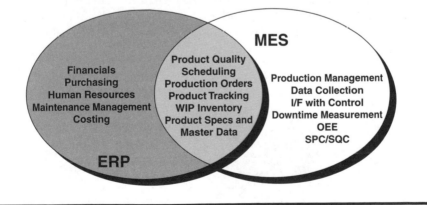

Figure 5.9   ERP and MES Functional Overlaps

reach into the plant has been limited and thus your plant is completely in charge of handling all manufacturing functions and you need detailed production management control at the plant level, you should choose a MES with a very robust production and work order function.

The same holds true for quality management. Who's the final arbiter of quality so that finished goods can be released for shipment? Some ERP systems are designed to maintain a firm grasp on this matter. If the product hasn't been "released" in the ERP quality control module, it's not going to get shipped, and that's that. But the manufacturing and laboratory systems will have to handle the details of quality management in the plant. A case like this requires an interface between the systems and a directive that clearly defines what ERP is responsible for and what MES is responsible for.

Product Lifecycle Management

The best way to get a good idea of product lifecycle management (PLM) is to see it in the context of MES (see Figure 5.10). Many of the functions handled by a good PLM system could be found in a good MES. But, while all of the functions handled by MES are related to the flow of work, the focus for PLM is the product itself. In any number of ways, MES will help you improve your manufacturing processes. It might tell how well a certain piece of equipment is running or how much downtime a specific line experienced last month, but it doesn't necessarily give you the context needed to improve your products. And, after all, the products are the entire reason for the company to exist in the first place.

PLM can help with improving processes in some ways as well, but the point is to provide more specific help toward improving your products. To accomplish this, PLM traces every product from cradle to grave. It's a system that both accumulates and disseminates all the data about the products, starting with creation and development in R&D, continuing

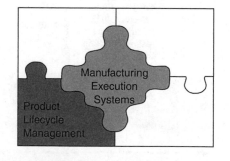

Figure 5.10 The Plant Portfolio — MES and PLM

through manufacturing, and staying with the products as they are used by the consumer. It's every piece of information you can get about every product you have.

Another important characteristic that distinguishes PLM from MES is that PLM is a functional concept, rather than a single product today. The system is assembled from various software programs, not purchased outright as a single commercial off-the-shelf product. The term *product lifecycle management* was coined by AMR Research because companies were already finding tools and programs to meet these needs.

Once assembled, a well-designed PLM system will manage product specifications and recipes, provide production histories, create complete product genealogies (in terms of materials and products and where they were made), and track total product quality. It's also essential that all four of these functions be done in conjunction with each other. A system where production histories and product quality are separate islands would not give you the complete picture. It wouldn't show you the relationships and give you the full analytical capabilities that you need. The separate functions have to talk to each other for the entire system to function properly. The real value of PLM is realized only when it's able to put context around all of your product data and all of your systems.

Where the Data Comes From

PLM is about organizing and correlating data that frequently is already being collected. Most companies have the data, even if it's on paper or spreadsheets. To explain this more fully, let's look at a list of areas that would be covered by PLM:

- Product and raw material specifications
- Production history for products, lines, and machines
- Comprehensive quality history for products
- Laboratory data collection systems
- In-line production and/or quality measurement systems
- Product development history (includes recipe history of various versions and revisions)
- Finished product quality reporting
- Field complaints (this is important because quality checking doesn't end once the product is shipped; field complaints and problems need to be part of this body of knowledge)
- Process analysis (this involves analyzing quality against the process variables at the time of production)
- Change management (this involves controlling the versions of recipes and formulas)
- Cost analysis

Putting the Data to Productive Use

The problem is that many companies don't have the tools to make good use of all this data. They don't have a method for using it in software applications, so it doesn't get put into a meaningful context, it doesn't get reported systematically, and it doesn't help people make better decisions. With the right PLM systems, there are several groups within a company that can put this data to wonderful uses.

Production, process engineering, plant operations, and technical or R&D groups gain valuable tools for improving products and production practices. Through careful analysis of the data, along with additional experiments that are borne out of that analysis, production and process engineering can take some big steps forward. The key is having all of the information in context. If you want to improve your quality process or your material yield process, this body of information is vital.

This means that the plant operations personnel, the people who are actually running the plant, can go into the system and obtain critical information about how the product performs in the process, and use this information to improve the process. For example, if you're making chocolate chip cookies, you can look at everything that happens with making the cookie dough: the raw ingredients, the recipe, the machinery used, the short-term and long-term history of the dough-making process, the quality, and more. You can see what has worked well and what has not, along with the root causes for good or bad performance. A plant manager or production supervisor can review the data and be able to say, "I didn't realize this till now, but when our reactor is set at 125°, we get better dough than at 120° or 130°."

Or say that you have three plants and you want to compare how similar products are being made at all three plants. Maybe the limited information you have tells you that Plant C is producing smaller quantities than your other two plants. Good PLM functionality will help you get to the root causes of the problem. It does this by providing performance data in the context of a specific product, not just in the context of the crew or the line. If you have a corporate-wide PLM system, you can bring a broad array of data together and compare it. What's causing the lack of production at Plant C? The answers don't always come out as you might expect. If Plant A made 800,000 cases, Plant B made 600,000 cases, and Plant C made 500,000 cases, it makes perfect sense to assume that Plant A is the best, but a look at extensive data reveals that Plant A uses twice as much material and Plant B uses twice as much labor, so Plant C has the lowest cost per case. PLM gives you this sort of visibility. And this is just the tip of the iceberg. PLM will give you visibility into why Plant C avoided the excess waste and labor, so that you can use that information to improve production at the other two plants.

For technical and R&D groups, an important question is "Are we producing the products and formulas that match our manufacturing capabilities?" PLM data and analysis provides them with a scorecard to measure their efforts and helps them begin to understand the plants' limitations. Having a clear picture of the company's manufacturing capabilities allows them to make better products and improve existing products. If you're designing a new product and you know the challenges faced by the plant, you might be able to find a way to make the product easier to make. For example, one danger with processing many food items is the danger of burning. Maybe a slight change in the formula that increases the butter fat content will reduce the chances that burning will occur.

Here's another possibility. Maybe there are two different substances that serve the same purpose in a formula, but only one is needed and either one could be used. You look in the PLM database and see that one of these ingredients has a history of being difficult to obtain because the supplier is unreliable. So you make the formula using the other substance and this makes life easier for the plant's procurement people and for production itself, given that production schedules are shot whenever a raw material isn't in stock when it's supposed to be. As this sort of information accumulates, it makes the entire R&D process more efficient.

PLM also comes into play with marketing. If the marketing department is planning to put together a campaign for the new 18-pack of Product X, there are some essential bits of information that must be shared by everyone involved. There needs to be a common understanding of production capabilities, costs, pricing, sales strategy, and so on. PLM can give everyone the full context, so that a marketing campaign is well-coordinated throughout the company.

Collaborative Manufacturing

We've already talked about the importance of vendor relationships. PLM has a major role to play here. Some manufacturers are now using PLM to give extensive feedback to their suppliers about product performance. Companies that are suppliers to other manufacturing companies need to know how their products are performing at their customers' plants. Having this information is critical to their efforts to reduce or prevent problems and it helps them make important product innovations.

Imagine that your company makes brake components for a major automotive company and you want to improve your product for a new car that's being designed. The first step is to have an extensive exchange of information about the design specifications: the exact size and shape needed for the new brake to fit into the design of the new car. At the same time, you're sharing information with some of your suppliers, perhaps the companies that provide you with springs or brake pads. You hear back from your brake pad supplier and he tells you that the pads he makes won't fit. He can make a pad that does fit, but it'll cost a good bit more to rework his equipment. Instead, if you can change your design ever-so-slightly in one way, he has a pad that will fit. So you go back to your customer and share this information. The customer says, "Fine, if it will save us some money. We'll have to adjust the design of the struts, but that won't be a problem." This is the story of today's efforts at collaborative design. A well-designed PLM system makes this process work at its best.

There are plenty of other examples and they're not just from discrete industries like automotive. PLM is used in process and hybrid settings as well. You could be a paper company and you have ideas about making newsprint differently, but you need to work closely with newspaper companies to see if the new product will work on their printing presses. Or, if you're making several different food products that use nonfat dry milk, you will always be interested in any way to reduce the expense of this essential raw ingredient. It may be that one supplier is experimenting with nonfat dry milk formulas that cost less, but in the process of changing the formula, the protein and mineral content changes. For some of your products it doesn't matter if the protein content changes, but the mineral content must stay the same; for others, it's the opposite; for even others, it's okay for both protein and mineral content to change, but it must still be within certain parameters. Without the tools provided by a PLM system, this entire process is 10 times more difficult.

Think about making pipe for use as casing in extremely deep gas or oil wells. In this situation, a product failure can cause huge setbacks and mean massive extra expenses. If any piece of pipe cracks or fails in any way, the pipe company will be desperate to know why it failed and to pinpoint which aspect of the manufacturing process was at fault. This information is essential so that it can make sure it recalls any other pipe made in the same way, given that it could have the same flaws. For the company to be able to trace an individual piece of pipe back through production, it needs to have documented everything that occurred: where the iron ore was mined, which blast furnace was used, which caster, what products were made from each batch, who bought the products, when each product was shipped, and all of the multitude of test results done on each product, among other things. In many cases, companies have to supply much of this information at the time they ship the products. This is done by submitting a COA with each product shipment. Here again, PLM is the tool for meeting these needs.

Collaborative manufacturing is only going to increase and it could go a lot further. It's clear that in some cases the paradigm will shift so that manufacturers will not pay vendors simply for however many tons or gallons were shipped, but that the pay will be based on the manufacturer's actual yield as determined by the performance of the raw materials supplied by that vendor. While this step has not been taken yet, if you want to have truly collaborative relationships with your suppliers, there is a lot information that you will want to share with them, and you will want to share it in a comprehensive way. Implementing PLM concepts is the vehicle for doing this.

Some of the future of e-commerce is becoming clear, and it's moving in the direction of greater collaboration between companies through communications over the Internet on a variety of levels. With more buying and selling being done electronically, it's becoming increasingly important to have information about such things as specifications and as-built quality available in a place where the buyer and the seller can communicate and make it part of the transaction stream. Many companies don't have a single place where all of this information is consolidated today, but they will need this capability if current business trends continue. If you have a PLM strategy fully integrated into your IT structure, you're a step ahead of the game.

The Role of PLM in Contract Manufacturing

PLM also can have a role to play with contract manufacturing. You may want to integrate co-manufacturers with your PLM system so that they can work with you on formulation and recipe management and on quality management. There are several matters to consider. Does the co-manufacturer have different warehouses, different formulation systems, different lab testing systems, and different quality measurement systems? You have to decide if you want to make certain parts of your systems available to them, so that they can perform the necessary functions. You also have to decide if you want to establish interfaces between your systems, or if you want to create another layer of systems, just so that you can provide a basic information exchange between you and them. There isn't really a universal answer to these questions. It's something that must be addressed on a case-by-case basis.

Discrete PLM vs. Process and Hybrid PLM

Despite what some vendors may say, the same PLM package will not work in both discrete and process and hybrid environments. In fact, there are some significant differences between an effective PLM package for a discrete manufacturing company and one for a process or hybrid manufacturing company. While it's accurate to say that both versions are centered around the use of data for the product, that's where the resemblance ends. They have entirely different structures and patterns of use.

For example, a PLM system designed for a discrete environment will focus on work orders. It will coordinate information starting with identifying the specific product being made. Then it will access any relevant drawings concerning that product; produce associated work instructions; and tie in with the BOM, the part number, and the SKU. In essence, it's making sure everyone is on the same page when manufacturing this particular product. A PLM system for process and hybrid, on the other hand, will focus on formulas and recipes. It will coordinate raw material data, quality data, data from testing for process optimization, genealogy data, and more to facilitate the manufacture of the type of products produced in this environment.

Another way to show how PLM functions differ depending on the manufacturing setting is to look at the specific sources of data in both cases. With discrete companies, a PLM system will gather information from the following systems:

- CAD systems
- Product data management (PDM) systems
- ERP or MES for work orders, BOM, and SKU
- Systems that provide work instructions

Compare that to the systems within process or hybrid companies that provide information to the PLM system:

- ERP or MES for specifications, raw materials, WIP, finished goods, and inventory
- Laboratory information management systems (LIMS)
- Process quality systems
- SPC/SQC
- Genealogy systems
- Research and product development systems
- Systems that record consumer complaints
- Cost analysis systems

The main point of making this distinction is to emphasize the danger of trying to fit a PLM package designed for discrete into a process or hybrid environment. Just like with MES, assembling the right PLM requires that you know how you want the package to function for your business. In order to pick the right software, you need to know beforehand what you want that software to do.

Decision Support Systems

The people running manufacturing companies face a constant onslaught of business and production decisions and challenges. They have to decide how to work around equipment failures, which supplier to use, when to launch a new product, and a multitude of other things. The challenges they face can range from how to increase yield to how to decrease equipment downtime and from how to monitor quality more efficiently to how to detect the root causes of waste streams. In every case, the more informed the decision-makers are, the better their decisions will be.

Decision support systems (DSS) provide the valuable information and knowledge that managers and supervisors need to make intelligent and informed decisions. By collecting a wide array of data and then analyzing it and putting it in context, information and knowledge are created. The goal of DSS is to make information readily available to all of the people in the company that need it.

This part of the Portfolio (see Figure 5.11) is similar to PLM in that it is a functional concept, rather than a single COTS product. But while the COTS applications needed to build a comprehensive PLM infrastructure are commercially available, DSS require more creation than just assembly. In this case, we're back to the toolkit era. There are no COTS on the market that will adequately execute the functions we want to include here for every manufacturing environment.

To get an idea of the scope of DSS, consider all the mountains of information that come from manufacturing operations. The following are only a partial list of the places where data is being constantly created:

■ ERP
■ MES
■ Lab data systems
■ Production quality systems

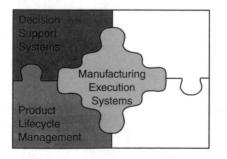

Figure 5.11   The Plant Portfolio — MES, PLM, and DSS

- Process control systems
- Process history systems
- Product specifications

Now think about all of the people who are consuming that data. For example, inside the ERP and supply chain systems, people need data based on actual manufacturing events. Production operations people need data that will enable them to visualize production status and understand historical performance and that will provide comprehensive context for informed decision making. The quality and process engineering people need comprehensive product and process data, such as specifications, as-built quality, and production status. The idea is to create a mechanism that brings all of this information together in one place so that it can be retrieved and viewed in context.

Here are four things DSS should do:

1. *It should integrate data from multiple sources (or applications) and apply context that transforms the data into useable information* (see Figure 5.12). The raw data has to be sorted and combined in ways that give you what you need to know.
2. *It should provide a historical as well as a real-time perspective.* When this is done well, you'll have both a snapshot perspective and a long-term perspective, which is important for analytical purposes.
3. *It should have tools, ranging from the sophisticated to the simple, that allow access by every user within the company that can benefit from using it.* Most manufacturing companies have people who fall all across the spectrum in terms of computer literacy. For this system to work, it has to be accessible to people who can't do much more than use a very simple Web browser and click on links to see static reports. At the other extreme, you may have someone in process

Manual Entry	Labs
■ Applications	■ LIMS
■ Data Collection Points	■ Instruments
	■ Formulas

Automation	Scanners
■ PLCs	■ Handheld
■ DCS	■ Fixed
■ Embedded Systems	■ Vehicles

Figure 5.12   Valuable Data Sources

engineering who wants to do an advanced analysis and needs to extract the data in order to use it in another program like Microsoft® Excel. The DSS needs to be constructed in such a way so that it accommodates both extremes, as well as everyone in the middle.

4. *Finally, it should be supportable.* Maintenance must require only mainstream technical skills, which means that the systems should not be built with any proprietary programs. Stick to standards-based products and technologies. You don't want to be dependent on staff who could leave at any time. Keeping the design mainstream also makes it easier to modify the system as needed. It has to be able to grow and evolve as your business grows and evolves.

Three Levels of DSS

Data collection and analysis can be handled in a variety of ways, but there are three main generic concepts for approaching this task. They are the *process historian*, the *repository*, and the *data warehouse*.

Process Historian

The process historian, which is a class of COTS, collects data from automation and control systems such as PLCs and DCSs (see Figure 5.13). Then it provides a limited amount of context data, such as time, location, type of data, and value. A typical example is temperature. If you make cookies, you may have a temperature probe stuck in a mixer for your cookie dough. Control mechanisms are set to collect values from the probe once a minute, so at 10:00, you know the temperature was 87°; at 10:01, it was 87.5°; at 10:02, it was 86.5°, and so on. The historian will collect massive amounts of data like this and archive it forever. It also can make certain calculations, such as providing the mean temperature over a set time period. Ninety-nine percent of the process historian's data consists of measured and calculated values from real-time measurement and control systems, which makes it a very useful tool for long- and short-term analysis. Every single source of data, such as the temperature probe is known as a point. The ability of process historians to handle hundreds of points per second is similar to the ability of the flight data recorders used on aircraft to record every aspect of the operation of a jet.

Process historians came into being in the 1980s and they were horrendously expensive. An oil refinery might have paid $500,000 to use one. Paper mills, refineries, and chemical plants are the main users of process historians, because they can justify the expense. Food plants, automotive factories, and general discrete manufacturing don't find it to be worth the money. In fact, process historians don't even make sense in a lot of discrete manufacturing. An automotive company won't make enough cars

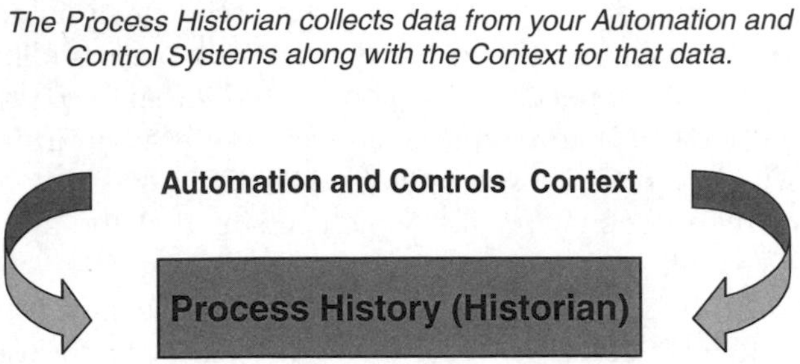

The Process Historian collects data from your Automation and Control Systems along with the Context for that data.

Automation and Controls   Context

Process History (Historian)

Figure 5.13   Process Historian

to justify the expense, but a parts supplier might make enough parts for it to be worthwhile. All of this may change, however, because the price is coming down. Previously, it cost about $10 to $15 per point, so if you have 100,000 points in your plant that you wanted to monitor that would cost at least $1 million. Recently one vendor slashed the price to around $1 to $2 per point. The technology has changed and the prices are dropping. So it may be a viable option for a broader range of companies now.

The benefits of a process historian are that it can handle huge volumes of data from multiple sources and report the data in real time. This means it gives you the ability to notice real-time trends by allowing you to do such things as charting the temperature and then overlaying the pressure and the flow rate. You can also get the data out and put it into other applications, such as Excel, for further analysis.

It does have shortcomings, however; the main one being that it provides only limited context to the data. It'll give you the temperature at 10:03, but you don't know what else was going on in the plant at 10:03, such as who was running the batch, when the batch started and stopped, how the cooker was running, what material was in the cooker, how much material was in the cooker, etc. This means that a process historian's reporting and analysis options are limited. Although it could be considered a database in a very primitive sense, it doesn't offer the traditional database's power of providing structure and showing relationships.

Repository

A repository expands on the work of the process historian by providing more definitions and context to what the data means, and by doing this produces a comprehensive manufacturing history (see Figure 5.14). It tells who did what, why it was done, when it was done, where it was done, which products were involved, and much more about all manufacturing events in the plant. In order to do all of this, the sources of data have to be expanded. In addition to getting data from a process historian, a repository also collects data from scanners, labs, and through manual entry. The focus is manufacturing events, such as starting and stopping batches, and that this batch was run on this piece of equipment and the mean temperature was such and such. The additional sources provide additional data; this means that repositories can provide plant-specific and product-specific context. They function much more like traditional databases, transforming the data into information that supports operational requirements. Essentially every computer software application that is an operational application has some type of repository, but one of the leading ways to implement a repository is through a MES application.

All in all, a repository is a critical step up from a process historian. By providing more context, it turns data into even more useful information. This information is easily accessible for making reports about manufacturing events that deal with such subjects as genealogy, tracking, batch records, performance, and production control. At the same time, repositories require some assembly, because they don't exist completely as COTS. It can be part of a MES package, but even in this case, it will be necessary to handle the integration with other systems. If you want a repository that connects to LIMS data, you will need to make an interface. Sometimes people try to take a process historian and stretch it into a repository, but this is ill-advised, given the limited technology of process historians.

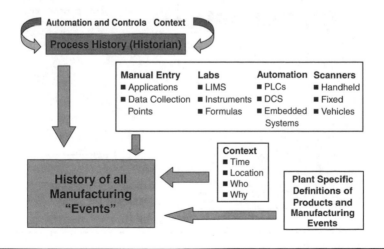

Figure 5.14   Repository

Data Warehouse

The data warehouse is the most sophisticated level of DSS. It gathers data from all potential sources, including process historians and repositories, and integrates it all to provide even more extensive context (see Figure 5.15). While repositories are geared toward operational requirements, a data warehouse takes the repository concept a step further. Data is transformed from being purely operational to having multiple dimensions that support analysis. The idea of multiple dimensions is that the data is gathered and organized according to highly specific perspectives, and this provides windows into all kinds of important issues beyond the realm of operations. The ongoing day-by-day, hour-by-hour, minute-by-minute monitoring of the repository is now enhanced by the ability to perform sophisticated analysis involving broad or narrow perspectives about particular products, raw materials, quality, and everything else.

You have both real-time and historical perspectives. You need real-time data because there might be something wrong with a batch that can be corrected, but it won't get corrected unless you catch the problem precisely when it first starts happening. While real-time tells you a batch is having problems, historical data tells you that the batch you make every Thursday afternoon has something wrong with it. Then, through the analytical tools that provide context to this historical data, you discover that the raw material you use Thursday afternoons comes from a new vendor. All of your other batches use a raw material supplied by your standard vendor. And this is an extremely simplistic example; the software's capabilities are really quite complex.

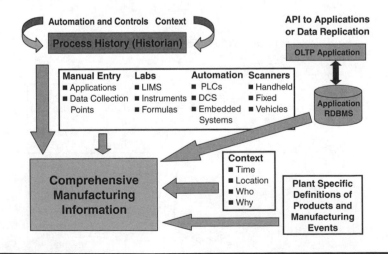

Figure 5.15   Data Warehouse

So the benefits of a data warehouse are significant. It allows you to gain access to information and knowledge in almost unlimited ways, and it's the foundation for building new applications as needed. As expected, however, it requires the most work, since it involves the most interfaces with both data sources and data users. Building a good data warehouse requires more design and maintenance work than process historians or repositories. Every company doesn't need all three layers. The DSS needs of any particular company depend on the data being collected and the people using the data.

The Role of Key Performance Indicators in DSS

Decision support systems are worthless if they don't use the data in ways that support the business. What drives your business strategy? In order to construct a DSS, you have to be able to answer that question first. Once you define your business drivers, you can express them in terms of KPIs, and your manufacturing strategies can be seen as KPI goals. These goals translate into tactical actions. They affect your work processes and produce specific results.

Throughout this process, the DSS is collecting data on everything that occurs, and then analyzing and transforming the data into metrics that provide visibility into what is really going on. This knowledge is immediately accessible online or organized into reports, so that everyone from the shop floor to the corporate offices can benefit. In all cases, the analyzed data provides the critical information needed to make the whole array of important decisions, including real-time decisions as the plant processes are running and going all the way up through annual decisions about what products should be made next year, at which plants they will be made, and whether new equipment or even new plants should be purchased. This knowledge, which could be called the KPI results, reinforces the tactical actions of the plant through the decisions that are made. The ultimate goal, as illustrated in Figure 5.16, is to influence behaviors, change work processes, make actions happen, and get results that satisfy the original business strategies.

Keep in mind that the term visibility is misused when it refers only to the ability to display data. If you don't have analytical tools such as root-cause analysis, then you really don't have visibility into the way your company is functioning. Ultimately, to get the full use of your diagnostic tools, you also need continuous improvement programs (such as Six Sigma, TPM, RCM, OEE) in place. Otherwise, the knowledge you've gained will never be put to use.

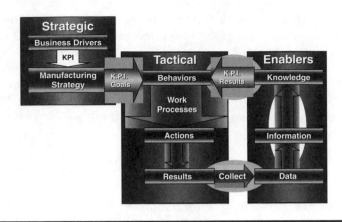

Figure 5.16   KPIs — The Big Picture

KPI Use Cases

People at all levels of a corporation can benefit from the use of KPIs. In general, the types of users can be broken down into these five categories (see Figure 5.17A):

1. Plant floor operator
2. The operator's supervisor (line supervisor)
3. Mid-level managers (functional managers, quality managers, production managers, operations managers)
4. Plant managers
5. Corporate executives

The task is to define the KPIs so that all of these people can use them (see Figure 5.17B). The fundamental question that provides a focus for the content of KPIs is this: What do all of these people need to know to do their jobs well? While a specific answer to this question varies according to each company and each individual, the broad answer is that everyone needs information on costs, quality, efficiency and productivity, and schedule adherence.

In order to help people gain access to the knowledge they need, KPIs commonly function by providing:

■ Awareness and visibility
■ A call to action
■ Analysis and diagnostics

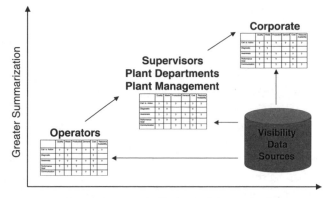

Increasing complexity due to data aggregation

Figure 5.17A Users of Manufacturing Information

	Quality	Waste	Production	Demand	Cost	Resource Availability
Call to Action	■	■	■	■	■	■
Diagnostic	■				■	
Awareness	■				■	■
Performance Goal	■	■	■		■	
Communication	■		■	■	■	■

What are Quality Call to Action KPIs?

Example: Quality Call to Action

- 5 different defined SPC alarms
- 3 different defined SQC alarms
- Contamination detection of any type
- Lot release not processed in 72 hours
- Lot quarantine not lifted in 24 hours for any single lot
- Missing or incomplete vendor COA
- Vendor COA revision or change
- Vendor COA verification sample failure

Figure 5.17B Aligning with Business Goals and Metrics

The fundamental function is to provide visibility or awareness into all aspects of the company. But this alone is only part of the role of KPIs. They also provide a call to action. The nature of the action depends on the responsibilities of the person involved. For the plant floor operators, those are mostly alarms that concern a specific part of a line. The alarm may be based on an event, a trend, a measurement, or some other real-time data. For the supervisors, the scope increases so that they can look for larger issues that may cut across the entire line. Then the focus continues to broaden as the person's responsibilities increase. KPIs also provide analysis and diagnostics, which are driven by either a call to action or a quality improvement program. This involves looking at root causes.

You can use a matrix to construct an effective KPI system. Examine what each person needs and how KPIs can provide this for them. For example, the calls to action and the type of analysis needed will be almost entirely different for the five different categories of users.

The point is to emphasize that for each category of user, there's a difference in granularity of KPI data and in the number of sources that supply data. All of the data for the plant floor operator can come from one or two systems. As responsibility broadens, more systems are involved so that the corporate executive is looking at data from every system being used.

Who Decision Support Systems Work for and Why

DSS works everywhere. What was true about MES is inversely true here. While you have to have the right MES for each company, the same DSS concept works everywhere. Think of a DSS as a dashboard. All kinds of vehicles — buses, tractor trailers, cars, trains, and planes — have dashboards. Driving each of these requires access to different types of information, but no one would try to drive any one of these if the dashboard didn't work.

DSS is process independent, not process specific. Some type of DSS can be put into any continuous improvement process in any manufacturing environment. The principles are universally applicable, because this is an area where the process is largely irrelevant. It's also technology independent. There's no need to have any particular vendor's database in order to apply the concept and the principles. You can use a DSS at the HMI/SCADA or PLC level or with a giant corporate-wide system.

All of this makes the DSS truly ubiquitous. It could work at a bank or an insurance company as well as in manufacturing. It will have to be constructed differently in different situations, but the overall concept works everywhere because everyone can benefit from knowing more about how their business actually works.

Advanced Planning and Scheduling

Everyone has to schedule and plan (see Figure 5.18). The difficulty of this task depends on both the complexity of your manufacturing processes and the size of your company. If you have only one plant that produces a small variety of low-value products on dedicated lines or machines, you

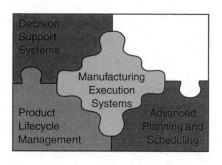

Figure 5.18   The Plant Portfolio — MES, PLM, DSS, and APS

have few changeovers, and you aren't capacity constrained, then something simple like a manual planning board or Microsoft® Excel may be entirely sufficient for your needs. In fact, you would be hard pressed to get a reasonable ROI on the money spent for more sophisticated software.

At the other extreme, if you have several plants producing a wide variety of high-value products on multiple lines and machines, requiring you to make frequent, costly changeovers, and you are at 100% capacity, then you do need something more sophisticated than the old white board or Excel. The potential savings from tracking and reducing waste streams is in the millions, but you have to have the right tools for this job. Advanced planning and scheduling (APS) programs will cost a lot more than Excel, but for large companies that are involved in complex manufacturing, the ROI is usually there.

Planning and Scheduling Paths

APS is a sophisticated, computer-based, optimization model that allows companies to manage planning in complex situations. To get a picture of how it works, think about the entire process of production at a typical manufacturing company and the planning paths involved, as illustrated in Figure 5.19. Everything starts with the forecasts and orders coming from an ERP or supply chain planning system that isn't a part of plant scheduling. The forecasts and orders affect demand planning, which is the basis for plant scheduling. Inventory planning is in turn affected, because you have to make sure you have the materials needed to fulfill the demand.

The next step is rough scheduling and capacity planning. The point at this stage is to take the given demand, fit it into your capacity constraints, and draw up a rough plan for getting the goods made. Then finite scheduling takes the rough plan and works out all of the specific details. As the actual production proceeds, there are feedback loops to finite

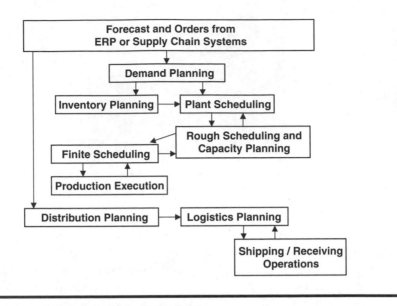

Figure 5.19   Planning and Scheduling Paths

scheduling and then on the rough scheduling and capacity planning. The process of sending real-time information back up the planning path is critical, due to the fact that production rarely proceeds exactly as planned. Without the ability to adjust and revise plans, the schedules already produced become meaningless.

At the same time that planning proceeds down a production path, the original forecasts and orders from the ERP or supply chain system also set plans in motion along a distribution path. Distribution planning comes up with rough plans from the orders and sends these plans to logistics planning, where a detailed shipping schedule is created. This detailed schedule is then used by shipping and receiving operations and warehouses. Once again, a feedback loop is needed between shipping operations and logistics planning, so that changes in the plan can be made as needed.

The Potential Complexity of Scheduling

All of this may sound complicated, but the general description is perfectly simple compared to some of the specifics. Say that you supply widgets to other manufacturing companies around the world. Your European customers want them to meet certain European Union restrictions, your Asian customers need them made slightly differently for the products they make, and your domestic customers are another matter entirely. Due to strict laws in California, you have to make a special widget just for the companies selling products there. In total, including all of the different demands coming from all of your customers, you have over 20 versions of basically the same widget.

Then consider that you have three plants and multiple lines at each plant. Each plant has the ability to make almost all of the widgets, but you've found that it makes the most sense to let each plant specialize in the versions it produces. So orders and forecasts come in and you have to make 30,000 A widgets, 30,000 D widgets, 25,000 G widgets, and 5,000 K widgets in the next week. In addition to dealing with inventory issues, you set up a rough plan that takes into account that lines 3 and 4 at Plant A are down because of maintenance work, all of the lines at Plant B are currently working overtime to make up some rush orders, and Plant C is struggling with a personnel shortage.

In finite scheduling, every detail is nailed down so that you know which line at which plant at which time with which crew will be producing which widget. Of course, once production starts, the need for the feedback loops kicks in. One of the lines at Plant C goes down after a machine part breaks. You don't have a spare part, so you have to have it shipped in overnight. So you shift the production from that line to one of the lines at Plant A. It turns out that another line at Plant A can't get started because a vendor didn't make a delivery on time, so you set that line up for a different widget. You didn't want to do this changeover because this widget doesn't run as efficiently on this line, but it was still the best option you had. All of these changes put crimps in your schedule, so you decide to run some of your lines on the weekend.

Even this scenario doesn't show the full complexity many companies face on a daily basis. Cereal companies sometimes have many different box designs for the same product, so there can be a lot of changes concerning packaging. Paper companies have a history of being highly capacity constrained, so downtime is minimized in every way possible. Automotive companies and their suppliers work on strict just-in-time schedules, so they have to be able to respond to demand in a moment's notice. Many different food manufacturers often use ingredients that can spoil easily and must be used quickly, so their schedules constantly have tight deadlines with little flexibility.

Taking everything into account can be a massive chore. APS software provides the tools you need to make sure you produce the right products at the right time in the right quantities and ship it to the right places. Likewise, it keeps you from making things that you can't sell or don't need.

A final point concerning complexity is the fact that companies involved in contract manufacturing run into scheduling challenges with their co-manufacturers. The challenge is not only integrating co-manufacturers with the scheduling and production planning process; there's also the need for feedback from them to update the status of inventories and to coordinate the execution of the overall production plan. This is complicated by the fact that co-manufacturers may be running different systems, which could cause some systems integration issues. To avoid these problems, companies sometimes choose simply to put their co-manufacturers on the same system they themselves are using.

Determining Your Company's Needs

As we said at the start, a company's need for APS depends on the complexity and the size of the business. The thing to remember is that size alone doesn't imply a need for this type of software. Some large pharmaceutical companies don't have difficult scheduling issues. They produce batches of highly expensive products, but they aren't capacity constrained, they aren't dealing with multiple product lines, and they aren't making frequent costly changeovers. On the other hand, a small specialty paper maker might be a good candidate for an APS system. If they have only one plant and are involved in frequent changeovers to produce a wide assortment of products on several lines that are running at full capacity, the scheduling can get messy really fast.

The need for APS is also something that doesn't break down according to vertical industries. Many food manufacturers definitely need it to handle the scheduling of their multiple products at multiple plants, but if you simply make a limited variety of potato chips, corn chips, and snack crackers all at one location and in the same quantities week in and week out, then you can manage easily enough without it.

For those companies that do need APS, the return on investment can be substantial, as illustrated in Figure 5.20. The savings add up through reduced material waste, reduced labor waste, increased production efficiency, and increased distribution efficiency.

Computerized Maintenance Management Systems

The need for maintenance is something easily understood by just about anyone. Houses and apartments routinely need repair, and every car has to spend some time in the mechanic's garage. When you call a plumber in or you pick up your car from the mechanic, the bill explains what was wrong, which parts were needed, and how much labor was required to make the repair.

Similarly, every plant has physical components of all sorts. There is the building itself, which means walls, door, windows, and a roof, and there are building-related systems, such as air conditioning, steam systems, compressed air systems, chilled or hot water systems, and hydraulics that

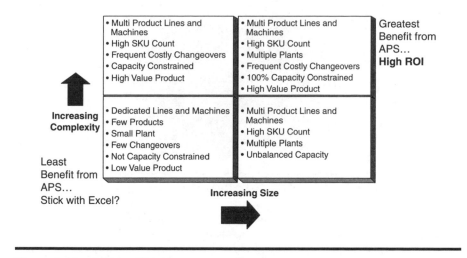

Figure 5.20   APS Justification

run everywhere. Then there is the equipment used in production. This includes process systems, assembly lines, packaging lines, and untold other types of machinery. All of these things are subject to failure of some kind. The roof leaks, the pipes or fittings start leaking, the machine stops running, or the machine keeps running but starts damaging products — you name it, it has probably happened in some plant at one time or another.

In a nutshell, computerized maintenance management systems (CMMS) are designed to handle all of these situations — everything connected to maintenance in any way (see Figure 5.21). In the days before computers, maintenance was handled by having a guy with a toolbox and a clipboard. He walked around, and if someone said a machine wasn't working, he came in, fixed it, and wrote down that he spent 3 hours fixing such and such. A CMMS replaces the clipboard with a system that can increase maintenance efficiency, decrease downtime, reduce maintenance costs, prevent breakdowns, and coordinate everything with other relevant systems.

The Role of Work Orders

Here is how this plays out in a simple scenario. First, CMMS would provide the means for someone to report an equipment problem instantly, so that it gets dealt with promptly. In response to this report, the system would issue a work order, which is a central part of the program. For one thing, work orders function as dispatch mechanisms and as such they drive the action. They define the maintenance activities that will be undertaken. A

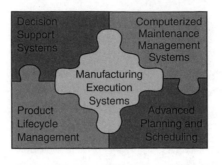

Figure 5.21   The Plant Portfolio — MES, PLM, DSS, APS, and CMMS

mechanic doesn't just go out and start using his wrenches somewhere; he has to have a work order in hand before he leaves his office.

Work orders also prompt the mechanic to make a record of his actions, and this data can be used in several ways. Let's say the repair required 2 new brackets, a new rod, 10 bearings, and a tube of grease, and that 2 hours were needed to complete the work. The mechanic would record all of this information, creating a labor and materials history to be used by accounting. The parts record would also help inventory maintain its stock of maintenance supplies and replacement parts. In the past, inventory consisted of someone manually keeping track of every item needed for maintenance, and if the part wasn't in stock, it would have to be ordered. Today, the inventory is kept online, so it's easy to determine if any part is in stock, or when it will arrive if it's been ordered. Sophisticated systems go a step further. They notice when any particular item is below a certain level in the bin, automatically do a search for the best price, and then order more.

In the process of entering his data, the mechanic would also indicate which machine was involved, how long it was out of commission, and the date, creating equipment history. The specific repair actions that were performed, such as replacing the brackets or calibrating the timing mechanism, would be logged in as well, creating a history of repair. Accumulated data of this sort can be highly beneficial. A close examination of a machine's history might alert you to a pattern of breakdowns and help you find ways to prevent the problems in the future.

Work Plans

Maintenance activities should also be driven by a work plan for each activity. This part of the maintenance program can be done manually with paper and folders, because it doesn't have to be tied in to anything else electronically. For these plans to be successful, they must have all of the information needed by the people actually performing the maintenance in the plant. This information will include documentation from equipment vendors, lists of replacement parts and of other necessary materials, step-by-step work instructions with drawings that describe how to do the job, and safety instructions such as lock-out and tag-out requirements. Without this information, maintenance workers often are forced to reinvent the wheel each time they handle a particular job, which means that it takes them a lot longer to complete the work. In successful maintenance management operations a great deal of effort and time is put into the work planning process by experienced planners. This work always pays off by ensuring that the team in the field doing the actual work has what it needs, knows what it needs to do, and can do it effectively and safely. The best maintenance management software applications make provisions for this work planning process and support the planners' efforts in ways that integrate the work plans with the work orders.

Preventative Maintenance

In the more mature versions of CMMS, work orders have one other critical function — they work as a mechanism to drive improvement processes. In some plants, every piece of equipment is included in a strict regimen of preventative maintenance (PM) and this accounts for 95% of their entire maintenance workload. All PM actions are time-based, condition-based, or usage-based. If they're time-based, then they happen every 2 weeks, every 3 months, or at some other regular interval. If they are condition-based, then they happen when the lubricating oil measures as having a certain amount of dirt, when the belts register as having lost a certain amount of elasticity, or when some other limit is reached. In many cases, sensors sound alarms when the conditions for preventative maintenance have been met. Another way that condition-based maintenance can be triggered is through the occurrence of too many finished products failing to meet quality standards.

PM actions that are usage-based occur when a certain amount of work has been done, such as after 100,000 units have been produced. Within the usage-based category, there's also the idea of planned usage. You may decide to perform maintenance work just before you begin a particularly long production run, changing all of the gaskets and lubing all of the bearings just to ensure that everything is in excellent shape before you get started.

Various approaches to deciding when to change the oil for your car provide a good way to illustrate the difference between these three categories. If you change the oil every 6 months regardless of mileage or how dirty the oil is, then you're using the time-based method. If you change the oil only when it looks dirty or is getting low, then you are relying on a condition-based approach. If you change it every 3000 miles, regardless of the time it takes you to put those 3000 miles on your car, that is usage-based, and if you change just before taking a long trip, that is planned usage-based. You measure different things in each case. If you change oil every 3000 miles, you measure mileage, not the quality of the oil.

The point of setting these time, condition, or usage limits is to establish when preventive maintenance chores should occur in order to keep all of the equipment in perfect running order. By coordinating PM with production scheduling, you can find ways to fit maintenance tasks into the general flow of work. For example, CMMS would give the operations planner a schedule that might indicate the need sometime in the next 12 days to do 4 hours of work on Line 1 to handle this task, 5 hours on Line 2 to handle that task, and so on so that everything is worked into the master production schedule.

The Relationship between Maintenance Philosophies and Maintenance Systems

Two philosophies or frameworks for approaching the task of maintenance are reliability centered maintenance (RCM) and total productive maintenance (TPM). RCM takes the position that reliability of assets is paramount and so it focuses in on measuring the availability, the uptime, and the reliability of assets, such as a piece of equipment, a line, or an entire plant. The overall concept is that reliability provides an indication of the success of the total maintenance program.

TPM operates with the goal of maximizing the effective utilization of maintenance resources. It addresses the challenge of evaluating your total resources in terms of money, people, and time, and then allocating them in such a way that put them to their best use. In other words, it helps you decide which pieces of equipment and which maintenance tasks will give the best return on your investment of resources.

Both of these philosophies can be integrated into a maintenance program. But in order for them to succeed, there's a certain amount of measurement and analysis that must be supported by a CMMS. If you're on one of these tracks or planning to pursue one of them, you need the IT to support it. This means asking vendors how their CMMS products support TPM or RCM.

Four Levels of Maintenance Management

Although everyone has to deal with maintenance, not everyone handles it in the same way. This only makes sense, given the vast array of manufacturing environments. Some companies want to avoid unplanned downtime at all costs, so they take a very aggressive approach to maintaining their equipment. Other companies are less concerned about downtime and have relatively simple machinery that can be repaired easily whenever problems occur, so they don't bother with maintenance tasks until something goes wrong. There are a multitude of approaches to maintenance, but we find it helpful to group them into four levels in terms of their maturity:

1. Reactive
2. Preventative
3. Mature
4. World Class

Reactive

People at the reactive level follow the paradigm "When it's broke, I'll fix it. Until then, I'm not going to tinker with it." At the simplest level of plant maintenance, such an approach often actually makes sense. If the equipment isn't overly complex and production scheduling is well under capacity, there may be no particular advantage to being any more aggressive about maintenance issues. The only IT requirements are usually some form of work order tracking for labor and materials consumed so that you know how much maintenance is costing and something to keep up with spare parts inventory and procurement.

Preventative

While the reactive level fills the bill at some plants, it can be a disastrous approach to take at plants where equipment failures cause huge headaches. As you move up in terms of equipment complexity and capacity demands, it becomes clear that you want to be actively looking for problems before they happen, so that you can prevent equipment downtime. This is the predictive level, where you begin to think about preventive maintenance and other efforts that will put you one step ahead of breakdowns.

The software used here is designed not only to handle accounting and inventory, but also to use work orders as a dispatch mechanism, to provide work instructions with task lists, and in some cases to create equipment and repair histories. The historical data can be used to spot trends and nip small problems in the bud before they become serious. A CMMS at this level may also have the ability to provide supporting documentation with the work instructions and to coordinate basic maintenance planning.

Mature

At the mature level of CMMS, every effort is made to develop ways of anticipating problems long before they happen. Through such mechanisms as load analysis, vibration sensors on high-value equipment, and the monitoring of run times, power consumption, and quality degradation, trends can be spotted within whatever measured parameters are established. The thinking at the mature level is "We're going after every minor variance with hammer and tong, because for us, the number one priority is preventing breakdowns and stoppages." The IT requirements become very sophisticated at this level and include histories from multiple perspectives, extensive planning, inventory and procurement optimization, and labor management.

World Class

The highest level, world class, is still somewhat theoretical. It encompasses all of the concepts defined in the earlier levels, and it applies these concepts in ways that make all maintenance practices part of an ongoing maturity process within the plants. The difference between world class and mature is that while mature is a steady state, world class is a constant effort to be continuously optimizing, improving, and evolving.

Finding the Right Fit

In our experience, every time someone has had a maintenance management system that failed, it has failed for one of two reasons. First, the level of the system didn't match the level of the company's needs. If your company needs a system that functions only at the reactive level, you're wasting your money on anything more sophisticated. On the other hand, if your plant is the type that needs a mature level system, you should definitely spend the money to get one. The ROI is there.

Second, failure can come from the lack of sound operating practices in the organization, regardless of the computer software being used. If work practices are sloppy and ineffective, or if scheduling and planning are incomplete or haphazard, equipment will not be well maintained. Unfortunately, many companies allow adversarial relationships to develop between the operations staff and the maintenance staff. A lack of coordination between these two groups in a manufacturing plant will undermine any efforts to build an effective maintenance program. No amount of information technology can counter these problems.

If you do have sound practices in place at your company, the next step is to make sure your maintenance management software matches your maintenance environment. Determining your plant's needs may require some work, however. Like planning and scheduling, a company's needs don't follow from the type of industry or the size of the company. Clearly, one of the biggest issues is equipment downtime. Some paper mills have machines that run around the clock and are generating over $200,000 an hour in revenues. This means that they are willing to spend a lot of money on a mature CMMS. They are also willing both to invest in a large, on-site inventory of spare parts and to employ repair technicians to be there around the clock, even if the technicians don't actually work on the machines very often.

In contrast, many newspaper companies operate their printing presses at night so that papers can be delivered in the early morning. Even if they use the presses for some additional dayshift runs, it's not unusual for the equipment to sit idle for long periods during the daytime each week. This gives them a window of opportunity to perform preventative maintenance on a regular basis. At the same time, newspaper companies face a daily deadline. If you're making cereal and the equipment breaks down and stays down for 12 hours, you can probably make up the lost time on the weekend. Newspapers don't have that luxury; they have to get the paper out everyday, one way or another. So, their needs aren't exactly opposite of the paper mill. Even though they have regular periods of downtime, when they are printing the paper, they have to be able to fix any problems quickly. They are also willing to spend money to keep a good supply of spare parts in stock.

In the end, it's no simple matter to find the right balance. The whole point of maintenance is to support operations to make the plant run more efficiently. Only the hobbyist does maintenance on a car just for the sake of doing maintenance, and there are no hobbyists in plants. ERP systems, which are ledger driven, can help companies reduce the money tied up in a maintenance inventory, and they can consolidate the purchasing of maintenance supplies and spare parts. But they will not be much help in structuring maintenance so that downtime is minimized, so most companies can benefit from using a CMMS at some level.

The fundamental issue, apart from ensuring that your organization has sound maintenance management practices in place, is making a good match between the maintenance philosophy your company is pursuing and the maintenance management information systems that are employed. The key to an effective system is to make sure your maintenance practices match the functionality you're trying to implement. Maintenance management systems that don't fit the needs of the company are destined to fail. If you're at the reactive stage, then don't spend a lot of money on the most expensive COTS products for maintenance management. On the other hand, if you need mature maintenance program functionality, don't expect it from simple inexpensive software programs. As with the other four parts of the Portfolio, your ability to choose the right CMMS is contingent on your ability to define your company's IT needs clearly and thoroughly.

CONCLUSION

Many manufacturing companies are faced with a large gap. Their plants are lacking solid manufacturing IT solutions, because on the one hand, the corporate IT systems provide only limited functionality in support of manufacturing operations. And on the other hand, they haven't found the manufacturing IT systems that could handle the chores. However, it's possible to build a portfolio of manufacturing IT systems that can function as a bridge over this chasm. Well-guided use of manufacturing execution systems, product lifecycle management, decision support systems, advanced planning and scheduling, and computerized maintenance management systems will allow companies to mine the gold that is waiting in their plants.

In the end, everything comes down to getting a real payback on your manufacturing IT dollars. The ROI can be demonstrated, because these systems have a real and clearly established payback. Demonstrating that you can get a solid payback from using the Portfolio is critical to the entire purpose of this book, so we have devoted an entire chapter to providing examples. Read Chapter 6 for stories of the ways that companies have benefited from implementing these systems.

6

ACHIEVING PAYBACK WITH
THE PORTFOLIO

In Chapter 4, we gave an overview of the ways that payback can be achieved and in Chapter 5, we presented the portfolio concept — a group of five types of applications that can be used individually or in combination to get this payback. Now in this chapter we'll demonstrate that these ideas are more than theory. The possibility of getting a solid, measurable return on your manufacturing IT dollars is real, not imagined. Intelligent use of the Portfolio can have a huge impact on capacity utilization, materials and inventory, throughput and uptime, quality and yield, and labor costs. Improvements in any of these areas can create significant savings. We know this is true because we've seen it happen. We can give you some examples. First, we'll list figures from some of the projects we know about. After that, we'll give more detailed examples of how companies have put the Portfolio to good use.

SNAPSHOTS OF SUCCESS

Here are some quick examples of solid gains made from various IT implementations:

- A major food and beverage manufacturer used OEE as part of a MES package, starting with a pilot project involving 64 production lines at 3 plants. By using KPIs in such areas as downtime and throughput, the OEE metric provided visibility into the relationships between individual pieces of equipment and the plant's total efficiency. Over 3 years, the pilot project saved the manufacturer $1.6 million dollars through improved productivity and yields. Another pilot project brought it $300,000 in savings and a 3% increase in uptime. The manufacturer followed this with a more extensive application of MES and OEE to many of its North American plants, which brought it *savings in the first year of $14.6 million*. This success led the manufacturer to consider taking a different approach to meeting increased demand for one of its products. The manufacturer had assumed that three additional lines would be needed to increase production in response to the product's rise in popularity. It turned out that by using OEE to increase efficiency on the current lines, the manufacturer was able to meet the demand, thus saving the money that would've been spent on installing the three new lines.

■ In a similar fashion, a major coffee manufacturer was able to avoid the cost of capital expansion by improving the production capacity of its existing equipment. Effective implementation of the right systems gave operators process-to-process visibility and coordination. This enabled the manufacturers to detect and eliminate a bottleneck in their production process, *the result being a throughput gain of 21%*.

■ Another major food and beverage company used production tracking software to gain visibility into every detail concerning the records of finished goods. Previously, this was handled on paper, which meant accuracy problems and delays. Sometimes production in one shift would begin without a definite record of what the previous shift had produced. With the new software, the company could see instantly at any point exactly how many products were coming off the lines and knew exactly where these products were stored or shipped. The company could also see if it was ahead of schedule or behind schedule for any given shift. Having exact counts in real time gave them visibility into all aspects of production and allowed the company to save $800,000 annually.

■ A major chemical manufacturer found that its MES freed up about 6 hours a day of a process engineer's time. On top of this, it also eliminated 38 clerical hours a week in collecting data and producing reports for regulatory compliance.

■ We have seen chemical, consumer products, and other manufacturers achieve close to a complete reduction in order fulfillment errors by automating their warehouses. In the process, they also have reduced the need for labor to fill the orders, they have reduced the movement of warehouse materials, and they have gained significant clerical savings. Shipping errors are one of those aggravating problems that we can now virtually eliminate. If you're still fighting this difficulty, you don't have the right software — or it's not implemented correctly.

- A major food manufacturer took the step of integrating its process, material, and laboratory information at the plant level. This allowed the manufacturer to correct some misunderstandings about the relationships between line speed, product temperature, weight control, and filling machine settings. By adjusting the equipment, the manufacturer was able to increase its first pass yield by nearly 5% over the course of a year.
- One manufacturing company used OEE along with PLM and a program that gave it quality control in real time. After implementing these systems at all of its 21 plants, the company found a savings of $4 million in the first 9 months. Of the $4 million in savings, approximately $3 million came from improvements brought about by leveraging OEE.
- When talking about ROI, there's always the issue of how quickly you can expect to recoup your outlays. A Fortune 100 food manufacturer used MES, PLM, and DSS to bridge the gap between its ERP system and its plants. On an investment of $4.1 million dollars for one plant, it gained *$4.3 million in savings in the first year*. The investment at another plant was $4.5 million and *the first year savings there were $5.3 million*.

EXAMPLES OF REAL PAYBACK

We have selected some examples to show how some manufacturing companies have used parts of the Portfolio to improve their businesses. We will start with an example of a company using all five parts of the Portfolio and then continue with examples that illustrate each piece individually.

Using All Five Parts of the Portfolio

A Fortune 500 chemical company with plants all around the world sought to reduce inventory, improve resource utilization, and improve quality. Over the course of 5 years, it implemented a plan that used all five parts of the Portfolio. The company also connected all of its manufacturing systems to its ERP system. This provided integrated information for all manufacturing and distribution functions.

A critical facet of this project was that the entire effort to improve manufacturing IT fit into a larger strategy. In other words, the company looked at the big picture from the start and defined what it wanted IT to contribute functionally as part of the long-range plans. By creating a clear vision and making it concrete through well-defined functional requirements, the company was able to avoid being swayed by the sales pitches of vendors trying to sell something that didn't fit its needs.

The next step was to determine which pieces of IT architecture would provide these functions. Once the company had the specific pieces in mind, it could get a handle on the costs involved and compare these costs to the projected benefits. This approach allowed the company to see that every component of its plan didn't have to have a clear ROI, if the *entire* plan could provide a sound ROI.

One example of this is that the company decided to install plantwide networks to serve as infrastructure for other parts of the project. This work alone didn't have a specific justification or direct payback, but it played an important role in the overall plan, so it was justified in that sense. Looking at the project strategically also led the company to determine which areas promised the greatest payback and which areas promised the quickest payback, so that it could make these the top priorities.

This project was immensely successful, coming in under budget and on schedule. The company reduced overall inventory by 7% and high-value inventory by 5%. It improved resource utilization by reducing:

■ Clerical labor, 16%
■ Environmental tracking, 25%
■ Utility usage, 8%
■ Material handling, 4%

The evidence for quality improvement is a 9% increase in first pass yields and an 8% reduction in scrap. Did the company get a good return on its investment? Yes, considering that the 8% reduction in scrap was enough ROI justification by itself to pay for the systems implemented.

Manufacturing Execution Systems

MES Used in a Discrete Plant

This story, which involves a cellular phone plant, illustrates how MES can help ensure that you produce the product that you intend to produce and that you produce it accurately and to the specifications given by the design department.

One characteristic of plants that make cellular phones is that they're highly automated and often use robots. Robots operate according to programs that are fairly complicated, and part of the manufacturing process is making sure that the correct parts are in place for the robot to use. You also have to have the correct assembly in the robot, which means putting in various components such as a circuit board, and you have to equip the robot with the specific tools it will need to perform its functions. Finally, you have to have the particular software containing the assembly program, which directs the robot's movements.

This is complicated in a number of ways. First, consider that there are several models of the phone. Then for each model, there are different versions for different regions of the world. They may differ by only one component, which could be the frequency of the board chip, but these different engineering revisions drive the different models and versions.

The MES package helped the plant facilitate the coordination of getting all of the correct elements in place: the parts, the robot's components, the robot's tools, and the assembly program. If this wasn't done exactly right, there would be problems in production. MES provided all of the information to the plant floor operators and it verified that everything was in place. This significantly reduced the chance for human error.

The MES application worked by taking a work order, then taking into account what was currently loaded on the robot, then informing the operator of the changes that needed to be made. In some cases, MES would make the changes itself, if they involved only electronic adjustments, such as putting the correct program into use.

The result was an 8% reduction in rework and scrap and a similar increase in quality in terms of the percentage of perfectly functioning units produced. One example of the potential for human error is that test runs of future products were often done at night, so the robots were retooled and reprogrammed for the test runs. Then the next day, if everything hadn't been perfectly reset for that day's production run, problems would occur without the MES to catch the errors. In some cases, the problem would be obvious, such as the robot malfunctioning physically. But if someone simply put in the wrong chip, the problem might not be discovered until hundreds of units had been produced. With the MES in place, the plant always knows before the run starts if anything is not right, thereby avoiding changeover problems that can occur so easily. The overall reduction in rework and scrap was remarkable. On top of that, the MES system in this situation also has the benefit of reducing changeover time.

MES Used in a Regulated Discrete Plant

This electronics company had a business process that required it to prove that the radio it built for military use had gone through a predetermined series of steps and that all of the data collection had been gathered along the way. A packet of information demonstrating compliance with all of this was delivered with each radio. The company had to prove and verify to its customer that this device has gone through all of the planned routing steps and all of the unplanned routing steps, that it had successfully passed any rework or repair steps that were required, and that any particular type of quality information and any tests that had been performed on the radio had been adequately documented.

Before using a MES, all of this documentation was done by hand. Folders would be handed down along the production process so that people could sign off on each and every critical step of production. Basically, everything was done on paper, including all notes concerning test results. Putting together the packet that shipped with each radio meant collecting and assembling all of these different papers. It generally took them about 8 to 10 hours in each case to verify that all of the paperwork was in place.

The MES system automated this process, so that the work-in-progress tracking was captured electronically, and this included all of the subassembly work along with the main assembly work. History and quality data, done before on paper, was all collected electronically. When everything was done on paper, it was never instantly clear which tests each radio had passed and which each had failed. Once the MES was in place, if a radio failed some test and had to be reworked, all of this was electronically documented. There were hundreds of functional tests as well and MES would capture all of the data from each of these.

The overall result was a substantial reduction in labor and thus a reduced production cycle time for each radio. The process of gathering all of this information manually was relatively straightforward, but it was particularly time consuming. With the MES, the task of ensuring that all documentation was complete could be done at the touch of a button. An 8-hour process was reduced to a 1-minute process.

The MES also improved accuracy, which meant that it made it almost impossible for defective products to get out the door or for good products to get out the door without all of the necessary documentation. One other benefit was having immediate access to all historical data needed in case of a recall. The company could track down all of the places where a component was used, without having to go through the manual process of sorting through folder after folder of paperwork. It also made it easier for the company to analyze its business processes and find ways to reduce waste.

MES Used in a Process Plant

A company that makes coffee installed a MES package to handle yields, batch tracking, and material management. Before installing the MES, it was simply managing production as each shift occurred. There was very little planning ahead and there was also a lack of clear instructions concerning quantities. Each shift would simply try to make as much as it could of whatever was needed next. As could be expected, the lack of organization left the company with too much of some products and too little of others.

Finally the company decided to try to correct the situation and it used the MES to establish a new procedure that entailed giving production orders for precise amounts of each product. This meant that when the plant received an order for 50,000 cases of this type of coffee in 5-lb. cans, it expected the plant to make exactly 50,000 cases — no more and no less. So the first objective was to improve the ability to have production results match the production orders.

The company's next objective was to maximize yields. There will always be some loss, but it wanted to reduce waste as much as possible. The last objective was to reduce costs. Its biggest cost component was clearly the coffee beans used to make the coffee and the next largest cost component was the labor expense. As for the labor expenses, the main thrust was to increase productivity, primarily through increasing performance, quality, and uptime. The main approach to lower raw materials costs was to increase the yields. In addition to this, the company also could improve its procedures to ensure that it never made mistakes in terms of using the wrong beans for the grade of coffee being made.

Keep in mind that there are several different grades of coffee beans and they don't all cost the same. Some are much more expensive than others. The higher quality beans can be used to make lower quality blends, but if the company uses some of the more expensive beans when only the less expensive ones are needed, it is wasting money. This really comes into play with the blends of different coffee beans, because while the proportions of each bean were set, they weren't always being followed very strictly. It was easy for the higher quality beans to be used in greater quantities than needed.

The company succeeded in all areas through the use of its MES. The MES started with a schedule, which might say that it needed 50,000 cases of a particular blend of coffee. The first step by MES in response to this schedule would be to determine the resources needed to produce this order, checking which of these resources were available and which needed to be procured. Specifically, it would examine the recipe to see which coffee beans were needed and how many pounds of each were needed. Next it would check equipment availability to determine which roasters would be used, which grinders, and which packaging lines. Another part of this was calculating the number of batches of each coffee bean needed to produce 50,000 cases.

Out of this, the MES would produce an overall schedule for meeting the order. Operators would have the opportunity to review the schedule and make changes, such as changing from this roaster to that roaster for whatever reason. Then production would begin.

The MES was connected to the PLCs to make sure that everything was done correctly. The recipe was downloaded to the PLCs and then the

MES would monitor the controls equipment to ensure everything was done according to the plan. This monitoring process would involve gathering all kinds of specific information about scheduling, the grades and amounts of beans being used, the roasters and the grinders, the packaging lines, and more. For example, the MES would know how many pounds of beans went into each roaster and how many came out, how many went into each grinder and how many came out, how many went into each blender and how many came out, and finally how many pounds went into the cans in the packaging line.

This would give the yield results, plus it would give real-time information about how far along the plant was in the process toward getting precisely the right amount of each ingredient. If one batch produces more or less than expected at any stage, then quantity adjustments would be made in subsequent batches to accommodate this. The MES was constantly checking and recalculating so that the last batch of any product would produce just the right amount needed to finish the order. Although it's almost impossible to make everything come exactly right, the MES brought the company dramatically closer to producing precisely the amount of coffee needed for each order. Compared to what the company had been doing before, the MES was absolute magic.

The overall results of implementing the MES were dramatic. The company increased total throughput by over 20% by increasing yields. It reduced downtime from over 30 minutes per shift to less than 20 minutes per shift. It reduced costs 8% by making sure the plant always used the right beans in the right quantities. The company increased its success in meeting production deadlines and was able to produce just what was ordered.

The company also gained some benefits that it never expected. For one thing, it reduced inventory costs by 12%. In the past, the plant frequently produced more than was ordered, so the excess went into inventory until the next order came in. Now that it was producing just the amount ordered, the company didn't have these extra cases of finished products lying around. Customer service improved by leaps and bounds in several ways. One was that the company became much more reliable in terms of meeting demands for delivery deadlines. But it isn't only that it was more reliable, the company's increased efficiency made it capable of meeting tighter deadlines, as well. If a customer called in and asked for a rush order, the company could confidently agree to meet the demand. Another way that customer service improved was that it never had to deliver short, because the plant always made the right amount to fill the order. And remember that all of these improvements were made while reducing inventory and cutting costs. All in all, the MES brought this company a tremendous return on investment.

MES Used in a Hybrid Plant

The operations performed at many manufacturing plants are either strictly discrete, such as working with parts or components in a machining or assembly setting, or strictly process, such as working on batches or continuous processes. The production issues for discrete plants differ greatly from those at process plants, but in each case, the challenges are clearly defined and understood. All of these issues are present in hybrid plants, which contain both discrete and process elements, but there's also an added complication. Managers of hybrid plants have to handle the unique issues that occur at the transition from process to discrete.

This story concerns a paper company with mills that produce paper that is cut into sheets, not just shipped in rolls. This higher degree of finishing gives these mills a combination of process and discrete elements. The work of taking the pulp and transforming it into a continuous sheet of paper is process manufacturing, but the task of cutting the paper into sheets and packaging it for sale in boxes is discrete manufacturing, so the mill could be characterized as a hybrid environment. The transition from process to discrete occurs as the continuous sheet of paper is cut.

As the company looked into the use of a MES system, it determined that the standard approach of using MES for production management and scheduling wasn't the point. This part of the mill management was relatively stable and didn't require a new sophisticated software package to maintain or improve it. Instead, the focus was on manufacturing performance and root-cause analysis of problems. To this end, the MES package the company used involved some historian functionality, some PLM functionality, and some product tracking at the end of the process. The real payback came in the area of operating performance improvement through the use of OEE.

One example of how this MES helped to improve operating performance involves the paper mill phenomenon known as "sheet breaks," which is illustrated in Figure 6.1. Paper is produced in a continuous sheet that is either wound onto a roll or cut into sheets at the end of the process. Before it gets to the end point, it moves through the machinery for some time as one unbroken sheet. If the sheet breaks, the massive and expensive papermaking machines have to be shut down and restarted to get another unbroken sheet going again. Sheet breaks are a hybrid issue, not just a process issue, because the discrete elements of cutting and packaging the paper are affected. Data obtained from monitoring and analyzing the process operation is used in managing the discrete operation and vice versa.

This mill had a problem of too many sheet breaks, so with the installation of the MES, it launched a campaign to reduce them. The task was to analyze the data surrounding a sheet break in the context of other

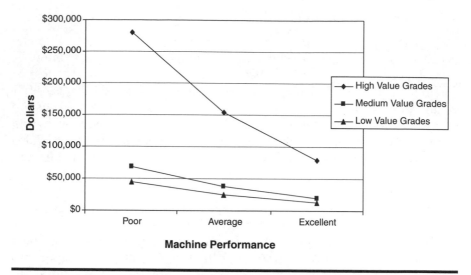

Figure 6.1   Average Weekly Cost of Paper Machine Sheet Breaks

variables, such as the products it was running and data from lab tests. These efforts paid off. The mill was able to reduce sheet breaks to one per day from four per day. To fully understand how significant this is, it's important to grasp the cost of downtime at a paper mill. Paper machines are extremely high capital expenditures, but they can produce at very high rates. So, every minute of downtime is time when a product isn't being produced. Each sheet break could cost the mill between 15 and 40 minutes. Eliminating three of those every day would mean reducing downtime by around an hour and a half per day. Add that up for each week, each month, and each year, and the total becomes significant. For example, depending on the grade of paper being produced, the savings could easily be tens of thousands of dollars in a week or hundreds of thousands of dollars over a quarter.

Another issue associated with downtime is changeovers. In the paper mill, this centers on changing grades of paper. The MES helped them minimize both material waste and the time required to make the changeover. Changeover times went down 50% to 60% (depending on the specific grade of paper involved). The combination of reducing waste and increasing productivity saved over $1 million in the first year, which meant that the capital outlay for the MES was recouped in less than 12 months after it was installed. This example of use in a hybrid plant shows how MES can be beneficial in ways other than the more common focus of production scheduling and product traceability. Here, manufacturing performance analysis provided the real payback.

It's important to note that the key to this success was the effort to focus on sheet breaks and grade changes. No software package will improve your business simply because you have it installed. You have to determine the areas where you know there's excess waste or where there's potentially higher productivity. There must be internal processes functioning within the company, such as continuous improvement methodologies, that generate initiatives for positive change.

Product Lifecycle Management

PLM Used by a Company Making Nutritional and Dietary Drinks

One food and beverage company that manufactures nutritional and dietary drinks has a PLM package that includes a LIMS program and a SPC program, with everything tied into its ERP system. The combination of the LIMS and SPC gives the company a PLM system that supports its efforts to manage production and quality from the raw materials through the finished product. At each step in production, the system accumulates and analyzes all kinds of data concerning the product. The LIMS supports the laboratory work and the SPC supports the shop floor.

An important part of this production process is analytical testing done in the laboratory. These tests include checking on the amount of protein, fat, sugar, and other components. The company also conducts sensory tests concerning the smell, the appearance, and the taste. Then there are microbiological tests to make sure nothing is in the drinks that should not be there. In addition to testing the product itself, the company tests the packaging to make sure the cans are sealing properly. All of this is handled by the LIMS part of the package.

Using LIMS made the entire testing process much more efficient and more accurate, so the company was able to increase productivity, while at the same time improving quality. The company improved productivity by taking less time to conduct all of the tests and improved quality by creating a more thorough battery of tests, which helped produce a better product. Improved testing by itself doesn't change production processes, but the ability to analyze test data can lead to uncovering root causes for production problems. This information is then fed back to production so that improvements can be made in the manufacturing procedures. As always, time is money, and an additional benefit of using the LIMS is that testing could be done quicker, which meant being able to correct problems faster. The production lines are running constantly while the testing is being done, so correcting problems more quickly means less product that has to be scrapped.

The SPC program helps monitor several critical elements of the production process. One example is the sterilization of the cans prior to being filled. This is clearly a top priority, since problems with sterilization can result in serious amounts of waste. SPC keeps a close watch on all sorts of data around the sterilization, so that at any moment trends can be spotted and addressed immediately. Prior to installing this system, the company was losing sterilization about five or six times every day on average, and it was costing tons of money with lost products and lost time. The SPC program cut the average occurrence of sterilization loss to about one time every other day. Improvements like this help software systems pay for themselves in no time.

Everything ties into the ERP system in a straightforward manner. The company decided that the ERP system will be its system of record for all of the inventory, which means that the lots of finished goods will be recorded there. All lot tracking and tracing will be handled by the ERP system; this is the system that will support the product recall system. In order to execute these functions, the ERP system has to know which lots have been produced and which lots have passed the LIMS tests. So an interface was established which would allow the LIMS program to tell the ERP system when products had been approved for shipping.

One result of installing this package was a reduction in inventory. Previously, some products were suspected of being below quality specifications, but there was no easy way to determine whether they were okay to ship or not, so they got put aside until someone could look at them more closely. This would have a domino effect. First, the company would have to make more to replace the ones put aside, so that it could make the current orders. But, the company also started making extra products in some cases, so that there were some on hand if the same situation arose again. This increased the inventory again. The LIMS software provided a more definitive method of determining quality and made it possible to meet orders without carrying a large inventory. This was not just a small change. With the use of this software, the company's inventory was reduced by over 10%. This also means that the company could be more reliable and provide improved customer service.

One other benefit was a better use of personnel. Much of the work done by the PLM system was previously done manually on spreadsheets and through other similar labor-intensive methods. Having this system made it possible to put people to work on other tasks that could add more value to the company.

PLM Used with a Focus on Specifications Management

This food and beverage company uses its PLM system in a variety of ways, but one of the system's most important functions concerns specifications management. Given that specifications pertain to so many different matters, such as raw materials, process materials, packaging materials, finished goods, tests, production processes, and equipment, it follows that almost everyone in the company uses specifications in one way or another. In general, people aren't allowed to create or change a specification, but they need to have access to them in order to do their jobs. In addition to people using the specs, other systems, such as LIMS, SPC/SQC, and weight control, use them to perform their functions.

An important part of the story is that this company has a huge assortment of products, such as mayonnaise and salad dressings, hot dogs and lunchmeat, crackers and dips, powdered drinks and canned drinks, and all kinds of cheeses. Specifications have to be managed around each and every one of these items. They all have different lab requirements, different limits for overpack and underpack, and different parameters for SPC and SQC. Add to this the fact that it takes dozens of different plants to produce all of these different products and it becomes clear that managing specifications across the corporation is a monumental undertaking.

The company set about to pursue two goals simultaneously that were potentially in conflict. The company wanted to use the implementation of this system to standardize procedures in many areas, but at the same time it wanted to design the system to be highly configurable so that it supported a variety of requirements. The balance between making the system flexible for configuration purposes and rigid for standardization purposes wasn't easy. On the one hand, the company wanted to standardize business processes. This meant that test procedures would follow the same format, no matter what the product was. Of course, the tests done on cheese would be different from the tests done on frozen pizza, but the method needed to be consistent. The aim was to have a specification management system where tests would be defined consistently, methods would be carried out consistently, instruments would be standardized, and data would be organized and stored in standard patterns. On the other hand, the company needed to construct the system so that it would accommodate the variety of different products manufactured, so it had to be flexible enough to work for both cheese and pizza, powdered drinks and coffee, salad dressing and hot dogs. It was a balancing act between standardization of procedures and flexibility of configuration.

In any situation where the task is this large, it only makes sense to start in one area and expand gradually. After piloting the system at key plants that were chosen for being representative of other plants, the company started to rollout the system to the rest of the company. This allowed the company to be certain all of the requirements were being handled. Extensive training accompanied the rollout, so that people could actually use the technology being made available to them. The company also was careful to make sure all of the components were integrated into one system so that it did not end up creating islands of automation. The project took 2 or 3 years to complete and it has been highly successful, providing millions and millions of dollars of savings.

PLM Used in a Paper Company

This story involves a paper company that had both process and hybrid plants. The process plants were the paper mills that produced large quantities of paper on rolls to be sold to other companies. The hybrid plant took some of the paper made at one of the mills and converted it to make consumer paper products. The company decided that it could benefit from creating a strong link between these two parts of its business and PLM was the tool it used to do this.

PLM provided the ability to unify the specifications from both the mill and the converting plant. Along with having specifications accessible in one place, the system brought quality data together, so that the converting plant could have complete visibility into the quality of the paper it was getting from the mill. This enabled the converting plant to evaluate the rolls of paper in terms of suitability for various needs, including being used in end products and being used in certain production processes. Having more information about things such as tensile strength, basis weight, or caliper, and having this data instantly and electronically available made it possible for the converting plant to make better and more profitable use of the paper through reducing waste and increasing yields. At one plant, raw material waste was reduced by 2.5%, which brought over a $1.5 million in annual savings the first year.

The advantages go beyond this, though. The sharing of information between the converting plant and the mill helps the product development teams at the mill to improve the quality of paper they produce. The first step is for the plant to specify all of the characteristics paper should have to make it ideal for being converted into end products or for being used in other plant production processes. This can get quite complicated, given that the specifications of these ideal characteristics will vary depending upon the way the paper is used. All of this information is taken by the product development people at the mill, who use it to find ways to alter or improve the production methods so that the paper produced comes closer to matching the ideal requested by the converting plant. The more they are able to achieve in this way, the higher the yields become when the paper is used at the converting plant.

These benefits all hinge on sharing specifications and as-built quality data through a PLM system. The plant and the mill also shared information on yields, efficiency, and profitability, and as a result of this, were able to integrate their efforts in a highly profitable way.

Decision Support Systems

DSS Used in a Pharmaceutical Company

A pharmaceutical company wanted to look at three different approaches for collecting data related to manufacturing. The first approach was to use a process data historian, the second was to use an operational data repository, and the third was to use a data warehouse. These are the three essential components of a DSS.

To get an idea of what each of these approaches entails, first consider how data is collected. It comes from many different sources, such as manual entry of data from data collection points; hand-held, mobile, and fixed bar code scanners; automation systems that use PLCs and DCSs; lab systems; recipe management systems; inventory systems; and more. Then consider how many different people need to use this data, such as quality personnel, plant management, line supervisors, research and development personnel, operations personnel, shipping and receiving personnel, and more.

A process historian is excellent both for collecting massive amounts of data from automation and controls and for providing context around the time, the location, the type of data, and the value of the data. Temperatures, pressures, and speeds are typical of the kind of data collected. Ninety-nine percent of the data is real-time data calculated or collected from control systems. The process historian typically does trending, charting, and reporting.

The repository functions as a relational database and will add more definition and provide more operational context concerning specific machines, products, shifts, schedules, and such. It provides real-time decision support, batch histories, manufacturing events and histories, and other application functions.

The data warehouse takes information from even more sources and adds even more context. It expands on the operational context provided by the repository and is organized to accommodate the people and applications using the data. To this end, it supports multiple perspectives and has the broadest range of analytical tools.

The company had several goals with this project. It wanted to provide decision support in all kinds of areas, such as quality, environmental, process development, research and development, product development, inventory, shipping and receiving, operations, packaging processing, and batch management. In order to do this, the company needed to collect the data, analyze it, report it, and make it easily accessible.

More specifically, the company wanted to have better batch and disposition reporting, quicker turnaround times, better real-time reporting of problems with batches, improved quality and accuracy, faster production start-ups, improved yields, and easier regulatory compliance.

DSS Used to Focus on Quality, Cost, and Delivery

This company decided to focus on a few fundamental key performance indicators concerning quality, cost, and delivery. The company's goal concerning quality was to gather information about quality on the following bases:

- Per hour
- Per lot
- Per batch
- Per product run
- Per shift
- Per day

This would involve data about first-pass quality and the loss of products due to rejects or rework. These were actually rather simple metrics, often given in percentages. For example, a 98% first-pass quality rating would mean a 2% rejection rate. And this rating would be broken out in terms of the batch, the line, the hour, the day, and so on.

The goal concerning cost was to gather information about yields broken down along the same specific characteristics as quality, that is, per hour, per batch, per shift, and so on. The point here is that raw materials are the company's largest cost component, so improving yields holds the potential to significantly reduce costs. For example, the company wants to track how much cereal comes out for every 1000 pounds of raw grain used.

Finally, the goal concerning delivery was to track overall productivity. This would mean gathering information about how many cases were produced and how long it took to produce the cases.

In all three areas, the idea was to have visibility into the data and to provide access to everyone who needed it. This is one example of the role of a DSS. In this case, the system isn't that complex. If the company looks at the data and sees that the yields are falling off, it may have some indication of what is causing that, but it also might have to do some research in other ways. This system wouldn't necessarily give a detailed analysis of why the yields dropped. The benefit of this system, though, is the extent of the visibility. When the yields go up or down even slightly, the company knows it immediately, so it can react immediately.

It is the same as the dashboard of your car providing visibility into your car's engine. You can glance down at the fuel gauge and see that you're about to run out of gas. The dashboard doesn't tell you to put more gas in, and it doesn't tell you where to find more gas. You've to do that part on your own. You can glance at the speedometer and see how fast you're going, but the speedometer doesn't tell you how many miles you have left in your trip and how fast you need to go to get there by a certain time. You have to make those calculations yourself. But if you'd been in the habit of driving a car that didn't have a fuel gauge or a speedometer and then you had them installed, you'd really appreciate the benefits of having these tools in your car.

This was the way this company wanted to run its plant. The company wanted the information available to people, so decisions could be made in response to it. The technology involved wasn't particularly complicated. The chore was to pull the data in from all of the different sources, gather it in one place, organize it and analyze it so that it could be useful, and provide a way to display it, make it accessible, and report it.

Even though the system wasn't that complicated to set up, it could provide all kinds of perspectives on the data that was being collected. The company could slice it or dice it in any way it wanted. The company could have reports that looked at data by hour, by shift, by week, by month, by quarter, by year, for 5 years, for 10 years, for the 1st quarter over the last 5 years, and so on.

DSS Used to Make Data Organized, Consistent, and Available across the Enterprise

This company has a general policy of using a "best of breed" approach when choosing software packages, which means that it doesn't go to only one vendor for all of its needs. Instead, the company buys various commercial off-the-shelf packages, picking the ones that best fit its requirements. If none of the COTS are exactly what it wants, the company might modify a COTS package or develop the software internally.

The DSS was connected with an assortment of systems, including several different manufacturing systems, source systems, planning systems, and delivery systems. The company's basic goal was visibility throughout the corporation. It became clear that, although the company had all of the data it needed, it didn't have it organized and accessible in the ways the company needed it to be. The DSS allowed the company to organize the data in every way it needed. The company could get reports based on customers, schedules, orders, plants, products, SKUs, time frames, and more. The company also created a variety of ways to access the data, providing visibility to everyone using it.

In addition to organizing the data, the company also found that it needed to standardize the data. For example, data coming from two different plants might be using different time settings or different units of measure. So the company created a data dictionary as part of the DSS. This entailed coming up with a standard method of defining data and a way to standardize data across different applications and across the corporation. For example, what is a shift? If you want to organize data from different plants around shifts, you need to make sure you're not comparing 8-hour shifts at one plant to 4-hour shifts at another plant. By creating this data dictionary, the company was able to establish standard terms and practices around its use of data. The entire process proved to be highly valuable. The result was well-organized data that was reported in consistent ways across the enterprise and was easily accessible to everyone who needed it.

DSS Used in a Consumer Products Company

This company has plants in North America, South America, Europe, and Asia. Having plants scattered around the globe like this presents all kinds of challenges. In an effort to bring everyone at all of these plants together as a cohesive single unit, the company came up with an idea. It wanted to provide all of the employees in the entire company with the ability to see and understand how their activities aligned with and contributed to the organization's stated strategic goals.

The company's approach to this was to establish key performance indicators that gave each employee a picture of his or her work in order to show how that work fit into the overall goals of the corporation. These KPIs involve information in many areas. For starters, the company uses them to measure financial matters, so it can see how different units, departments, plants, or divisions performed. It also has personal measures, which indicate the role played by individual activity within the company, and hourly, daily, weekly, monthly, quarterly, and yearly measures concerning how well all of the different units, departments, etc., are doing. Plus, the company has an assortment of other reports on such things as quality, maintenance, inventory, shipping, and more.

A project of this sort involved an immense amount of data coming from countless different sources. The strategy was to integrate all of the data into a DSS and arrange it so that everyone could have access to it as needed. Part of the way the company decided to make the data accessible was to present it as a manufacturing KPI dashboard, centering around customer service, cost-effectiveness, asset productivity, employee productivity, and occupational safety. A critical element of the plan was to have these key measures standardized across the corporation, so that employees in Saskatchewan used the same measures as the employees in Singapore.

Achieving standardization was a difficult and ongoing process, because there are so many different computer systems in place at all of the company's plants around the world. The company has a hodgepodge of applications and some situations where data is being collected manually, and on top of this, it uses different methods and procedures for reporting data in different places. The company didn't want to try to replace all of the computer systems, but it did want to standardize the reporting methods and procedures. This allows the company to establish standardized KPI dashboards throughout the company centered on the five areas mentioned before.

The company also wanted to extend the use of KPI dashboards beyond the five main areas and create more dashboards that provide visibility into plants, departments, groups of machines, specific machines, and ultimately individual employees. The result is a variety of perspectives, including views specific to maintenance of certain machinery, views specific to shift supervisors, finance views based on periods, product views, schedule views, line views, shift views, regional views, raw material views, and so on. The idea of the dashboards for individuals is that each person can have current information pertaining to all matters that are part of his or her job.

The point is to make the use of the data a routine part of everyone's work life. To achieve this goal, the company created a vision of how regular and routine use will look. It sees every individual, factory, group, customer, and supplier having access to the shared data, and it sees performance data being available on a timely basis. The company imagines that strategic plans will have specific and measurable objectives, and it imagines changes in business processes and production processes being driven by the analysis of shared data. They envision trends and relationships being discovered through analysis of the data and employees aligning objectives through sharing information. And it sees learning being promoted by managers discovering what works and what doesn't.

The company realized that it needed technology to make this vision a reality, and it developed general requirements for this technology. The technology needed to:

■ Provide all of the employees with access to performance data in a format that is easy to learn and easy to use.
■ Guarantee the quality, integrity, and accuracy of the data.
■ Show results of the improvement initiatives.

- Show each employee how his or her performance helps the organization achieve its goals.
- Provide various views of the data to support intuitive learning.
- Support the employees' decision-making process.

Intelligent business decisions require real-time responses to current situations. This means having tools, metrics, and analysis capabilities. Data must be transformed into information and information must be transformed into action. The KPI system that provides all of this includes data collection and storage, information analysis, and real-time reporting. All of this is built on business and operations context. This is put into a Web-enabled, manufacturing KPI monitoring and reporting system that has automatic data collection, business and operations context built into it, historical and real-time perspectives, and allows for analysis of data and customer reporting of data. It has business rules that create calls to action, meaning there are alerts or alarms. It has low maintenance and support costs and is accessible across the entire enterprise.

Data is collected from sources in the plant and in corporate offices, from the shop floor to the ERP system. Basically, data can come from anywhere and should come from everywhere. Three separate and distinct activities go on. Multiple tools accessible throughout the enterprise provide visibility, reporting, and analysis. Visibility means real-time, instantaneous, up-to-the-second access to all of the data needed to do any job. Reporting means being able to focus on specific areas, such as a time period, a product, a shift, or more. Analysis means comparing all sorts of data to discern patterns and relationships.

The architecture consists of a KPI database and an application server with Web technology that supports the entire enterprise. Then there are multiple KPI displays across the enterprise that are all Web-based, thin-client technology, which is available on desktop and laptop machines. It's just like going on the Internet — click a few times and you have the information you seek. On the data collection side, data is being collected from the shop floor, ERP system, supply chain systems, finance systems, human resource systems, payroll systems, inventory systems, warehouse systems, scheduling systems, and more. Standard interfaces are used to collect all of this data and get it into the KPI database.

Advanced Planning and Scheduling

APS Used to Upgrade a Company's Entire Scheduling Operations

One company that makes a refrigerated food product had a problem coming up with accurate forecasts. This was a serious problem, because it left the company sitting on the fence debating whether it should be a "make-to-order" company or a "make-to-stock" company. The company had basically been operating under the assumption that it was a make-to-stock company, so it had inventory targets, which were based on forecasts of expected orders. These inventory targets would dictate the manufacturing schedules.

The difficulty was that the company had people who had access to information concerning customers' orders and these people would look at the inventory targets and find problems. In other words, the people setting the targets didn't always have all of the actual order information or the order information would change after the inventory targets had already been set. So, when new information came in, people would try to change the production schedule to either increase production or decrease it, depending on the nature of the new information.

But often the person wanting to change the production levels didn't have the whole story. One person might be aware that a new order had come in, but not that another order was canceled. In the end, there were too many cooks in the kitchen — too many people who were trying to influence the production levels. The entire situation was complicated by the fact that the company makes lots of different flavors of its basic product. If you missed your forecasts, you could end up with way too much or way too little of this flavor or that one.

Part of this problem can be tied to poor business practices, so the company addressed that issue and improved its planning procedures. In addition to this, it saw a chance to use an APS to provide a more sophisticated way of making forecasts. One of the ways the APS improved things was by collecting information from a broad range of sources. This meant that the forecasting mechanism was considering all aspects of the business, all orders, all marketing promotions, all seasonal adjustments, all holiday adjustments, plus historical records that let the company know how much it produced last year at this time.

The company also used the APS for demand planning and scheduling. This involved taking the forecasts and then setting weekly production levels for each plant. The next step is finite capacity scheduling, where the lines are scheduled with start times, end times, changeovers, and quantities produced. For example, this schedule would tell operators that they will be using line 3 to make 460 cases of one flavor from 4:10 P.M. until 8:45 P.M., then they will need to change the line over to another flavor, and the changeover will take 20 minutes, so that the next run will begin at 9:05 P.M.

So there are three layers to the system. The first is the forecasting, where the total quantities needed are determined. The second is the demand planning and scheduling, where these quantities are divided up to different plants over each week. The third is the detailed plan from finite capacity scheduling, where everything on every line for every shift is spelled out. Through the combination of improved business practices and the technological advantages of the APS, the company was able to make a complete turnaround concerning its scheduling problems.

APS Used to Relieve Capacity Constraints

A different food and beverage company had a similar problem. Forecasts were being made, but people in the plant didn't have faith in them. The situation became more difficult as a result of the company's success. As demand grew, production facilities became more constrained and this made scheduling tighter and less flexible. Constrained capacity puts a strain on both sales and production. Sales wants to be able to respond to customer orders at the drop of a hat, but if the plants are running nonstop already, there's no easy way to squeeze in a rush order. Production also has a hard time because problems in meeting production goals cannot be corrected so easily. If a machine breaks down during a run and you're not capacity constrained, then you can find a way to make up the lost time. But if you're already feeling the pinch just getting out the main orders, equipment failures become big headaches. This sort of environment is ripe for the benefits of an APS and this company found the benefits to be lifesavers.

Computerized Maintenance Management Systems

CMMS Used to Reduce Equipment Downtime

This company felt a pressing need to increase productivity, particularly through a reduction in equipment downtime. Its objectives were completely straightforward. It wanted to increase equipment uptime and reduce the cost of maintenance. The main cause of downtime was unexpected breakdowns, and the company had been in the reactive mode of maintenance management. When things broke, it would fix them, but not before.

So the company's approach to increasing uptime was to become more aggressive about catching problems ahead of time and performing preventative maintenance tasks. Another cause of downtime was the lack of spare parts and the time it took to have them delivered. The company wanted to improve on this front as well.

The costs associated with maintenance were not only the labor and parts involved in repairing machinery, but also the inventory of spare parts needed to make the repairs. As we just mentioned, the company didn't always have every spare part it might need, but it did routinely keep a sizeable store of parts on hand. Reducing this inventory would free capital for other uses.

The company hadn't been using any sort of CMMS, handling everything on paper instead, but it decided to install a good software package for managing maintenance. The system the company used was set up to manage work orders, schedule preventative maintenance tasks, look for indications pointing to the need for predictive maintenance, and handle inventory.

In order for the system to determine the nature of the predictive maintenance needed, it was necessary to collect and analyze data from many sources. An example is having data from vibration sensors. It could be possible to detect a trend concerning vibrations that indicates the beginning of a problem, which would cause a breakdown if ignored. Once certain trends were spotted, the specific nature of predictive maintenance tasks could be mapped out.

By working out a preventative maintenance schedule, the company could determine a large part of its need for spare parts and have them delivered just in time for the repairs. The system could also look at the production schedule and fit the maintenance schedule in around it, so that uptime was maximized. For example, a quick look at the production schedule might reveal that Line 6 will be idle all afternoon on Thursday. So the company would plan to use this time to do the routine preventative work needed on Line 6.

Another aspect of the system was keeping maintenance records and equipment histories. Having this sort of information meant that the maintenance supervisor could go to the production supervisor and say that maintenance needed to have 2 hours to work on Line 3 sometime in the next week. It might be easy for the production supervisor to provide 2 hours, if there is an entire week to work it in. The production supervisor will be happy to do it, given that it reduces the likelihood that the equipment will break down in the middle of a run.

The maintenance records could also show which parts were needed most frequently and which were rarely, if ever, needed. On top of this, the system would give accurate, up-to-date information about which parts the company did have in stock and which parts it didn't. As a result, the inventory of spare parts could be managed even more efficiently.

In the end, the CMMS installation helped the company decrease its maintenance costs by 42% and increase its overall uptime by 35%. That is tremendous, all by itself, but there is even more. The maintenance work performed didn't just serve to prevent breakdowns; it also improved the machinery's overall performance. After the company had been on a preventative maintenance schedule for a while, it noticed that it was able to run the equipment at higher speeds with no ill effects. In the past, operators were reluctant to push the speed up too high, in fear that something might fail. Now, they are running at higher speeds without concern.

CMMS Used to Increase Asset Utilization and to Reduce Material Costs

This company wanted to become more aggressive about asset utilization and material costs, so it implemented a CMMS that tied into both materials management and accounting. Materials management was helping with inventory and purchasing, which in this case involved more than just maintenance. It included everything with maintenance, repairs, and operations (MRO), meaning everything a plant buys that is consumable, from repair parts and lubricating oil to work gloves and cleaning supplies.

One of the first results was savings from the consolidation of suppliers, because previously the company hadn't standardized its purchasing practices. Then it worked on improving asset utilization by tracking work orders to find out how long machine repairs were taking and how much the repairs were costing. The CMMS used was mainly focused on creating financial histories and not on managing the maintenance personnel. This is a narrower range of functionality than many other companies pursue, but it was a good fit for this company and brought the results that the company was seeking.

Using a Variety of Systems in One Company

We stressed all along that manufacturing industries are immensely varied. It follows that there are all kinds of ways that IT systems are used. In the following examples we look at the ways various IT systems have been used in a steel company, a bearings company, and a couple of plastics companies.

IT Systems in a Steel Company

Scheduling

This steel company used a continuous caster. Molten steel would be poured into a long cast that was about 2 ft. deep and 2 ft. wide. Continuous casting meant that the ladle would pour more molten steel into the caster before the last bit had cooled. In effect, this produces a continuous strand of steel that's then cut into pieces as needed. In order to produce the molten steel, the company started with scrap metal and melted it in an electric arc furnace. Next, it had other processing steps involving the addition of alloys and testing for certain properties. The steps in the process made it difficult to coordinate everything so that the ladle could be filled on demand.

The challenge was timing the production process so that the ladle could be filled as needed to avoid breaking the strand. Each time the strand was broken, there was a lot of work needed to set up the equipment again before the next strand could be started, and in the process, a good bit of finished steel would have to be scrapped. So, a break in the strand would cost the plant both time and materials. The process of filling and pouring each ladle of steel took about 2 hours. The plant was routinely able to do about three or four ladles without breaking the strand, which meant it frequently went about 6 to 8 hours on each strand; the company thought this was fairly good.

Nevertheless, the company wanted to improve the process, so it installed a scheduling application. This system was highly interactive and required an operator to be engaged with it on a regular basis. Using this system tripled the amount of ladles the plant could pour without breaking the strand. The plant went from about 3 or 4 ladles to about 10 or 12, which translates into a productivity increase of 15% on average.

Level 2 and Level 3 Systems

In order to describe the details of the scheduling application that was installed, we will refer to the CIM Pyramid model. The steel industry is a good example of a manufacturing segment that embraced this model and its idea of clearly defined levels. It may be that the strong influence of the engineering departments at many steel companies is the reason for this development. This particular company had what it called "Level 2" systems, which were area computers in charge of various parts of the production process. Some computers were responsible for the area where the electric arc furnaces were located, others were responsible for the ladle area, others for the casting area, and so on. This was all part of a large supervisory control system that was set up to manage recipes, set up instructions, and process instructions, testing, and data collection among other things. The system would maintain recipes and download them to the PLCs, and at the same time it would collect data back from the PLCs. Since this company didn't have other systems to handle such things as test specifications or set-up instructions, the area computers would maintain this data locally. Another matter handled by these computers was additives. If the plant needed to use powdered nickel in a recipe, for example, this would be managed by the area computers. A bar code system would help them keep track of when it was needed, how much was used, and how much was left in inventory.

All of the data collected about what happened and when it happened would be sent up to the "Level 3" system, which was a plant level computer system. This system was responsible for coordinating the scheduling. It would take in all of the data about raw materials on the one side and the casting process on the other side and determine how the ladles needed to be scheduled. It would also keep track of the inventory of raw materials, work in process, and finished goods. This system also kept track of all of the master recipes, master routings, standard operating procedures, and master work instructions. Each of the area computers would have specific recipes, routings, procedures, and work instructions that pertained to each area, but the plant-level system would maintain records that applied to the plant as a whole. The Level 3 system also managed all of the specifications, and these would play a role in process management. Each customer order would bring up the product specifications required to fill that order.

Asset utilization throughout the mill was very important. For example, there were three different rolling mills, so the plant-level system was responsible for adjusting the schedule to make the optimal use of the equipment. The point was to avoid having one rolling mill idle while another one was backed up with work. It was also important to keep track of every part of production. If some problem arose in one area, this could affect how work would be handled in a different area. The plant-level system allowed the company to look at production at any place in the plant and see how every order was progressing.

The Level 2 systems collected data and the Level 3 systems grouped the data into one production history. This allowed the company to see everything that happened with all of its products and to provide a complete genealogy, including quality assurance testing data, to each customer.

Being concerned with minimizing downtime and maximizing through-puts and yields, the plant level system would track material in and material out to determine yields. Although the company didn't have a maintenance management system, it could use the plant level system to track downtime and eventually it moved into an OEE system.

The plant level system was responsible for interfacing with the business systems at Level 4 and Level 5. Orders came in from the business systems and were executed by the Level 3 systems. Then once the orders were completed, the Level 3 systems would inform the business systems that everything had been done. The Level 3 system also handled the BOM and tied it into the recipe and specifications.

By making intelligent use of IT applications, the company was able to increase productivity without any corresponding increase in labor costs. The company had more ladles per shift while reducing the overall cost per ladle. This had the added benefit of making the company more flexible and thus more responsive to the needs of its customers. It reduced the lead time required to start any specific product and enabled the company to adjust production more easily during any particular shift. For example, if the company needed to change to a steel mix that used higher concentrations of nickel and cadmium, it could make this change in less time and for less cost.

IT Systems in a Bearings Company

This company makes bearings in many shapes and sizes. In addition to ball bearings, it makes high-tech, tapered, roller bearings, which have a cone-like shape, being larger at one end than the other. These are much more expensive because their use in autos, trains, and aircraft can affect human safety in critical ways should they fail.

Quality Assurance Data Collection

Given that the roller bearings are used in ways that can affect human safety, they must undergo extensive testing procedures to ensure their quality. The bearings have to handle a lot of stress and they have to fit together perfectly, so the steel used in the bearings is tested for its composition and the bearings themselves are tested for size tolerances, which can be exceedingly tight.

All of the testing data is collected and organized by a quality assurance system. This system also collects data from customers who report back about how the bearings actually perform when they're used in various products. For example, when routine maintenance is done on an aircraft, a report will be made that indicates the level of wear found on the bearings. The company then compares the data in these performance reports to the test data and to the original recipes with the intent of finding ways to improve the quality of the bearings.

Work Instructions

There are a variety of bearings made by this company, and the differences between some of them are minute. However, even though the differences may be small, the tolerances for error are also minute, so it's critically important that each bearing be made precisely to its specifications. In the process of making different bearings, the production processes can also be strikingly similar, differing only in one or two steps out of the entire sequence. Another element that complicates matters is that specifications can change frequently in response to the constant efforts to improve the products and in response to changing customer requirements. The result of all of this is that the shop floor operator who is in charge of making the bearings has to be extremely careful. It's very easy to make a slight error concerning the specifications or in the manufacturing process and end up producing the wrong bearings.

The solution is detailed work instructions that are updated regularly and that must be matched against the customer's specifications and requirements. In order to ensure accuracy and to promote efficiency, the work instructions are presented in a format that operators find easy to use. Given that changing the equipment settings to set up for a new bearing may mean only extremely small adjustments, the work instructions have to be very clear and precise about each order.

CAD and CAM

This company used computer-aided design (CAD) to produce drawings of the bearings and computer-aided manufacturing (CAM) to translate these drawings into automated instructions for machinery. The process of machining the bearings can involve drilling, cutting, and shaving with reference to multiple angles. As changes come in from the customer, the CAD system is used to modify the drawings. This creates modifications in the CAM instructions, which are downloaded to accompany work instructions for an order.

Finished Product History

It was important for the company to know several things about its finished products:

- Where the steel used in each product originated
- Which machines were used to make each product (this means a detailed history of the routings through the plant)
- Which shifts and which operators worked on the products

The company used this not only to address problems as they were happening but also to deal with any customer feedback. One example of feedback from a customer could be that their tests show some bearings exhibiting more wear than others that were installed at the same time. The company would get feedback on virtually all of the bearings used and this is one of the reasons that it had virtually no failures. Some bearings may show more wear, but that doesn't mean that they failed in any way.

Scheduling and Routing

This company also makes bearings that are used in all sorts of rail cars — subway cars, light rail vehicles, box cars, and engines. Here again, the company had a wide variety of products, which translates into a complex scheduling challenge. Part of the challenge was that products were manufactured in precisely the quantities ordered, as opposed to being made in large lots and put into inventory. The nature of the production process is that there are several steps that involve different machines and there are various paths that any one product can take through the plant.

In order to manage the scheduling of production runs, the company used a system that matched the specifications of each product with the pieces of equipment needed to produce that product. Bearing A might require the use of Machines 2, 3, and 10, while bearing B might require the use of Machines 2, 3, and 14. So there was some overlap and some variation in the machines needed by different products. The scheduling program would check the availability of the machines and find the optimal approach to queuing the production runs.

SPC and SQC

When this company started using a SPC/SQC system, it was so successful that the company kept expanding the ways in which it was used. With cone-shaped bearings, there is a diameter measure on each end, a slope angle, and a length. The company had discovered certain problems that tended to arise during production in terms of size variances. So the first step with its SPC/SQC system was to track three measurements: the diameters at each end and the length. This allowed the company to determine the source of the problem and make adjustments as necessary.

At first, the company wasn't set up to test every bearing that went through, but eventually it was able to do this. Before the company installed this system, it would simply keep producing bearings until it discovered one that was outside the specification parameters. Then the company would stop to make adjustments and scrap some bearings in the process. With this system, the company was able to spot trends and make adjustments before the bearings ever became too far outside of the specifications.

Parts and BOM

The bearings for rail cars often were sold in a housing. Some of the bearings measured from 6 in. to 10 in. The housing could be up to 18 in. long and weigh up to 50 lbs. The company used a BOM system to ensure that all of the parts were matched to each order.

Maintenance Management

As business increased, the company ran into maintenance problems. It responded by adopting a RCM program. Part of this was unplanned downtime analysis. The company collected all kinds of data concerning every aspect of equipment failures. The company eventually expanded this to an OEE system, because it was discovering that many of the machines weren't performing as well as they should. In many cases, operators had decided to run the machines more slowly in order to ensure quality and avoid breakdowns. As the company worked on the problem, it found ways to increase the speed without increasing breakdowns or decreasing quality. It could also see ways to conduct maintenance in ways that supported overall plant reliability.

One of the most important overall gains this company made through its use of IT was the ability to develop a broader range of products, while simultaneously increasing productivity and reducing costs. In most cases, companies experience a drop in productivity and a rise in costs whenever they enlarge their product line, so this was a dramatic benefit. This change of offering more products built upon itself, because as customers saw the company's increased flexibility, they began asking for an even broader range of options in terms of the product specifications. As a result, the company gained a reputation for being able to accommodate many different requests and it stood out against its competitors.

IT Systems in Plastics Companies

DCS Use

Making plastic can be a challenge. This company makes plastic that is sold to other companies that mold it into all kinds of different products. An important characteristic of the company's IT environment is extensive use of DCSs, which makes it possible to collect a lot of data through the control system. In effect, the company was able to use its DCS to do much of what HMI/SCADA normally does, plus trending and charting of data. The company also had PCs and minicomputers connected, which allowed it to create a database for a process historian. All of this provided a great source of data for all of the other IT systems, so the control system was running the plant and at the same time feeding data to all of the other applications.

Specifications Management

At another company, the process entails taking plastic pellets, which are about 2 sq. mm each and molding them into sheets and films of various sizes. The products vary in length, width, and thickness, and are made to each customer's specifications. Making the various sizes requires different additional ingredients to be added to the plastic pellets, and different products have different quality tests associated with them. This meant that the company had product specifications and quality assurance specifications of many sorts, and managing these specifications was an important part of the manufacturing process.

The solution to managing the specifications was a simple application. It allowed the company to tie its specifications to each work order. When a client requested certain materials, the sales department could confirm all of the specifications with the client. Then the plant would have all of the information needed to produce the product and test it exactly according to the required specifications.

This ability is critical, because this manufacturer has so many different products that it produces. One customer could place an order for several different products at once and sometimes customers would request that something be changed. They might want a plastic sheet to be harder or softer, more opaque or more transparent, stiffer or more flexible, and so on. This meant a change in existing specs and additional testing. The entire operation could become exceedingly complex.

Bar Code and RFID

The company that makes raw plastics has a process that involves mixing several chemicals in pellet and powder form in a large vat. The main ingredients are added in bulk, but some of the additives and fillers, which are a small part of the total formula, are added by hand. After everything is mixed, the plastic goes through an extruder, which heats it and forms it into strands. As the strands cool, they are cut into square pellets. The pellets are then packaged and stored while quality testing is done. Finally, the pellets will be shipped in a variety of ways, from 50-lb. sacks to railroad cars.

The production process in this plant involves about 50 larger tanks with bulk material and about 200 small tanks with additives and fillers. All of these tanks feed the mixing vats, which support about 20 extruders. One of the biggest dangers is that the wrong ingredient will be put into the mix, because once the wrong ingredient goes in, the batch has to be scrapped. There is no way to get it back out again. In many cases, the mistake will not be found until tests are run, which means that the potential for wasted time increases also.

To help ensure accuracy, the company installed a bar code system and used it in several different ways. First, when materials were delivered, the system would make sure the bar code on the material being delivered matched the bar code on the tank to which it was transferred. To ensure that the system was used, the company installed an interlock mechanism that prevented anyone from putting material into and taking material out of a tank without matching the bar codes. The company also uses this system to manage its raw materials inventory.

In order to manage the storage and shipping of the finished products, the company installed a radio frequency identification (RFID) system. As the pellets were finished, they would be put into containers, each of which had an RFID tag. This would be programmed with information about the product ID, the lot number, the weight, the date of manufacture, and the line that it was made on. The container would be put in an automated warehouse until it was needed for shipping, at which time the tag would be used to find exactly the product needed for each order. The RFID application made certain that the right product got shipped to the right place. Tracking finished products became entirely automated and shipping errors became virtually nonexistent. After shipment, the tag would be reprogrammed to indicate that the container was empty and needed to be cleaned. After cleaning, it would be reprogrammed again to indicate that it was ready to be filled once more.

Recipe Management

Plastics can be made to meet many different specifications with respect to thickness, hardness, color, viscosity, melting point, shatter point, and so on. For each type of plastic there's a different recipe and given the number of variables involved, managing recipes can become quite complicated.

The difference between a recipe for a product and that product's specifications may not be readily apparent. In this case, the specifications indicate the characteristics that the finished product must have, such as the melting point, the hardness, and the color, while the recipe is the list of ingredients and the manufacturing instructions that must be used to produce a product with exactly the specifications needed. A recipe might say that these ingredients are mixed first in these quantities, then this amount of these other ingredients are added and mixed together on this piece of equipment for this long, at this temperature. Recipes often have to be adjusted and this complicates matters further. Different pieces of equipment may have different qualities that affect the production process, so producing a specific product on two different lines may involve slight changes to the basic recipe.

One aspect of this company's approach to recipe management was to tie its recipes to its product specifications. This way, when an order came in, both the specifications and the recipes connected with that order were automatically tied to it through the work order. The company's system also ties the recipes into its control system, so that operators on the plant floor have all of the information needed to produce the correct product. One aspect of this is that operators can use the system to verify each step in the production process as they proceed, which helps to ensure that no mistakes are made as they go along.

Scheduling

In this plastics plant, the extruders were generally the busiest pieces of equipment and could become bottlenecks for the production process, so scheduling was a primary concern. The company had a finite capacity scheduling application which started when an ERP system took orders from the clients and downloaded them into a MES. The MES would then look at the best ways to group the orders and designate which pieces of equipment should be used in which order.

The challenge of scheduling involved several factors. Some products required the use of specific extruders. Products of different colors needed to be run in certain sequences, mainly going from lighter colors to darker colors. Cleaning and maintenance activities figured in as well and the entire effort was framed around the need to keep the extruders running as much of the time as possible.

Downtime Tracking and OEE

Part of the company's effort to keep the extruders running as much of the time as possible involved a MES application tracking downtime. All downtime was carefully analyzed. The company looked at unplanned downtime in order to get at the root causes. The company also looked at planned downtime, such as changeovers, cleaning, and maintenance to see how it could reduce the time spent on these activities. This was part of its continuous improvement program and the downtime application eventually grew into an OEE application so that the company could look at quality and performance in greater detail. One thing the company discovered was that slowing the extruder down slightly made it easier to manage and improve overall performance.

Cleaning Management

There are a number of concerns around cleaning the extruders. One is that they have to be cleaned really well whenever they are changing from a dark color to a light color. Residue from the dark color could contaminate the light color. Another matter is that different products require different cleaning solutions, so the plant has to be certain that it's using the right cleaning products at the right times. The cleaning management system helped ensure that the operators were following the cleaning procedures exactly as needed.

Product History and Genealogy

The company used a product history and genealogy system to collect data from all of the DCSs, the bar code system, and the RFID system. One part of this was the ability to give a COA to the customers indicating that the products met all of the required specifications. Another part was the ability to track down the source of quality problems. When a customer filed a complaint about any product, the company wanted to be able to find the cause of the problem. The system could tell them how each product was made, which materials were used, which lines were used, even which containers were used, and how long it stayed in the warehouse.

Quality Assurance

Testing for quality is an integral part of the production process and the company has several laboratories where it tested the products for color, density, viscosity, and more. To manage the testing data in its labs, the company used a LIMS system and then fed this data into its product history system.

SPC

The company used these applications to adjust the temperature and the speed of the extruders, based on the results coming out, such as a high viscosity reading or a small pellet size. The company had targets and whenever the readings got outside of a certain range, an adjustment would be made.

Scrap and Rework in Scheduling

When the plant was changing from one color to another, it wouldn't turn off the extruder. This means that the company would have some scrap produced that couldn't be used for either color, but which could possibly be reused later for black or some other dark color. The company used a scheduling application to plan the reuse of this scrap. This involved data concerning specifications and inventory of the scrap. This application was a hybrid of scheduling, inventory, specifications, and recipe management systems.

With both plastics companies, the benefits gained from the use of IT applications echo those of the steel company and the bearings company. In all cases, productivity and customer responsiveness increased while costs decreased. For the company making plastic sheets, this meant being able to provide an incredible array of different products in terms of thickness, hardness, opacity, color, and more, and being able to provide these products more quickly and more efficiently. This company was also able to offer the service of cutting the sheets to customers' specifications, which was something it hadn't done before. The company making plastic pellets gained the ability to make subtle changes in the different grades it offered, thus providing its customers with valuable options not previously available. In both cases, the companies gained significant competitive advantages in terms of their customer service capabilities.

CONCLUSION

We have explained where the gold is, laid out the mining tools, and shared stories of others who have had success getting the gold out. Knowing about the opportunities for savings in the plant and about the tools needed to make use of those opportunities are the first steps, but the process of putting this knowledge to practical use is complicated and arduous. First, you have to determine the specific opportunities that are available in your company. Next you have to decide which tools, should be used to take advantage of those opportunities. Then you have to implement those tools, and finally you have to sustain an ongoing effort to support and improve what you have done.

At every stage in this process, there are difficulties of all shapes and sizes. That's why we've devoted the rest of the book to the challenge of actually doing the work. In the next five chapters we will provide you with strategies and insights that will assist you as you navigate the passage from theory to reality.

7

HOW TO MAKE IT SOLUTIONS A REALITY

Our focus to this point has been on understanding why IT has developed in manufacturing the way it has and where it is today. We've shown that there are tremendous opportunities for using IT to improve manufacturing, and we've examined the tools needed in order to make use of these opportunities. Now comes the hard part — how you actually make IT solutions a reality in your company. The final five chapters of this book are our answer to the question "How?"

There are important reasons why the process of using information technology in manufacturing plants is difficult. We'll examine those in the first part of this chapter. After that, we'll lay out the four stages of a project's lifecycle: strategy, framework, implementation, and support. The next three chapters will examine these stages in depth, and our final chapter looks at the pitfalls that can undermine all other efforts for success. Our goal is to provide the knowledge you'll need to handle all of the challenges that lie ahead.

WHY THE PROCESS IS DIFFICULT

The fundamental reason the process is difficult is that manufacturing IT is an exceedingly complex field. This problem is compounded by the fact that people frequently fail to acknowledge this complexity. It's as if choosing the right IT solutions for a manufacturing plant were no more trouble than choosing a new washer and dryer to do laundry in your home. With household appliances, you can go to a store that has every-thing under one roof. If you don't know that much about how washer and dryer technology has advanced recently, you might need to spend

30 minutes or an hour discussing your options with a salesperson. But that's all it would take. You could be ready to choose in an hour.

With software systems, the options are much more varied and complex. What if washers and dryers weren't all standardized in so many ways? For example, imagine that some dryers ran on 220 volts, some on 110 volts, and some on three or four other voltages and that homes sometimes were wired for one voltage and sometimes for another. Then consider that water wasn't provided in consistent ways. In some homes, maybe the water needed to be filtered before being used and some homes needed a washing machine that comes with a filter. Say that no company had developed a washing machine that would handle all kinds of fabric, so you needed different washing machines for cotton, nylon, blends, and so on. What if electrical power to your home wasn't always reliable and that you needed a solution that could also work when the power was unavailable? Finally, imagine trying to buy the right washer and dryer when no one store sells everything you need to do your laundry at home, yet all salespeople insist that their models will definitely do it all, 100% guaranteed.

This analogy barely scratches the surface in terms of illustrating the complexity of software options. Matters can become remarkably confusing, and it leads people to engage unwittingly in some absurd decision-making processes. For example, no one would try to decide between buying a dishwasher and buying a toaster oven in an effort to find a solution to dirty dishes. Yet, there have been many cases where the software systems being considered as specific IT solutions to problems in manufacturing plants have every bit as much functionality in common as a dishwasher and a toaster oven.

Making matters worse is the fact that in virtually all situations, the solution that works best is an assembled solution. That usually means dealing with more than one vendor. Being able to discuss your company's needs and the software solutions with vendors is critically important, but these conversations will not be productive unless you have a firm grip both on your requirements and on the scope of technology available. And getting a firm grip on these matters is no simple task.

Given how quickly technology changes, there may be a temptation to wait 6 more months or a year in hopes that the one-size-fits-all IT solution will appear on the scene. Dramatic advances in software capability are unlikely, however, because the manufacturing industry is simply too varied. There's software currently available to do just about anything you need done, but it takes work on your part to make sure you get the right tools.

One additional difficulty is that there's no single source for gaining the knowledge needed to navigate the process. No one is presenting the big picture of the entire spectrum of IT solutions for manufacturing companies. You can learn a lot about specific products from vendors. You can learn more about specific types of information technology from some industry groups, but there's a distinct lack of an overarching perspective from anyone. We see this book as a step toward filling that void. You can use the information here to achieve an encompassing viewpoint, so that you can survey the entire panorama of possibilities and make intelligent choices.

THE PROJECT LIFECYCLE

A fundamental aspect of the big picture is understanding the lifecycle of IT projects, which is illustrated in Figure 7.1. Every project can be seen as a process through four stages:

1. Strategy
2. Framework
3. Implementation
4. Support

You begin with a **Strategy** of *what* you want to pursue and *why* you want to pursue it. The idea is to pinpoint the ways that manufacturing IT investments can bring value to your company by articulating the benefits you expect to achieve. Do you want to reduce material waste? Improve equipment uptime? Have better visibility into production processes? Eliminate scheduling headaches? Reduce maintenance costs? Answering these questions involves several things. You'll want to conduct an honest diagnosis to identify the opportunities for improvement, and you have to do this within the context of the systems already in place at your company. Then you need to translate the opportunities into a detailed set of functional requirements.

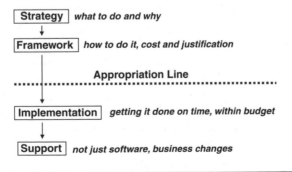

Figure 7.1 The Project Lifecycle

Your requirements are the basis for everything that follows, so their importance shouldn't be underestimated. Part of the Strategy stage is using the requirements to begin sketching out an idea of the architecture you will want. There will often be several different ways to structure your IT solutions and people within the corporation are likely to have opposing views on the best approach. The key here is to keep the focus on using the right tool for the job. In Chapter 8, we discuss requirements thoroughly and we look at all of the essential steps you should take to form a solid strategy.

In the **Framework** stage, you start to examine the technological solutions using both the requirements and the basic architectural plans you've made. The point now is to answer *how* your goals will be achieved. You are transforming the vision into concrete terms. There's a lot of hard work involved in educating yourself so that you can competently evaluate the applicable software. Various standards and models can be valuable educational tools in this effort. The point is to map your IT landscape, to settle on the precise architecture you'll use for your additions and changes, and to select the vendors and the specific products you need.

Part of the work at this stage is that you must get your project funded before you go on to the Implementation stage. There's a line here that can be thought of as the "appropriation line." You must cross it before you can continue. Without a solid plan that can demonstrate either hard paybacks or clear advantages based on new capabilities, the project may never justify funding. Given that in most companies many projects and programs compete for the same dollars, some proposals are destined to never make it past the initial stages. This is particularly true in light of senior management's general skepticism about getting a payback on IT expenditures. But if you can show how the software you want will do such things as reducing labor expense, saving material costs, or increasing capacity utilization, you stand a good chance of getting the funds you seek. Chapter 9 presents a discussion of evaluating technology, a review of important standards and models, and some critical advice for getting your project funded.

Once your project has been approved, you enter the **Implementation** stage. This can be a long and complicated process, but there are all sorts of ways to manage an implementation so that it goes as smoothly as possible. Above all else, remember two things. First, be careful not to underestimate the challenge of implementing software systems. Tremendous problems can occur when the resources committed to the project are short of what they should be; these are the sorts of problems that don't happen when the right amount of attention is given to the implementation from the start. The other thing to remember is to remain flexible. No plan remains unchanged once it meets reality, so the ability to adapt is essential.

Finally, you come to the **Support** stage. The systems are installed and running, you're getting the benefits you hoped for, and everything is finally working exactly the way you envisioned. The problem is that your success will not be sustained without adequate support. Training isn't just a one-time, initial affair that occurs during the implementation. It's an ongoing process, because personnel are always changing and people learn things in stages, not all at once. The matter is also complicated by the fact that, for most companies, the manufacturing process is not static. It's subject to all kinds of changes, which means that your software will need to do more than just keep running the way it is. It will have to adapt along with your business. In Chapter 10, we look first at a variety of ways to ensure that your implementation process is a complete success and then we examine the essential elements of establishing and maintaining support.

Support should also be viewed in the broader context of continuous improvement. One of the ways to support ongoing development is to be aware of the many pitfalls that can endanger your success. Hidden dangers and difficulties lurk within every project, so in Chapter 11, we list the most common pitfalls, discuss how they can be avoided, and suggest strategies for getting out them if you do fall in. We also give a list of why companies succeed. Under "Seven Habits of Highly Effective Manufacturers," we present our ideas for creating a corporate culture that is supportive of and conducive to successful IT projects.

Through these final four chapters we describe the lifecycle from the perspective of starting a completely new initiative, but you may already be managing projects at any of the lifecycle stages. The point is to recognize each stage as it occurs and handle it in the manner appropriate to that stage.

Using the Project Lifecycle

A New Plant

One company that used this approach successfully was building a new plant and needed to determine which IT systems should be installed there. In line with the project lifecycle concept, the people within the company who were responsible for the project started by defining their strategy and establishing a framework for achieving it. This meant looking at the big picture, seeing everything they wanted to accomplish, and determining which systems would fit the bill. This is analogous to having work to do that requires some sort of vehicles. Based on the specific tasks you have in mind, you might find that you need a pickup truck and a minivan, but you don't really need a sports car or sport utility vehicle. After evaluating their functional requirements, they decided which software packages would work best.

Continuing with the Framework stage, they went into more detail concerning the requirements and they used this information to design the architecture for integrating all of the systems. They also developed a project plan that included the scope of the project, the resources needed, the estimated cost, and the schedule for the implementation. When the plan was submitted for funding approval, everything was laid out in detail and the project was approved. This put them across the appropriation line.

After the implementation was complete, they arranged technical support for all of their IT systems, which includes maintaining the database and all of the applications. Additionally, the systems are monitored proactively, so problems can be detected quickly.

The process works. The success of the entire project couldn't have occurred if any phase of the lifecycle process had been given short shrift. Money had to be spent up front in order to do all of the work necessary to thoroughly define all of the functional requirements. Without good requirements, it's impossible to design the framework appropriately. Even with perfectly defined requirements, if you don't give enough attention to the framework, your project plan will be either vague or inaccurate. This can lead to two possible dangers. One is that you can't get the project funded, because the plan can't demonstrate a solid ROI. The other danger is that you do get your project funded, but your plan's budget numbers and implementation schedules are way off the mark. This just sets you up for serious problems later on.

A Plant Expansion

A poultry processing company decided to build a materials handling center as a plant expansion. The new center was designed to include a new packaging line, a new sorting system, and a new warehouse with a new shipping dock. The goal was that as boxes of poultry came in, they'd be sorted according to SKU. Next they'd be palletized and put into a warehouse. In the warehouse, customer orders would be put together, which typically involved gathering boxes of several different SKUs. These would then be loaded onto one pallet and put into a truck for delivery.

The company had a distinct idea of what it wanted to achieve physically with the facility. It knew what size the warehouse needed to be, how many sorting lanes would be needed, what the packaging lines should be able to do, how the palletizer would operate, and how the labeling stations should function. What it didn't know was how to fit all of this into its IT environment.

The first step was to develop an overall strategy for the IT architecture based on high-level requirements. Once the strategy was done, the company was in a good position to start looking at the various pieces that would fit into that architecture.

Once the company knew how the pieces would fit together, it could take the next step which was creating a framework based on functional requirements. The company could see how each part of the entire system would function and how each would be interfaced with others. Having a well-defined strategy makes this step much easier. It becomes a matter of filling in details, which allows you to examine your options more effectively. With your requirements set, you can evaluate various solutions for each area and pick the one best suited for your purposes. In other words, this company was in the position to use systems from different vendors or write its own programs, whichever made the most sense in each case.

For example, for the warehouse system, the company chose to use an internally developed legacy system. This system had most of the functionality needed and there were no problems maintaining it, so the company kept it and enhanced it to fit the new situation. In other areas, the company bought COTS from an assortment of vendors. By using different vendors, this company avoided being locked into a single implementation approach. In some cases, it chose to manage the implementation internally. In other cases, the company contracted for implementation services along with the software product.

CONCLUSION

Even though it's difficult to make IT solutions a reality in your company, it can be done. Companies are successful all of the time, but these successes are no accident. It takes a great deal of work educating yourself and others within your company so that you can make the right decisions and handle all of the problems that can arise. Using the project lifecycle as our guide for the next four chapters, we present a guidebook for success.

8

STRATEGY

Strategy is the first stage of every successful IT project and the foundation for devising a good strategy is a good set of requirements. Once you have your requirements, you can begin to sketch out broad solutions. In order to do this, you have to consider both your requirements and the systems already in place. As your basic IT architecture takes shape, you may encounter opposing points of view concerning the best approach to take, because there's a natural tendency within various departments to see their own systems as the best. All of these challenges are part of the Strategy stage, so we start off this chapter by looking at requirements in depth, explaining why they matter, and how to create them. Then we discuss the challenge of using your requirements to begin creating the overall IT architecture you will need. Next, we examine different approaches to IT architecture and explain why we recommend a balanced approach. Finally, we stress the importance of involving the end users from the very start.

WHY REQUIREMENTS MATTER

Imagine hiring a contractor to build a house and having no discussions whatsoever about how that house would look. The idea is obviously absurd, because the house could end up being anywhere from 1,000 sq. ft. to 10,000 sq. ft. It could have no windows or entire walls of glass. It could be made of cement blocks, or it could even be a straw hut. If you want the house to meet your needs, you have to tell the builder what those needs are. The same holds true for IT projects. If you want computer software that solves certain problems, you have to describe those problems in detail. Otherwise, you're almost certain to end up with something other than what you actually need.

A well-written, well-constructed list of requirements will help the project stay on track and help it deliver the expected benefits. Lack of good requirements will at the very least cause cost or schedule overruns. At the worst, it will cause the project to fail by delivering the wrong functionality. A solid definition of your requirements is the first step to completing projects on time, on budget, and with the endorsement of both management and the user community. For example, scope creep is an ever-present danger for IT projects, but clearly defined requirements guard against this. When your needs and goals are described only in vague or general terms, it opens the door to efforts to expand the focus. Creating and using a requirements document to guide the technology selection and the ongoing project activities ensures that your project objectives are met and that the final result is a solution that can be used. It saves time and energy and it results in a finished product or solution that meets all the desired requirements.

GENERAL GUIDELINES FOR CREATING A LIST OF REQUIREMENTS

Here are some basic ideas to consider as you approach the task of defining requirements:

- *Don't lose sight of your business objectives.* Think about what you're trying to achieve in the broad sense, not just what you're trying to achieve technologically. If you're a college student who has to produce a term paper, you would want to have a computer with a word processing program. In this case, your requirement is a term paper and the word processing software is your tool. In other words, requirements aren't about defining the technology you need; they are about defining what you need technology to do for you.
- *Define the role of technology in meeting your requirements.* In order to produce a term paper, you may want more than just word processing capability. You may want to be able to use your computer to do research, so you would need a connection to the Internet and Web capabilities. On the other hand, perhaps you are studying in a field where the computer isn't a valuable research tool. In this case, you don't need additional technology other than word processing. Remember to focus on using technology to do what it does best and let people do what they do best. Computers are remarkable tools, but they aren't so remarkable when their functionality doesn't fit their application.

- *Document your requirements, enumerate them, and make them measurable.* Document the requirements in terms of specific jobs or specific uses. For example, a requirement could be processing a purchase order. Also document where each requirement came from, why it originated, what it's trying to solve, and how technology is going to address it. Then don't just list your requirements; enumerate them and make them measurable. This means that you've broken them down into individual components and they are numbered for tracking purposes. When you are implementing the project, you'll be able to see if a specific, detailed requirement has been met or not. If it hasn't, you'll know what else needs to be done, because you'll be able to trace these individual components back to the functional source. This methodology allows you to map your requirements against your deliverables. In the software industry, this is called "requirements traceability" and its importance to your project is every bit as significant as tracking and tracing is to your manufacturing effort.
- *Distinguish between functional and operational requirements.* Functional requirements address the actual work that needs to be done by a software program. Operational requirements address how people will be using the software. This means looking at the number of users, the daily schedule for use, the types of interfaces, the expected life span of the system, the plans for the evolution of the system, the degree of detail required, and the timeframe for collecting data, among other things.

BENEFITS OF REQUIREMENTS

To the users, the project team, and other individuals, good requirements should provide several specific benefits, such as the following:

- *Requirements establish the functional baseline.* They provide the basis for an agreement between the users and the project team on what the system will perform. They enable all parties to be clear about what's supposed to be accomplished. A complete description of each of the system functions assists the potential users to determine if the system meets their needs or what additional modifications are required to meet their needs.
- *Requirements reduce the project effort.* The preparation of requirements forces the various concerned groups to consider all of the requirements before the project begins. Careful review of the requirements can reveal omissions, misunderstandings, and inconsistencies early in the project when these problems are easier to correct.

- *Requirements provide a basis for estimating project costs and schedules.* The description of the system is a realistic basis for estimating project costs and can be used to obtain approval for bids. It allows the project team to obtain more accurate bids from prospective hardware, software, and service providers.
- *Requirements provide a basis for definitive testing, validation, and verification.* Organizations can develop their test, validation, and verification plans more productively from good requirements. As a part of the project, requirements can provide a baseline against which compliance can be measured. The final system is acceptable only if it passes the agreed upon acceptance criterion.
- *Requirements serve as a basis for support.* Requirements can be used as the mechanism to measure future changes to the system's baseline. This allows the business to assess impact to proposed changes. Requirements provide a foundation for continued enhancements.

THE REQUIREMENTS DOCUMENT

A requirements document is used to describe the necessary capabilities of an application or system. It's a collection of all of the specifications required for a system and it describes how a product will work functionally, giving this description entirely from the user's perspective. This means that there's no concern for how the solution is implemented. Instead the document talks strictly about features, functions, constraints, and other items that any user of the system would need. It states what a system should do, not how it will do it.

Users have a high-level perspective of what they want an application to accomplish. The requirements document takes their perspective and provides details of what it should do, how it will be used, and what it will look like. The document creates an overview of the project, which and it saves time and reduces costs. It's much easier to change functionality in the beginning of a project than it is to redo the project after someone discovers that a critical piece is missing.

There's also a natural tendency to lose focus on the requirements themselves and to start thinking about highly specific solutions. This is one of the biggest pitfalls that people encounter while developing a requirements document. To avoid falling into this trap, concentrate only on what the system needs to do and refrain from considering how these needs will be met. Defining the solutions in broad terms is the next step of the Strategy stage. Defining solutions in greater detail is part of the design work that is done in the Framework stage. A requirements document and a design document are two separate and distinct items. Success in creating a good design depends upon a solid and thoroughly researched requirements document. The design team will use the document to create the design and to determine if various proposed solutions do an acceptable job of satisfying the requirements.

USING REQUIREMENTS TO SKETCH OUT BROAD SOLUTIONS

Your requirements tell you what needs to be done, so the next step is finding ways to satisfy these needs. In the Strategy stage, you want to look at solutions in general terms. Don't forget that the requirements are born out of your business goals, so the solutions you choose must be aligned with those goals. Decide what role your ERP systems will have and whether you need a CMMS, a MES, a DSS, or all three. But don't get preoccupied with acronyms or the names of the various systems. The point is to keep a clear focus on the functions that these systems must address and to avoid worrying about the fine points. At this time, it's not necessary to know how the selected systems will interface with the ERP system or how the screens will look for each user. Details of that nature will be addressed in the Framework stage. The task now is to look at the systems you already have in place and determine which systems you need. The result is a sketch of how your IT architecture should look in broad terms.

The task of choosing systems to handle requirements is analogous to choosing gardening tools to handle landscaping chores. Imagine a suburban neighborhood with houses that have the standard variety of shrubs around the houses, some trees, some flowerbeds, maybe some fences along property lines, and lawn everywhere in between. It may be that every single house in the neighborhood has most of these features, but it also is likely that no two houses have them in the same proportions. One house may have a chain link fence around the perimeter, but another may use a hedge of bushes to mark the boundary between houses. One house may be positioned on a steep slope, while the plot of land another sits on is perfectly level. The owners of some houses may pursue gardening to such a degree that there's little lawn left around the house at all, while other houses could have wide expanses of grass.

Likewise, each house will have the appropriate tools for the type of yard work being done. For example, if you have extensive flowerbeds with only tiny patches of grass left, why bother to own a motor-powered lawn mower? A manual reel mower will suffice perfectly. It's less expensive to purchase, less expensive to operate as it requires no gas or oil, and less expensive to maintain since it's a much simpler mechanism with fewer moving parts. Plus, given the small lawn, a power mower has no real advantage in terms of saving labor. On the other hand, if you have a large lawn, it may be that a power mower allows you to cut the grass in half the time it takes you with a reel mower. The extra expense may be well worth it. If you have a few bushes, you may want to own a pair of hedge clippers. If you have a long hedge, you may want to own some power clippers. But if you have almost no bushes at all or the ones you do have don't require trimming, then this type of tool would be completely useless for you.

Your immediate task is to decide which type of tools you need. Do you need a lawn mower of any kind? Do you need any type of pruning shears? Settling on the specific type of mower and the brand will come in the Framework stage. It's at that stage that you will evaluate and select the precise products that you will use. But even at the Strategy stage, when you're sketching out your architecture in broad terms, it's important to understand two ideas that will apply more pointedly when you reach the Framework stage.

No Single Solution

The first idea is that there's no single solution that will work in every situation. Think about your particular landscape. If your facilities produce expensive drugs, then your quality system needs are quite different from a plant producing rubber worms for fishing. If you produce products in all different shapes and sizes that are packaged in different ways for different regions of the country or the world, then you shouldn't be using the same tracking and tracing software used by a different manufacturing company that makes only one product and sells it in only one region of the country. The same goes for companies that are highly regulated vs. those that aren't. Manufacturing industries are incredibly varied, which is why no single solution will work for everyone.

This is one of the most important ideas to keep in mind when approaching the Portfolio. Despite what you may have been told, in most cases, no one single vendor can supply all of the systems you need. Imagine if the person selling you a riding lawnmower said that this was the only tool you needed to do all of your yard work. When you mention that you thought it might be good to have a weed eater to take care of the grass growing along the edges, the salesperson replies that there is an attachment that can be added to the rear of the lawnmower to handle edging. All you have to do is back up the riding mower to where the weeds are. Well, of course, this is absurd. The beauty of a weed eater is its ability to be easily carried everywhere and turned in all directions and used at any angle to get into all of the nooks and crannies where bulkier and heavier equipment is useless.

You may encounter claims from certain software vendors that are similarly misleading. Clearly the idea of using just one vendor for all of your IT needs has tremendous appeal, but a single, integrated solution for manufacturing IT simply doesn't exist today. ERP companies were able to create a single product that handles financial matters, but that's a different story. The types of transactions handled by ERP are much more uniform across the business world. Manufacturing industries are too diverse and the manufacturing IT demands of these industries cover too wide a spectrum for any single product to handle it all. Although technology is constantly changing, it changes on its own timescale, one which is distinct and unrelated to the rhythms of your business. A single integrated solution will not be available from a single vendor in time to help your current projects. This means that, by definition, every good solution is an assembled solution. The Portfolio that meets the needs of your company will have several, if not many, components.

The tools you need do exist, however. In this domain of manufacturing today, a lack of good technology isn't the issue. For all practical purposes, there are plenty of tools to do anything and everything you would want to do. Prices certainly vary, but the software products are there. Plus, in almost all cases, the products are commodities. You just go buy them off the shelf. Though you may be forced to use toolkits to address the functions of decision support systems, in most other cases there are COTS that can handle the functional applications in manufacturing plants today. If you're busy writing custom code, then odds are either that you're just not fully aware of all the COTS products on the market or you haven't taken a close enough look at them.

Finding the Right Tools

The second idea is that success depends on finding the specific tools that fit the landscape of your company. Most software has been designed to address specific applications in specific industries. The solution that works well in one place can be an abject failure when used to address either a different application or the same application in a different industry. If you want to see such an abject failure, try taking a MES designed for an automotive company and putting it into a pharmaceutical company. It would be a disaster not because there's anything wrong with the software, but because it's just the wrong product in the wrong setting.

In making your choices, consider both your landscape and the tools you already possess. Don't spend tons of money on a riding lawn mower, if you only have a small patch of grass to mow. And likewise, don't expect a weed eater to efficiently handle a large lawn. Following this advice will prevent you from spending millions on an application that may bring only a small return on your investment. You will also avoid falling for the one-size-fits-all sales pitch. In most cases, the same application will not work equally well at both large and small plants. Determine precisely what you need and then *get the right tool for the job.*

VARIOUS APPROACHES TO IT ARCHITECTURE

Remember that the gap that exists between the plant systems and the corporate IT systems is a functionality gap. The functionality provided by enterprise systems doesn't adequately address the functionality needs of the plants. Our focus with the Portfolio has been the effort to bridge this gap between corporate-level, enterprise-wide IT systems and the plant. Just as there's no single software product that will work in all situations, there's no single architectural solution that will work for all companies. As you examine architectural options, it may be helpful to consider the various good and bad ways that companies implement and integrate all of their IT systems. It's very likely that you will encounter people in your company who insist on certain architectural approaches, and you need to be able to steer them away from making bad decisions.

Every company has a history of assorted IT projects and every one of these projects has had a sponsor who defined the needs for the project and took charge of getting it implemented. Generally speaking, the person or group in charge of an IT project would come from either corporate IT or plant engineering. In some larger companies, the sponsor might come from an operations department that is separate from both corporate IT and plant engineering. These three areas correspond to the three layers of the AMR model for how IT should function across the entire company: planning, execution, and controls. What often happens is that the project's design and implementation get slanted according to the sponsor's viewpoint.

This is hardly surprising. It's quite common to be caught within your own point of view. It takes a concentrated effort to expand your vision to see things from someone else's perspective. But expanding our vision is exactly what we need to do, because IT projects don't produce the best results possible when people approach them from only one point of view. This is commonly known as the "hammer and nail syndrome." If the only tool you have is a hammer, everything around you starts to look like a nail. Yet the fact is, although a hammer can be pretty handy in some situations, it has its limitations. You'll be better off if you use a variety of tools.

In manufacturing this translates into seeing all applications in terms of your own department. If you're at corporate headquarters, you see IT as a way to enhance your ability to do such things as conduct financial planning, manage the larger supply chain, and manage human resources.

If you're a plant engineer, you see IT as a way to run manufacturing more efficiently. And if you work in operations, you see IT as a way to get a better grip on what is happening in the plant and as a means of eliminating waste and inefficiency by attacking the root causes.

We will look at three common approaches that are intended to provide the vital functions of planning, execution, and control. While they all have some advantages, they have some distinct disadvantages as well. After that, we will put forth our idea of the balanced approach to a company's overall IT structure.

The ERP-Centric Approach

One way to approach your IT architecture is to view the solution from the point of view of corporate headquarters (see Figure 8.1). The theory is to take the best possible advantage of an existing or new ERP system by extending its functions all the way down to the shop floor. In this way, you leverage everything you possibly can with the ERP system along the way. A typical way for this to play out is with ERP managing work orders for the plant. The plant, in turn, collects batch or lot histories, quality data, and inventory data (such as inventory receipts, creation, and usage), which all get reported back to ERP. Depending on the sophistication of the plant level systems, this integration between the plant and a corporate ERP system may be manually intensive in terms of data collection and transactions with the ERP system.

Presuming that you have chosen the best ERP package for your business, there are some distinct benefits to this approach. You get a high degree of functionality all in a single, integrated software package. You are not creating a patchwork quilt of software programs from an assortment of vendors. Obviously, the fewer packages you have, the fewer integration hassles you will have to deal with and you also gain economies of scale in training and consulting services. What's more, control systems vendors are making heroic efforts to ensure that the interface between ERP and controls is simple and efficient. All of this saves you time and energy.

On the down side, ERP-centric systems usually require a significant number of manual transactions in the plant. If you don't have plant-level systems in place that can be integrated with the ERP system, or if you choose not to perform that integration, handling all of these transactions manually doesn't save you time and energy. Additionally, most ERP systems will require data that a control system can't provide. Either you enter this data manually or you have to construct another program to handle it. Another problem is that, depending on the type of plant operations, some ERP systems simply ignore many requirements and handle others quite poorly. This results in the need for custom programming or supplemental programs and processes to support manufacturing.

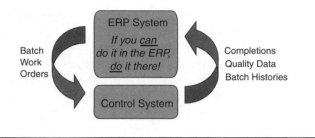

Figure 8.1   ERP-Centric Approach

The execution requirements that are outside of ERP's domain are often implemented by hand or done using spreadsheets and PC databases. Customization of the ERP system pushes up lifecycle costs and complicates upgrades. The use of office automation tools like Microsoft® Excel and simple database tools like Microsoft® Access pushes the plants into half measures that create isolated islands of data.

The Controls-Centric Approach

This is an approach usually taken by plants on their own initiative, often when a project gets started by plant engineering groups (see Figure 8.2). Sometimes this happens if one plant has such good results with a particular implementation that the company decides to use the same system in all of its plants. The result is one where the plant keeps control over information as much as possible and implementations are highly customized to meet the plant's specific requirements and desires. Anyone in charge of production has learned the hard way that systems failures know no time boundaries. In light of this, the production managers want a system they can handle easily at 3:00 A.M., when all of the corporate IT folks are sound asleep at home. The Controls-centric approach mirrors the ERP-centric approach by trying to do everything conceivable through a single system, but in this case it's a process control system or other architecture local to the plant instead of a corporate ERP system. The idea is to extend basic regulatory process control and HMI/SCADA systems by configuring them to provide additional functionality extending up to the execution level.

The evolution of IT budgets accounts for part of the reason that this approach developed. Plant engineers who found themselves with large budgets stemming from new capital projects would use the funds to expand the HMI/SCADA system so that it handled everything conceivably possible, including all kinds of execution and corporate functions from scheduling to data warehousing. It wasn't done out of choice as much as necessity. This happened at a time when corporate IT departments offered little support for new IT initiatives in the plant, so it was the only avenue

Figure 8.2 Controls-Centric Approach

available for improving functionality. Plus, vendors of HMI/SCADA systems were entirely supportive of the idea.

The pros and cons of this approach in many ways match the pros and cons of the ERP-centric approach. For one thing, it minimizes the number of software programs and vendors needed and it can produce sound, simple integration between controls and ERP. It also provides a simple way to handle the most basic execution level requirements. That is, it handles the execution level requirements that it deems necessary, but some requirements are completely ignored. Additionally — and this again is like ERP-centric systems — the use of a controls-centric systems often means you will be looking at custom programming, with its increased lifecycle costs and upgrade complications.

Another common characteristic of controls-centric projects is that they suffer scope creep. This is a danger with any large project, but it's particularly common with the controls-centric orientation. Many companies have systems already in place that are designed to handle the simple monitoring of PLCs and the tracking of a few variables. After the implementation of a new system starts and is well underway, new data requirements frequently arise. This creates the need to track more variables, so an attempt is made to find a new way to accommodate the additional data, and thus the scope of the original project has broadened.

Potentially making matters worse is the fact that in many cases, people choose to keep adding custom code to their original program and they end up with all types of functions patched in that could have been purchased from a COTS vendor. Custom code has the advantage of offering a perfect fit for the requirements, but it comes with a price. If you have a lot of systems running programs written by your own staff, you're dependent on that staff for development and support. Having people in-house who can handle problems is great, as long as it lasts. There's always the danger that the only people who know how to make changes in the programs will leave. One of the big advantages of buying COTS is the security of ongoing support.

The Execution-Centric Approach

This is the least common of the three approaches, because it's usually not the first one chosen. People gravitate to an execution-centric approach (see Figure 8.3) in reaction to one of two situations. One is when there is already in place a strong controls-centric system, but a weak or effectively nonexistent ERP system. The other situation is when corporate turf wars get out of hand. In both cases, execution-centric systems are seen as an antidote to an unhealthy condition.

With this approach, an effort is being made to restore balance and part of the idea works. For one thing, execution-level requirements are handled superbly, without requiring a sophisticated interface with the ERP system. On top of that, some of the ERP functions are easily accommodated and some higher-level controls applications can be implemented.

But the theory breaks down. Many execution-level systems are not designed to simply fill in their specific niches, but also to try and do everything with extended functionality up to the ERP level and down into the controls systems level. However, this reach exceeds the systems' grasp. Some of the ERP level requirements are completely ignored as irrelevant to the business of execution and others are handled poorly and without any flexibility. Plus, this approach has the same problem as the others we have examined of needing custom programming. Lifecycle costs once again go up.

The Balanced Approach

The idea here is simple. Use a combination of systems to create a balanced, integrated whole (see Figure 8.4). Let each system do what it does best and don't ask any system to go beyond its bounds. You achieve all of the benefits of the other approaches and at the same time you eliminate their shortcomings. This is the beauty of using the Portfolio.

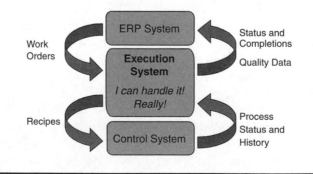

Figure 8.3   Execution-Centric Approach

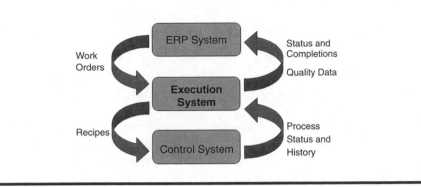

Figure 8.4 Balanced Approach

It may sound too good to be true, but don't forget that simple doesn't mean easy. The idea is simple, but implementing it isn't simple. A balanced approach does achieve all of the requirements. It does ensure that the strengths of each level are maximized. It does provide straight-forward interfaces between the levels. And it does lower overall lifecycle costs by using less custom code and more commercially available software.

However, a balanced approach will require more individual components in the complete system. This makes initial implementation costs higher, given that you have to license more packages and the different skill sets involved require more initial training. This is a tradeoff that must be considered carefully. The initial investment can provide a return far beyond its cost, but this must be decided on a case-by-case basis.

Also, to make the balanced approach work, you must handle one particular task carefully and thoroughly. The key to making this approach successful is the *correct allocation of requirements to systems*. You have to analyze every business need that you have and decide which package is best suited to handle each requirement. Some functions, such as financials and human resources, clearly should be handled by ERP systems, while others would obviously fit into the controls systems. But what about product quality, warehouse management, and production management? And what about inventory and material tracking? Or recipe management and execution? There may be some gray areas here and it will take some thought to determine the best package to handle such functions. The answer could depend on the nature of your industry or the specific systems you already have in place. But once you have chosen a package for a function, let that package be authoritative. For example, don't divide inventory functions over various systems. This will help you avoid creating complex interfaces between different systems.

Remember that the balanced approach is not the initial choice of many people. There are many cases where it isn't even a conscious decision to pursue an ERP-centric solution or a controls-centric solution. Rather it's a case of people being locked into a certain mentality. They use the tools that they know well and that are handy to them. In fact, some of these people deserve a great deal of credit for being able to accomplish as much as they have with tools that aren't specifically designed to do what they're doing. A hammer isn't a screwdriver, but some people find a way to make it work as one.

Another case is that people sometimes feel that they want the existing systems to do all of the work. After all, the argument goes, these systems are already paid for, so why spend more money? And there are people who choose to use systems that work fine in their particular area, regardless of problems the system causes for others. The challenge is to understand all of these different perspectives and enlighten others so that your company finds the best system to fit its particular needs.

INVOLVING THE END USERS AND THE STAKEHOLDERS

Nothing can be more aggravating than spending loads of money and expending tons of energy to install a wonderful new system, only to have the end users ignore it. It does happen — but it can be avoided. The cardinal rule is: *Involve the users from the very beginning.* Consult them about the concept, about the requirements, about the design, about the implementation, and about the support. Getting users to buy in to the project is critical, and one of the surest ways to encourage users to buy in is to communicate early and often. The point is not to take users' functionality requests as definitive descriptions of requirements, but to use them as starting points. Many people who'll be using a new system understandably have no particular knowledge about budget restraints, so they may ask for the moon. You may not be able to deliver everything they want, but at least you know what to shoot for.

There are plenty of people who hold a stake in the success of any project and they are generally eager to assist in any way they can. In order to tap into this source of support, you have to identify them and keep them informed about the project at every stage. It may be that the plant manager or the project manager at one of the plants has a big stake in your project. Even if they aren't sitting around the table helping to design the plans, they need to be included as the plans develop.

Continue to consult the users throughout the Strategy stage and into the Framework stage. As you consider different IT architectural solutions or different software packages, end users can provide valuable input about what will work and what won't. Some of the worst software in the world can be produced by a programmer neglecting to consult end users about the design. A programmer might not care that it takes 10 screens to enter one bit of data, but you can be certain that the shop floor operator, who has plenty of other things to worry about and is forced to deal with all those screens 100 times a day, cares deeply.

If you're in charge of designing a system, it's always dangerous to presume that you know what is best in every way. By consulting end users, you can get all kinds of critical information. Having them test drive an application will tell you whether the program is going to require extensive training or not. Some types of programs can be learned at first, but it may be hard to remember how to use them two weeks later. One feature of good software design is that it has an intuitive character to it. Even if you don't remember how everything works, do your guesses have a good chance of being correct? You have to test the program with the people who will actually be using it in order to answer that question.

Involving users in the Implementation stage is important because they need to have some knowledge of how the system is configured and they need to ensure the accuracy of the configuration in the first place. They are also integral to final acceptance testing, systems start-up, and training. It's always a good idea to have some users, who are highly trained and can help others, use the system after it's up and running. These people are called power users because they're the ones who will be using the system the most and they're the ones who will be instrumental in making the implementation a success.

How One Company Involved the Users in Two Different Projects

A pharmaceutical company needed a CMMS and it considered several options. One option was for the project team to handle it entirely by itself. While this may have been the cheapest approach, the team didn't really have the expertise or staff needed and it would have taken a long time. At the other extreme, the company could let outside consultants handle everything. This would have been the most expensive, but it would have been the way to get the job done most quickly and the consultants had all of the expertise needed to do everything right.

One other downside to using the consultants would have been that the system they create wouldn't have been as custom fit as one created internally. In other words, although the consultants were IT experts, they couldn't have complete knowledge of this particular business. That means that anything designed entirely by the consultants would reflect a lack of business knowledge in one way or another. In the end, both sides concurred that a joint effort would produce the best results. A key objective of the project became the transfer of knowledge from consultant to customer. The significant point here is that working together meant that the end users would be part of the implementation process in several ways. They would help define the requirements and help configure the system during the implementation, which would give them hands-on training with the product. A good cross-section of end users were involved, including people from each plant and even from different work shifts.

At the beginning, the consultants were doing 90% of the work and the project team was doing 10%, but by the time the implementation was nearing completion, those proportions had flip-flopped and the project team was doing 90% to the consultants' 10%. The project team understood the system, configured it, and maintained it.

Every project is different and the degree of end user involvement will and should vary. The highly technical nature of some work precludes the use of end users. Nevertheless, the benefits of having their input mean that they should be brought into the process to the highest degree possible or practical.

Another project at this same company demonstrates how end users can be a big help in defining requirements. They can show you exactly what they do and explain everything that's part of the job. When this company implemented a system for managing laboratory data, people from the project team spent days in the lab and were walked through all of the processes and procedures used there. They found out what was working well and what needed to be done to solve some of the problems there. By spending this time doing research on requirements and processes, they were able to ensure that they found solutions that worked.

CONCLUSION

The Strategy stage is the foundation of your overall success. If you start with good requirements and base your architecture on them, you have dramatically increased your prospects of achieving your goals. The next step is the Framework stage. This involves the challenges of designing solutions, evaluating and selecting software, and obtaining approval for project funding. We address all of these issues in Chapter 9.

9

FRAMEWORK

Once you've developed your strategy, you're ready to build the framework for your IT solution. Using your requirements as your guide, you have to design solutions, evaluate the available technology, and select the systems that will achieve your goals. In this process, you will come to firm decisions about your architecture and the vendors you will use. This is where matters can get extremely technical, so it's important to know as much as possible about every aspect of the software you're considering. Finally, you have to get your project funded and in order to do that you have to provide a hard justification.

This chapter begins with an examination of design and then proceeds to a discussion of how to evaluate and select technology. After that we discuss standards and models, since these can be extremely valuable in your efforts to define solutions and to choose systems. Then we finish the chapter by presenting some detailed advice on how to justify the capital investment in the IT systems you have chosen.

DESIGN

Design is the process of finding precise solutions to your requirements. Although creating the design you need is a separate process from evaluating and selecting technology, efforts you make in one area inform and affect the efforts you make in the other. Plus, a good understanding of standards and models will augment your ability to design solutions well. So, although this section on design comes first, achieving success in the Framework stage comes from working in all of these areas jointly.

In order to design solutions that address all of your requirements, you have to confront countless decisions and negotiate trade-offs at each step along the way. The countless decisions are unavoidable because there are always several different options for meeting any specific requirement.

The trade-offs are also unavoidable, because some design solutions are less expensive but more cumbersome; while others are more efficient yet less comprehensive; and still others are more comprehensive but more expensive.

Think about the analogy of taking a trip. You need to get from point A to point B. That's your requirement and there are several options that will satisfy your requirement. You could walk, ride a bicycle, drive a car, take a bus, ride on a train, or fly by a plane. If you only need to get from your office to a building across the street or if you need to go from Atlanta to Los Angeles, then certain solutions are obvious.

But what if you need to get from New York to Washington, D.C. and you also have requirements concerning the cost of the trip, the timing of your travel, or excess baggage? A train or a plane might work fine for many schedules, but what if you need to leave after midnight and arrive before 6:00 A.M.? Maybe your schedule is flexible, but you want to save money or you're willing to pay whatever it costs, but you have a truckload of furniture that has to arrive when you do.

You have priorities, such as a willingness to alter your schedule in order to save money, but there are also likely to be limits. You won't wait 2 weeks to save only $10. So, even though you can establish your preferences, the options presented to you may require further deliberation. Add to this the fact that various vendors, such as airline companies in the case of air travel, have any number of qualities that may make you prefer one over the other. Anyone who has tried to balance convenience, cost, comfort, reliability, and the risk of no refund while buying an airline ticket is acquainted with this trade-off calculus. Choosing solutions to your IT requirements presents the same sort of challenges.

The best way to start crafting solutions is by beginning with a high-level design. In discussing the Strategy stage in Chapter 8, we discussed using your requirements to sketch out your overall IT architecture. So, by the time you reach the Framework stage, you should have determined whether you're going to drive a car or take a plane. Now, the task is sorting through all of the options available within the category you've chosen. You have to decide upon the basic design elements that will fit within your overall architecture.

A high-level design is essentially a working plan for meeting the needs of the requirements. Gradually this design will be fleshed out in more detail, eventually becoming the project plans used for the implementation after funding has been approved. At the start, the point is to clearly identify the following critical concepts:

■ Assumptions and constraints
■ Data flow

- Process flows
- Timing and events
- System interfaces (corporate systems, plant floor systems, engineering systems, other legacy systems, external partners)
- Data migrations
- Archiving and data retention
- User interfaces

All of these issues must be understood thoroughly before trying to evaluate and select any particular technology or products.

Assumptions and Constraints

Good requirements provide detailed descriptions of all assumptions and constraints, and these must be kept in mind by the design team. For example, there could be a constraint that information must be available to an operator on a scheduled interval of 1 minute. If a proposed design is set to handle the information transfer only every 5 minutes because the design team regarded the constraint as arbitrary and chose to ignore it, there could be problems. The 1-minute constraint could be based on the fact that the operator on the production floor has a buffer large enough to handle only 3 minutes of material; so if the interval is every 5 minutes, there's the possibility that the production line could fill up or stop.

The goal of the design process is to uncover the solution that is the best fit within the context of all assumptions and constraints. The design team should take these parameters as gospel, respecting the fact that they came from the user community. If there's no design solution that can satisfy the requirements while accommodating the provided constraints, then the design team needs to raise a red flag and work to resolve it within the project team. Working together is essential in these cases. Unilateral decisions almost invariably produce frustrating results once systems are implemented.

Data Flows

The ability to move data around is fundamental to every IT design, so it's important to think about the information that will be produced and consumed. This will help you identify every data flow that will be created or affected by any new systems, including flows that are less prominent. IT systems always have hidden data flows and these must be taken into account as well. The design accommodates all of these flows, so this is a critical early step. There will be times when certain aspects of the design necessitate additional data flows that aren't part of the requirements. This isn't a problem in and of itself, but it's important that the design team avoid treating them as requirements. The point of design is to satisfy the existing requirements, not to create more of them. Knowing about the flows also helps with the process of selecting products and technology. One of the things to consider while looking at any particular product is how well it handles your data flows. Precise maps of the flows will be drawn as the high-level design is fleshed out into greater detail.

Process Flows

At the same time that you look at how data will be produced and consumed, you also need to examine step-by-step what people, equipment, or systems need to do in order to satisfy the requirements. These step-by-step procedures are the process flows, and although the design process may uncover alternative or better ways to implement a process, care should be taken to verify that any proposed change to the process meets the requirements. Changes in processes may be either intentional or the result of the need to accommodate a particular software product, but in either case there's the danger of adverse consequences. It's usually difficult to implement new processes at the same time as new systems, unless that's the stated intention behind the requirements. There have been many occasions when the original requirements could be satisfied by changing one part of a process, yet a design was crafted that changed several processes all at once. There may be justification for this approach at times, but it means a steeper learning curve and additional training, so think twice before making changes in process flows that aren't absolutely essential.

Systems Interfaces

Identifying data flows forces you to look at systems interfaces, but eventually you'll have to deal more comprehensively with how all of your various systems communicate with each other. This means looking at every system that is external to the proposed design and seeing which of those will be affected by the changes being planned. The list of systems that could be involved include corporate systems (such as ERP and supply chain systems), engineering systems (such as CAD, CAM, and PLM), control systems, and document management systems, among others. There could easily be incompatibility problems between any two systems and the design needs to address this.

There are other issues to consider about interfaces. One is the need to transform certain types of data in various ways as it gets moved around, such as changing a temperature reading from Fahrenheit degrees to

Centigrade degrees. Another is the issue of data storage in the event that a communications link goes down: Should the data be stored at all and if so, how? How will interfaces operate when any particular system is down? How will interfaces with external partners be set up? In all, there is a long list of questions to answer concerning interfaces. The goal is to have an exhaustive accounting of every way that various systems will communicate with each other. This means knowing the technological requirements of the interfaces and the timing, frequency, and volume of the transactions that will be conducted over them. This information will have a significant impact on the design and it's central to the work of evaluating and selecting technology.

Data Migrations

Frequently with the installation of a new system, large amounts of data will need to migrate from a legacy system to the new system. The requirements should clearly indicate if this is the case; if it is, there are several questions the design team must answer. Will it be possible to take a production system offline for 12 hours to migrate the data? Or will there be a parallel system running in place instead? Does the design include a contingency solution if the data migration cannot be completed as expected? There are potential problems here that can be big headaches if no one addresses them at the design stage.

Archiving and Data Retention

The design team should consider how long data will be retained, how it will be archived, who will need access to the archives, and how data retention and accessibility will change over time. Sometimes these requirements are already established and won't change with the introduction of a new system, but any changes that will occur should be addressed. Additionally, when implementing a new system, data archives of the legacy system may be required. In that case, provisions should be made so that those archives can be accessed in the future.

User Interfaces

If you want to avoid creating user interfaces that require plant floor personnel to go through six screens just to enter one bit of data, the design stage is the place to do it. Careful attention should be paid to this aspect of design, because all of the time and money spent on a new system is wasted if users ignore it. Consider who'll be using the system, especially if the proposed changes mean completely new users. New systems can also mean changes in technology, such as introducing a Personal Digital Assistant (PDA), bar code, or handheld device, so the design should reflect this. On top of this, determine whether there'll be different types of user interfaces or if the system will need to support only one.

In addition to all of these critical concepts, keep in mind during the design phase that new systems will need to be tested during the Implementation stage. Although verification and validation of new systems are not part of the design process, designers have all of the details at their disposal that will need to be tested, validated, and verified. Taking certain steps now will make testing easier and more thorough later on. The design team's knowledge of changes in systems, interfaces, and more should be used to help establish the extent and nature of the tests that will be necessary. If this information isn't captured during the design stage, it will have to be recreated later on and it will be more work to do it at that time.

Once the high-level design is complete, there'll be a need to start evaluating and selecting technology. This process should start before the high-level design is fleshed out into greater detail. A common approach is to break the high-level design into sections or modules and then focus on these smaller units one at a time. Standards and models can be excellent sources of vital information as you evaluate technology and flesh out the design.

GUIDELINES FOR TECHNOLOGY EVALUATION AND SELECTION

Here are some important ideas to keep in mind when trying to decide which software systems to use:

■ *Start with a good, solid set of requirements and map your IT solutions to these requirements.* We can't say it too many times — good requirements are the foundation for everything that follows. If they are done correctly, they will guide your technology selection, because the software must address the specific needs spelled out in your requirements document.

■ *Set up priorities and group requirements accordingly.* Distinguish between which requirements must be met and which are less serious. You might want to assign each requirement a value from 1 to 5, with 1 being top priority and 5 being the lowest priority. Having requirements classified in this way can greatly simplify the process of selecting the best software package.

- *Recognize that there are always trade-offs, no perfect solutions.* Products have other trade-offs besides the obvious one of a higher price for better functionality. You could call some of these "architectural trade-offs." This means that one product may cover some of your functional requirements really well, but cause problems interfacing with your other systems. Another product may fit perfectly with your other systems, but fall short in terms of functionality. This is an important example, because you need to determine how everything will fit together, including your legacy systems.

- *Evaluate both the products and the vendors.* Are you looking at a product that the vendor has been making for years or is this its first attempt? Is the product the vendor's specialty or is it a sideline? Has the product been used by 200 other companies or only by 2 others? How long has the vendor been in business? All of these questions, and more, should be pursued when getting information about products that might cost millions of dollars.

- *Avoid the* Request for Information, Request for Quote, *and* Request for Proposal *approach with vendors.* Sending the list of requirements to a vendor in this way generally elicits the same response in all cases. Most vendors are reluctant to ever admit that their products have any shortcomings, so the standard reply is that they can do everything you need. You have to examine what they offer and decide for yourself if it can handle your requirements.

- *Compare apples to apples.* Be sure you learn enough about all of the software you are evaluating to know which are comparable and which aren't.

- *Have vendors demonstrate their products for you.* Arrange to have vendors demostrate software products to see how they'll address your requirements, item by item, and involve a broad range of people in evaluating the demo. Good vendors will jump at the opportunity to prove the value of their products.

- *Use your instinct.* How does the product feel to you and to others, especially the users? Sometimes there are things that you like or don't like that are hard to articulate. You may not be able to express what makes you like or dislike a product, but that doesn't mean you should ignore these feelings. If the end users tell you they won't use the product, it would be wise to believe them even if they can't explain why.

THE VALUE OF STANDARDS AND MODELS

Standards and models are important bodies of knowledge that reflect the collective wisdom of the people who created them. There can be a great

deal of value in understanding how certain standards and models originated and what they seek to accomplish. They function as communication
tools that help you discuss very complex subjects. In many cases, they
provide the context for discussions with vendors and consultants. If you
don't understand the models or standards that apply to any given situation,
it can be very difficult to understand everything you're being told or to
defend your vision against people who criticize it.

Each standard and model has a different perspective or area of focus
and each tries to solve problems in its own way. Since each serves a
different purpose, you may benefit from using any of them at one time
or another through the course of a project, because they can help you
understand different aspects of a problem. You shouldn't use just one and
throw the others out the window. If you only use one, you will have the
benefit of only one point of view.

At the same time, it's definitely possible to succeed without using any
of them at all. Many people have ignored them over the years and
companies have successfully manufactured products without giving them
a second glance. Ultimately, if you stay focused on business issues and
solve the problems confronting you, you will succeed, with or without
standards and models. There are many examples of successful projects
that ignored them or even did exactly the opposite of what they suggested.
Standards and models can clearly be used to your advantage, but it isn't
the case that everyone should use them in every situation. It's good to
pick and choose where and how you use them.

STANDARDS

People are always seeking the ideal. In the realm of information technology, that translates into trying to establish a standard for the best way to
design and implement systems. Standards act as guides in the process of
choosing the right technology for your business and they can be tremendously useful. At the same time, a certain amount of caution must be
employed when dealing with standards, because they've proven themselves to be transient time and time again.

Standards have a role in the development of your Portfolio, because
they come into play any time you use manufacturing IT systems, so you
need to understand them. Standards can help you achieve success or they
can be a source of problems. The challenge is to use them in the right
context. By themselves, standards are neither good nor bad; it all depends
on how you use them. Don't ignore them completely or accept them
blindly. Being oblivious to standards can hamper your efforts to make
efficient use of current technology, but being ruled exclusively by

standards can have the same effect also. Our aim is to help you obtain a healthy perspective on the best use of standards, so that you can see them in their proper context and make value judgments based on your project's needs. It's important to be able to evaluate any particular standard and see what it is trying to accomplish.

Categories of Standards

Standards serve different purposes and originate from different organizations. It can be helpful to categorize them into five major groups. There are functional industry standards, technical industry standards, technical corporate standards, business process corporate standards, and vendor standards. Here are some common examples of each category:

1. Functional industry standards
   - ANSI/ISA-88.01-1995: Batch Control
   - ANSI/ISA-95.00.01-2000: Enterprise-Control System Integration
   - SCOR — Supply Chain Operations Reference model
   - OSHA 1910.119 — OSHA's Standard Process Safety Management of Highly Hazardous Chemicals
   - Title 21 Code of Federal Regulations (21 CFR Part 11) — Electronic Records; Electronic Signatures

2. Technical industry standards
   - MAP/TOP-802.4
   - OSF
   - X-Windows
   - DDE — Dynamic Data Exchange
   - Open SQL — Structured Query Language

3. Technical corporate standards
   - HMI design
   - Network
   - Desktop
   - User Interface
   - API

4. Business process corporate standards
   - ISO 9000 (quality)
   - Document for each corporation (safety) — an example is "lock out, tag out" for maintenance workers

5. Vendor standards
    ■ IBM SAA
    ■ DECnet
    ■ PowerBuilder

Ultimately, there are three factors that determine when a standard is created:

1. The market speaks — Microsoft® Windows operating system is a perfect example.
2. There is a mandate — all corporate standards are driven by a corporate mandate and there are standards mandated by the government, such as safety standards.
3. There is a consensus — something is acclaimed or championed.

Vendor standards come into being by achieving success in the market. Industry standards come into being by winning the consensus of people in the industry. Corporate standards come into being by management's dictation. Although some standards are solely corporate standards, any standard can become a corporate standard. The motivations behind the various types of standards are entirely different. Corporate standards are there to protect and benefit the corporation by reducing chaos and reducing overall lifecycle costs. Vendor standards are entirely self-serving, driven by the profit motive. Industry standards are generally altruistic and have many beneficial characteristics.

The Transience of Standards

Any time a company needs an IT product or solution, standards should come into play. The problem is that many people regard standards as solid, permanently established practices, when in fact, they're anything but that. Most efforts to create a lasting industry standard fail. In spite of everyone's best efforts, standards have proven to be transient. The market leader and dominant force today will probably be a historical footnote in 5 to 10 years, if not sooner.

Here is an example. In the mid-1980s, about 90% of all transaction processing, mid-range computers sold were based on proprietary operating systems and proprietary databases from three vendors — DEC, HP, and IBM. These computers featured DEC VMS and RDB, HP MPE and Image or SQL Image, and IBM® OS/400® and DB/400. *For all practical purposes, most of these don't exist in the market today and the majority are no longer supported by the vendor.*

Here are some examples of standards that have sunk below the horizon:

- DECnet
- IBM SAA (System Application Architecture)
- OSF and OSF/1
- MAP/TOP and IEEE-802.4
- X-Windows
- PowerBuilder

(To get a better idea of how standards come into being and how they pass out of existence, please refer to Appendix A, where we describe these standards as examples in more detail.)

Transience of standards is not necessarily a bad thing. Standards have different lifetimes. While there is no sure way to pick the winners and losers, here are some ideas to keep in mind as you navigate this storm:

- Stay tuned to the market. It's the market alone that decides which standards succeed and fail. Success has nothing to do with technical excellence, industry analysts, or standards-establishing bodies. Instead, it has to do with three things that rule the market: low cost or value for the dollar, reliability, and ease of use and implementation.
- Understand what's important about your technology infrastructure. Then, as you evaluate standards, focus on what's really important to your company and ignore the trivia.
- Establish company standards where it makes sense, but never to the detriment of the company's business goal. Sometimes an individual within a company takes the standards idea too far. Don't fall victim to this mentality.
- Avoid technical solutions that are clearly on their last legs. A product's functionality may seem to fit and the price may be right, but if you have to throw out the entire system in a few years because it can't be upgraded, you've placed your bet on the wrong horse.
- Be wary of costly changes that are driven by industry "fashion" cycles. Think of all the money spent on e-commerce solutions that resulted in no added value to the company. People would love to have that money back now.
- Put in place an *ongoing process* to investigate, evaluate, and reposition your company with respect to infrastructure and standards. Given that standards change, you can't rely on the evaluations you made 3 years ago. Revisit the issue on a regular basis.

The Benefits of Standards

This may sound like a lot of work, but it can pay off. When you use the right standards, there are benefits in all of the following areas.

Project Execution Speed and Acceleration

Time is money, and some industry standards can enable quicker starts, faster progress, and quicker closure. They do this by keeping you from reinventing the wheel and by limiting the amount of discussion and floundering you might otherwise do. They provide a framework for verification and validation, and they help define the complete domain of the functions. They may also suggest potential solutions for your project.

Communications

Functional industry standards give you a common terminology. Everyone is on the same page with nomenclature and definitions. When you communicate internally or with a vendor, you know that your words mean the same thing. This also serves to level the playing field amongst vendors by eliminating vendor-specific definitions. When you discuss matters with different prospective vendors, you can talk apples to apples, not apples to oranges.

Quality

Functional industry standards can serve as a benchmark. You match your system against the standard and see how it compares. Best practices may be established by, included within, or referenced by standards. This provides further guidance in the search for quality.

Reuse/Economy

Standards would have little value if they were highly specialized and could be used only in one situation. The neutral format of a standard makes it the common denominator for multiple projects. By having a generic quality, standards achieve broad applicability. This allows you to use the same standard in different plants in various locations around the world.

For all of these reasons, we encourage people to learn about and use standards. They can be an invaluable asset, if chosen with care.

MODELS

Models, like standards, are concerned with ideals. The point of a model is to provide a clear representation of how a process would ideally occur, how a system would ideally function, or how a company would ideally be organized. Models are always abstract and they're usually rather clean and neat, just the opposite of reality. Nevertheless, they can help you conceptualize valid and practical solutions to all kinds of messy problems.

(For descriptions of nine important models, please see Appendix B.)

The Wrong Ways to Use Models

Models can be valuable tools, but they can also be misused. Here are some ways that they shouldn't be used:

- Don't think of a model as an absolute. In most cases, models are starting points, ideals, or frameworks. If you're building a house, you could decide that you want more than the standard floor joists indicated by the blueprint. Maybe you own a grand piano, so you want to build the floor with double joists in order to account for the extra weight of the instrument. You're not bound by the blueprint's specifications, because you know that you want something different in this particular case.
- Don't use a model in the wrong context. If you have drawings for the electrical wiring of a house, don't use them to do the plumbing.
- Don't use a model just for the sole purpose of being able to declare that you used it. You may be able to say, "I'm S88 compliant," but that doesn't guarantee that you have the system functionality that you need.
- Don't assume that a model will ensure success. Success depends on many factors.
- Don't apply the wrong model in the wrong way.
- Don't assume the model is the real thing. Don't confuse the flight simulator with a real aircraft.
- Don't assume the model will give you something or do something for you that it won't. A blueprint isn't going to build your house for you. The most perfectly drawn blueprint in the world won't bring you a beautiful house if you hire lousy carpenters to do the work.

The Right Ways To Use Models

Here are the ways to use models if you want to get the maximum benefit from them:

- Use models as evaluation tools. They can help you see where you are, what you're doing, and where you're going.
- Use models as abstract tools to understand and discuss complex concepts. Models can give you both a framework for your own understanding and a common language for communicating with others. You can take a blueprint and discuss the design and dimensions of a house's kitchen. You don't have to build the actual kitchen to discuss it.
- Use models to give you frameworks, templates, and starting points. You may be struggling with something, but you don't have all of the details worked out. You can take a template from a model and use it to flesh out your ideas and complete your plan.
- Use models to define specifications. In working with other people, you can specify a particular model to establish your standards.
- Use models to understand the ideal.
- Use models to help define and refine functional requirements.
- Use models to evaluate software vendors.
- Use models to organize and categorize information.
- Use models as checklists.
- Use models to support your decision-making processes.
- Use models to classify your business processes into the functions that the model supports. The idea here is that you're basically looking to see if the functions that you are trying to address do or do not fit in the model. In this way the model helps you clarify your processes. You can see which of your functions don't fit in the model or which of the functions described in the model are still not enumerated in your business requirements.
- Use models to duplicate previous successes. If you build a house one time with a good set of blueprints, you ought to be able to use those same blueprints to build another house.
- Use models to build on past successes by improving the model. Even if you're very happy with the house you built from a set of blueprints, there may be some things you'd like to improve. Perhaps you weren't entirely satisfied with the way the electrical wiring was done. You can add more details to the blueprint that help ensure the wiring gets done exactly the way you want it.

JUSTIFYING THE CAPITAL EXPENSE FOR IT PROJECTS

Producing a solid requirements document is hard work, as is evaluating and selecting the right technology. But now it's time for another difficult task: explaining why spending a lot of money will be a wise thing to do. There are situations where the benefits of an IT project can be easily defined, but in many other cases, it can be quite a challenge. Let's say that you want to install software that will track your yields so that you can improve them and thereby cut costs. You must produce some numbers that demonstrate current yields and how much they would be improved. The catch is that without the software, you don't have those numbers, so it's very difficult for you to provide hard statistics about the changes you anticipate. You're forced to rely on long-term averages or perform manual computing in order to establish the estimated current state. Another example is using a new IT system to improve the overall quality of your products. This could translate into lower material costs due to less scrap, lower labor costs due to less rework, and higher sales due to greater customer satisfaction. Documenting all of this and assigning a dollar value to it is a formidable challenge.

Nevertheless, if you want your IT project to get funded, you have to find a way to spell out in hard detail exactly how it will achieve a payback for the company. All companies have limited resources and must prioritize expenditures on what they believe will give them the greatest return. Business managers are regularly presented with proposals that claim to improve their business through new information technology. Being able to properly compare, analyze, and evaluate these alternatives in order to determine where the company's limited resources should be invested is vital to the company's future. Each project in a company competes for funding. It's important to make sure that your project receives a chance to make its case.

In the late 1800s, economist and avid gardener Vilfredo Pareto discovered a principle, which is commonly referred to as the 80/20 rule or the Pareto Principle. He observed that 80% of the land was owned by 20% of the people. He also observed from gardening that 20% of his pea pods yielded 80% of the peas that he harvested. Thus was born the principle that has stood the test of time and has been demonstrated in many areas of business.

Opportunities abound for improving every organization. In order to recognize opportunities effectively, you need to understand the business in which your company is engaged. Put the 80/20 rule to work. Most companies receive 80% of the revenue from 20% of the products they sell and 80% of the cost from 20% of the operations. Focus on the 20% that's the most important to your company first. This is the part of your business that's most critical for your success and that means that this is where the biggest return will occur.

THE THREE MAIN WAYS TO JUSTIFY PROJECTS

As you work to identify opportunities within your company, bear in mind that they'll fall into one or more of three major categories:

1. Revenue expansion opportunities
2. Cost reduction and avoidance opportunities
3. Regulatory compliance

Revenue expansion opportunities include:

- Volume
- Operational flexibility
- Process debottlenecking
- Quality improvements
- Sales effectiveness
- Sales responsiveness
- New products
- Product enhancements
- Reduced customer returns
- Increased distribution
- Added brand value
- Improved market image
- Extended product life

Cost reduction and avoidance opportunities include:

- Reduced purchasing costs
- Reduced production costs
- Reduced downtime
- Reduced transportation costs
- Reduced overhead
- Increased efficiency
- Improved yield
- Improved materials management
- Maximized working capital
- Increased capacity with reduced capital outlay

Regulatory compliance includes:

- EPA
- OSHA
- FDA
- USDA
- Tax code

Don't allow these lists to cause you to think of opportunities as corresponding to only one of the elements mentioned above. In most cases, your project will provide multiple benefits to the company. For example, at some companies, the software programs that provide regulatory compliance also dramatically reduce labor costs. It's important to see all of the angles, because one way or another, you must establish a quantifiable return on the investment.

Before making your case, you have to formulate a solid plan that clearly defines the scope and the budget. This plan should provide extensive details concerning every aspect, such as a detailed schedule of how the project will proceed, the use of internal and external resources, and a timetable for when measurable benefits will be seen.

After you make your proposal, be prepared for partial success. In many cases, IT projects are funded incrementally. You may have to demonstrate benefits before additional funding will be approved. In other cases, the overall cost may simply be too much for any one budget. Part of your funding may be delayed until the next annual budget is considered.

THE IMPORTANCE OF BUSINESS STRATEGIES

Through all of this, keep in mind that your company's operating and manufacturing strategy should be the key factor driving your actions. Use your business strategy as the guiding principle in defining the functional requirements for the systems you need, without worrying about the technology or the vendor. Then your functional requirements will determine the applications you buy. These will in turn support your basic business plans in a synergistic cycle. You will be accomplishing goals with your IT systems that allow you to execute your manufacturing and operating strategy.

This may seem obvious, but it's easy to lose sight of your business plan when vendors hawk their latest wares. One sales pitch that many people have fallen prey to goes like this: "Your industry's best practices are already incorporated into our product, so it only makes sense for you to adjust the way you operate to the way we designed our software." Don't believe it! There are other vendors and other products. You don't have to live with a forced fit. It may be true that any COTS product will require some adaptation, if you compare it to a program written in custom code. Nevertheless, you should still be able to find software that supports your business plan. A forced fit ultimately limits or inhibits your operations and manufacturing strategy, because it fails to meet some of your functional requirements.

CONCLUSION

The Framework stage involves a great deal of work designing solutions and then educating yourself and others about the technology that can provide these solutions for your company. Plan to spend the time and money needed to address this stage in the project lifecycle. Part of the educational process is the understanding of standards and models. These are tools which, if chosen carefully and used in the right way, can be tremendously helpful in designing and implementing IT architectures and making major decisions about the Portfolio. Remember that good standards and models have a lot of blood, sweat, and tears behind their creation and evolution. Using them is a way to gain the benefits of years of experience from other professionals.

In order to proceed, however, you have to win funding for your project. Doing that requires that you show a hard justification for the IT dollars you need. Once your project is approved, it's time for the next stage, Implementation, which is followed by the Support stage. Those stages are the focus of our next chapter.

10

IMPLEMENTATION AND SUPPORT

IMPLEMENTATION

The third stage of the project lifecycle is the Implementation stage, and this means good news and bad news. The bad news is that repeated real-world experience shows that bringing a new software package into your company can be an incredible nightmare. The good news is that it doesn't have to be and the difference is largely within your control. Although IT projects necessarily involve a great deal of work, a great deal of training, and any number of people plodding through the hardest part of the learning curve, they can be managed to run smoothly and efficiently. Making use of the advice we offer in this section on implementation can be the key to greater efficiency, which means saving time, reducing costs, and increasing overall success. The point is not that we think everyone should follow every suggestion we offer, but that all of them deserve consideration. You have to decide which practices apply to your situation.

Do Your Homework

You want to have a complete project plan that exhaustively accounts for every aspect of the implementation. The plan should describe what you're going to do, how you're going to do it, how long it's going to take, and how many people will be needed, among other things. It's a given that this plan will change as the implementation progresses, so it's impossible to be completely accurate about everything from the start, but it's still of great value. You have to start making these estimates at some point. Once you have a base to work from, you can adjust your figures as you go along.

One critical part of this plan is establishing milestones that will demonstrate the value of the project. Many projects are funded incrementally, and future funding is contingent upon demonstrating payback early on. Look for ways to fulfill this demand and put them into your plan.

Also, give some serious thought to ways in which an implementation can change your company. Is it part of a change in business practices? Will you have to retrain people for different jobs? Will some of your manufacturing processes change? Are jobs going to be eliminated? Will the new software have an impact on company culture? Does the project fit in with other corporate initiatives? Doing all of this homework may seem to be a chore, but it's time and energy well spent.

An Example of How Doing Your Homework Can Pay Off

In this case, a company had decided to replace a legacy system with "mobile data entry," which was a solution to collecting data by using hand-held and fork truck mounted terminals that were RF-based. The application, which involved packaging and storage, wasn't particularly complex. As the products came off the line, they would be put into cartons. The cartons would be put into cases, which would be stacked onto pallets and shrink-wrapped. A pallet of finished goods would then be put into a warehouse, where it waited to be shipped to a customer, which would involve being put onto a truck and taken to a distribution center.

The legacy application needed to be replaced, but the people in charge of this project weren't sure exactly what they should use instead. After some deliberation, they realized that they didn't need to concentrate on strategy, because their focus was narrow. What they did need to do was define their functional requirements.

This conclusion led to a plan. They would look at the data and the interfaces, at their current technology and how their IT architecture was structured, and at the software applications that could satisfy their requirements. Then they would choose the right systems and implement them.

The project people submitted this plan to the managers who were overseeing the entire effort to find new IT solutions; these managers responded by expressing two concerns. First, they thought that gathering all of the data needed would take too long and second, they doubted that they could make a quick decision about which systems to implement. The project team assured them that the data could be collected within a reasonable amount of time and that everything would be laid out clearly. The project team would present all of the pros and cons of each system along with the costs involved, so that everything needed to make a decision would be there.

Upper management agreed to this, so the project team did all of the homework and presented all of the options. Every possible question was addressed. Everything was documented and laid out. The team did what it took to get all of the information lined up, so that all upper management had to do was examine it and decide. By doing all of this work beforehand, the project team was able to provide exactly what upper management needed and a decision was made on the spot.

Use an Incremental Approach to Solutions

In too many cases, companies will try to solve all of their problems at once. When you see this happening, you can bet that a vendor has convinced them that one single product will meet all of their needs. Besides the fact that one product will not solve all of any company's needs, we think it wise to avoid the mega-project. Don't try to solve everything in one grand swoop. It may be wise and appropriate to *envision* a grand solution, but don't try to *implement* all of it at the same time. Instead, use an iterative or incremental approach. Implement projects in manageable units of work and forget the Big Bang theory of accomplishing everything with a single project.

Clearly, some applications and projects are very narrow, so an incremental approach might not apply. But if you're looking at a project that addresses downtime, quality, product tracking, and genealogy, you would typically want to go in and handle downtime first, because that's often a place where there's quick payback. Although it will require a capital investment, there's not a lot of service investment. Downtime improvements are also very visible, so the payback can be easily observed and advertised. At that point, you have some of the infrastructure in place for working on the next phase. The incremental approach might say that this year you do downtime, next year you do quality, and so on.

A Big Bang Failure

A steel company decided to build a new steel mill and wanted it to have sophisticated automation and information technology systems. But advanced automation was something new to the company. In theory, there's no reason that the plan couldn't have worked, but the company chose to use technology that had never been used in a steel mill before. Instead of piloting the systems and using a gradual approach, the company went for the Big Bang approach. The company wanted everything installed from the start, so that when it turned on the switch to put the mill into production, all of the highly sophisticated IT systems would be fully operational. If an information system was designed to have 20 functions in one particular area of the mill, the company wanted all 20 of those functions up and running on Day 1. When you realize that there were 20 areas, each with 20 different functions, you see how tremendously ambitious this was. The company was really reaching for the stars.

Indeed, the project's complexity and goals were somewhat similar to a space shuttle launch. There's no way to put the space shuttle into orbit incrementally. It has to be done at once. Everything has to be perfectly in place. There can be no pilot program of any substance. But what you can do — and what NASA does do — is spend years testing and retesting every component of the entire system. The problem at the steel company was that it was not taking years to test and retest before the blastoff date. Even though the company didn't have to take the Big Bang approach, it was somehow convinced that was the best way to proceed.

When the time came to turn on all of the systems, it was an absolute fiasco. Many of the systems failed to function properly and the frustration about these failures poisoned the entire project. In the end, almost every information system in the entire steel mill was shut down, as the company threw the baby out with the bath water. Millions of dollars went down the drain and not because the objectives were wrong. The problem was a terribly misguided implementation approach. If the company had been willing to take more time to see what actually worked and what did not, what fit perfectly and what needed some tweaking here or there, the project could have been a huge success.

An Incremental Approach Success

One example of using an incremental approach involves a food and beverage company that wanted to install LIMS across the entire company, which in this case means scores of plants. The company started by devising a project that targeted only four plants. The first phase of this project was a pilot program at just one of these plants. The pilot was a success, so the company implemented the system at all four plants, and this also went well.

The next step was to try the system in a different division, so the company piloted at one of the plants where it made ready-to-eat food products. After working through whatever kinks came up, the company rolled out the system to all of the other plants in that division and continued with this pattern across the entire company. Each time the company did a new pilot, it taught them something about how the software should be configured in each setting. The company could use this accumulated knowledge as it moved along.

Another example from the same company involves the implementation of a SPC/SQC system across the company. In this case, the company chose one key representative plant from each of several divisions — a canned food plant, a ready-to-eat food plant, a dessert plant, and a drink plant. Then the company piloted the system at all of these key plants simultaneously. After gathering information from the pilot, the company installed the system at the other plants, one by one, continuing with the incremental approach, because no two plants are the same. The company realized that every implementation project taught them something valuable about making it work better the next time.

The aims of the incremental approach are multidimensional. The first part is to make sure that the system actually functions in the way it should. Another part is to see if the expected payback is really there. In other words, even if the system functions perfectly, you could still conclude that the benefits don't justify the expense. If the payback is actually there, the pilot also functions as a way of providing documentation. You can take the results to upper management as hard evidence that will justify further implementation of the systems involved. With the incremental approach, there's also the potential for the project to become self-funding. The paybacks established early in a project can pay for the cost of extending the project.

Use Proof of Concept, Conference-Room Pilot, or Live Pilot

Every situation is different, so every project is different. This means that it's impossible to have an ironclad plan from the beginning. You learn and adjust as you go along; the more you can learn at the beginning, the more successful the project will be. Proofs of concept, conference-room pilots, and live pilots are all about gaining more information before you move ahead to the next stage. The valuable information they can provide helps reduce the risk that your project has serious design flaws. Each of these tools has a different role to play. You may want to use only one of them or all three, depending on the specific nature of your project.

At the very beginning, when you're still creating the vision of what you want to do, it makes sense to consider more than one solution or concept. Maybe you have to decide which way of constructing an interface works best. Maybe you see several different viable solutions to a particular problem, but you need more information before you settle on the best option. Use a **proof of concept** to compare these different ideas to see which one works best. A proof of concept is highly focused on techno- logical issues and is often conducted in an IT lab by IT specialists, without the involvement of end users. The results could be that one method involves nine steps, while another method involves only three. If every- thing else is equal, you have your answer: Use the method with fewer steps. However, matters are usually more complicated and you'll have to consider some trade-offs. For example, the nine-step method may be more secure and if that's a high priority, you might choose it over the three-step solution.

Also, in many cases a new software program takes the company into unfamiliar terrain. You're doing something new and no one's familiar with this new technology, or it could be that you're mixing technologies that you have never mixed before. How much time is required of these people doing those tasks? How would this specific technology affect these specific people? Running a proof of concept can help you see how things might play out in your company's environment. At this stage, failure is not necessarily regarded in a negative light; it's just more information. The whole purpose is to see what works and what doesn't so you can adjust your plans accordingly.

Once you have a fairly firm sense of the approach you are taking, it might be advantageous to conduct a **conference-room pilot**. With a conference-room pilot you take a package and build a prototype of the application that you're going to try to deploy. Then you see how that solution should be configured or arranged in a specific situation. The methodology involves an iterative process, in which you build the prototype, judge it, then go back to modify the requirements, then judge it again, and so on. You get evaluations and then you modify and expand. The conference-room pilot process can take you through the full life cycle of requirements, testing, and delivery in small chunks. It allows you to make assumptions about what the system should be without knowing all of the requirements. In fact, that's part of a prototype's utility — it helps you define your requirements.

A typical conference-room pilot might go like this: You get the production manager, the people who run the line, the quality manager, the instrument control group, and put them all through a training class. Then you start hammering out the prototype together, building screens, configuring things, bringing products in, and so on. You train everyone for three or four days, so they know what the product is, then you all get in a room for several hours a day, every single day. The goal is to come up with a prototype system, so you can say, "This is what our system will look like when we deploy it." This process may take anywhere from 2 to 6 weeks.

A **live pilot** can be useful at a later stage, once your requirements are set and you're ready to perform a scaled-down or limited-scope trial run of the project. It's much more complex than a conference-room pilot and it yields much more information. In a conference-room pilot, you're not actually connected to other systems, so you mimic the interfaces. A live pilot is the real thing, but on a limited scope. You run the system in a certain area or with limited deployment to see if particular solutions fit the needs as projected. For example, if everyone likes the way the prototype looks, then you take 1 line in the plant out of your 32 lines and install it on that line only, not across the whole plant. You train the operators on that line only and get it going there. The point here isn't to help define the requirements or modify the design. Those things should already be set. The goal of a live pilot is fine tuning and risk reduction. It gives you an opportunity to test or seek boundary conditions. A live pilot, if successful, can end up being the beginning of the implementation. There will always be matters that cannot be explored before the full implementation, but a live pilot takes you as close as possible.

In some cases you could skip the conference-room pilot and go straight to a live pilot. You could configure the system on the line, then tune it, adjust it, and tweak it as needed. In order to determine if a conference-room pilot is really needed, consider how complex the system is. If it includes quality, data collection, genealogy, tracking and tracing, downtime monitoring, and production order control, then a conference-room pilot is in order. On the other hand, if all you're doing is downtime tracking, a conference-room pilot may be a waste of time and resources. In this case, you can just go ahead to a live pilot on one of the lines.

A conference-room pilot is traditionally in order when the new system means a fundamental change to your business processes, because it allows you to validate and substantiate your requirements. Changes in business practices could include workforce reduction, changes in the production process, and changes in quality control, such as changing the criteria for whether a product gets out the door or not. The elimination of jobs is a serious matter. If you're going to need only two people on the line instead of six, because you're automating a section that was done manually in the past, you need to reduce the risk that the system will not perform as expected. Once you've eliminated jobs, they're gone. If the new system doesn't work, that can be a serious problem.

This entire approach of using a proof of concept, conference-room pilot, and live pilot should be part of every company's thinking. Don't count on the vendors to suggest it, because there's no advantage in it for them. Salespeople get compensated for sales, not for pilots. It may cost you something to conduct a pilot, but it's a wise use of funds.

Use of Pilots by a Paper Company

As we mentioned before, paper companies are one of the industries that must be concerned with environmental regulations known as the Cluster Rules. While engaged in an effort to improve its ability to handle regulatory compliance, a paper company chose a software package that was fairly new. So the company's management was dealing with regulations that were still rather new and they were planning to use a new system to help it. Wisely, they decided to pilot this system before rolling it out across the company.

In this case, the pilot served several purposes. For one thing, it helped to flesh out the requirements. Even though the company's management had the rules from the EPA, they didn't know exactly what it would mean to be in compliance. There are matters of interpretation and variations on how companies could respond. So, piloting the system would help them view their options and give them more information about the best way to design their IT architecture in support of compliance. It also gave the company an opportunity to train a core group of people, who would later be the main users of the system. An added benefit of training these people is that, in the case that system shows promise, there's a good chance that they will become advocates for the system. It always helps to have as many people as possible to provide support for a broader implementation. On top of all this, piloting the system helps the project designers to work out the kinks and bugs so that it functions the way it's expected to function. Once the pilot was successful, the company's management rolled out the system to all of their mills.

Leverage the Rollout Process

Rollouts can range in size from simply a few more lines in a plant to scores of lines in scores of plants all over the world. No matter how big or small your rollout process is, there are some basic practices that can serve you well.

Have a Comprehensive Plan

Make sure that you've thought about everything you might encounter and define your problem areas and domains. Know what you're attacking and what you're planning to do before you roll it out. Maybe Line 1 was built in 1977, Line 14 was built in 1998, and Line 22 was built last month. There will be differences. Then you have 20 plants. You bought that plant from XYZ, Inc., back in 1974, you bought this plant from QRS, Ltd. back in 1986, and this other plant you built yourself back in 1992. Also, two plants are in North America, one is in South America, and one is Europe. One is in Louisiana and one is in California. There are tons of issues. You have to have a plan to account for the differences, which can be very subtle or quite significant.

Many times the process in various plants is the same, but how it is achieved is different, because you have different equipment, different people, different plant floor layouts, and different timing, among other things. For example, making paper cups involves taking a roll of paper that's got a plastic extrusion coating on it, printing a layout on the paper, punching out the cups according to the layout, and then putting them into a machine that forms them into cups. Then they're stuffed into bags and the bags are put into a box — maybe six steps in all. But you have four plants that do that same process in about six different ways. Sometimes it's all done on a single machine. There's a roll of paper at one end and boxes of cups at the other end. At a different plant, one machine prints the layout, but then the printed sheets are stored in a warehouse temporarily before they're put into the next machine, which punches them. The entire process might be done in such piecemeal fashion, so the way a new software system gets used will be different in this case.

Look for Ways to Achieve Early Payback

At the beginning of a rollout, build momentum by starting with something that really shows the payback. Realize that rollouts can be really complicated. You may choose to rollout downtime at five plants, OEE at eight other plants, quality at seven others, and so on. Early payback can mean seeing that Plant 6 has a problem and doesn't know what's going on, so you do it first and really show the benefits of the system. Another example is if you're planning to roll out four systems at 10 plants, with each plant taking 4 weeks, so it would take most of the year to complete the roll out. Instead you could roll out only downtime at all 10 plants in less than a month and you've got systemwide payback on downtime.

Get Contributions from All Sources

Put people from other plants on the design team and have them work with the conference-room pilot. Use a team approach, pulling in resources from all affected areas.

Use Templates to Define Common Terminology

A lack of common names will cause all kinds of problems during a rollout. Templates can be utilized for gathering information from the field and then for communicating and disseminating the information in a concise manner, so that everyone involved can absorb it. You want a template in your communication structure, in your data structure, and in your reports. The use of common terminology across the enterprise dramatically increases efficiency.

Know Your Requirements and Objectives

In the case of Cluster Rules, it was EPA regulations. It doesn't matter that your plants on the West Coast do things entirely different from your plants in the Midwest. It doesn't matter that some of your plants are 50 years old and others were built last year. All of your plants have to follow the same EPA rules.

Plan Change Management

Change management starts with including the inevitability of change into your plan. If you don't plan to handle change, it will handle you. Strive for continuous improvement of your management plan.

Establish a Program Office

When a system is being rolled out across many plants, it becomes a series of individual projects. Program is the term used to describe the overall endeavor. A program is an immense undertaking. If you're dealing with 30 different plants, then you have 30 different plant managers, 30 different quality managers, 30 different production managers, countless line supervisors, area supervisors, and foremen, plus corporate people, consultants, hardware suppliers, and software suppliers. The amount of coordination required is intense. Doing nothing more than making sure the right hardware and the right software gets delivered to the right location at the right time can be a full-time job for one person.

In order to facilitate communication and coordination, you should establish a program office to act as a repository of knowledge and be both a collector and disseminator of information. In the rollout of the first plant, you'll gain a lot of knowledge that can be used as you move on to the following plants. Say you start with Plant A and it's going fine. The next step is Plants B, C, D, and E. It may turn out that Plants A and C have the same special interface that requires a lot of extra work. If your program office is functioning as it should, you won't have to reinvent the wheel at Plant C. Use what you learned at Plant A about this interface and Plant C becomes a snap.

This is one of the main ideas of the rollout. Find out what works in one situation and duplicate that success in subsequent situations. Use the knowledge of what's already worked to save time as you continue. And remember that plants that are down the list in the order of the rollout don't want to be left in the dark about how things are going. There's no reason they can't be learning about developments as the program proceeds.

Measure and Evaluate as You Proceed

Establish some metrics to be used as measuring tools and then put them to use. Go to Plant 1 and record the results. Go to Plant 2 and do the same thing. Determine what's working well and what isn't, and use this information to adjust your approach. Something may be taking longer than it should, so you want to find these problems as quickly as possible. Always seek continuous improvement.

Maintain Consistent Project Management

An old adage states that too many cooks spoil the broth. A good way to make implementations even more difficult than they already are is to have too many staff changes during the process. The more stable the project management team remains, the better. Part of the point here is the establishment of a good communications matrix. You want to clearly define how vendor specialists will interact with people in your company. The specialists in a given area should talk with your person responsible for that area about issues or items in that area, but not about topics outside that area of involvement or expertise. You don't want someone in finance debating DO loop decisions or someone in engineering trying to nail down cost models. You also want to make sure you get the right people for each task. Remember the advice that came out of the AMR survey: *Put your best people on implementations.* This may mean that you'll need to bring in temporary help to pick up the slack, but doing so will pay off in the long run. Use your most talented people and make sure everyone is committed to making the project a success.

Manage Risk

Most people neglect to include risk management as part of managing the project. Instead they handle it in an ad hoc fashion. In effect, they're opting for crisis management instead of risk management. There's a wide range of problems that can arise during an implementation. It's true that some fires are so minor that it takes more effort to prevent them than it does just to put them out once they occur. But there are plenty of more serious risks that deserve your attention. This is particularly true if you're attempting to do something at your company that you've never done before. In this case, it makes sense to develop a formal approach to handling your risks.

Start by identifying as many potential risks as possible, recognizing that you won't anticipate everything. Think about what could go wrong and what the consequences would be. Next, analyze the risks and partition them into categories, such as schedule risks, technical risks, expense risks, personnel risks, and so on. Now, decide what would cause these problems to occur — determine the contributing factors. After that, develop a plan for monitoring the risks and preventing them. For example, if you're worried that a particular interface might fail, have someone alerted to watch it carefully and at the same time try to think of ways to make it more secure. You'll also want to rank or prioritize the risks, so that you treat each risk with the appropriate amount of attention. Not all risks pose the same magnitude of danger, so look at each and determine both how serious a problem it will be if it does occur and how likely it is to occur. In addition to having risk-monitoring procedures, you should have backup and contingency plans. Know in advance what you'll do if any specific problem materializes. When you do have to take action in response to a problem, keep good records of everything you do. Then learn from the experience and incorporate any relevant knowledge into your entire risk management program.

Invest in Training

Training needs to be seen as a part of change management. Bringing in a new software system normally means changes in the way the business functions, which means changes in the way people do their jobs. People who are working in quality, in labs, in the warehouse, on the shop floor, or in the offices are subject to having their duties change significantly. The challenge is to train them so that they feel comfortable with the new technology. It's not just a matter of helping them become proficient, because good training also includes giving people the reasons for the changes and showing them how the technology can be a positive change for both them and the company.

Don't think of the project from the technological point of view; think of it from the point of view of all of the people who'll be using the technology. What will they be getting out of it? What needs to be done to make sure the users get what they need to make everything work smoothly? Thinking in this way empowers the users and helps the project achieve its goals.

The training should involve more than just how the software works. It should address how the technology fits into the company's plans and what benefits it will bring. In many cases, this may be obvious and the changes may be totally welcome, but not in all cases. Sometimes people are extremely wary of the changes, and they may specifically fear that their job status is threatened. While there can be no question that technological advances eliminate jobs, the smart companies today seek to find ways to retain employees. They try to build upon the investment in the people they already have working for them. Companies are always trying to increase productivity, and new technology is one of the ways to accomplish that goal. Given that employee bonuses are often tied to profits and increases in productivity help bring about increases in profits, there can be good reason for employees to welcome new technology.

The need for training may be a given, but there are good ways and bad ways to handle it. Here's our list of training best practices:

- Keep the "train the trainer" concept to one generation. That means that the people at your company who are trained to give other people instruction in the new software should do only that. They shouldn't be involved in training more people at the company to be trainers.
- Recognize that training is an ongoing challenge. Every company is subject both to personnel changes and to changes in work practices. In other words, your staff and your software will evolve, so training will always be needed in one form or another.
- Both classroom training and on-the-job training have a place, but train on the actual system as opposed to a demo system whenever you can. The danger here is that demo systems don't match implemented systems exactly in any case and aren't even close in some cases. You want people to learn the system as it really behaves in your company's environment, not as it functions generically in a made-up situation. To this end, it's best to use real data whenever possible. Using test data that doesn't resemble real data can cause trainees to lose confidence in the system from the start. Conversely, using real data fosters trust and helps trainees retain more of what they're learning.
- There are different levels of training requirements. Some people are going to be more computer savvy than others, and some people will have more experience with new applications than others. Understand the needs of the people in each of the areas. Develop a common set of training materials and then tailor them to each specific situation.
- Focus on power users. These are the people who will be using the system more than anyone else. They can promote the use of the system and be instrumental in helping others learn how to use it. Make sure that they are as up to speed as training can get them before the system is turned on.
- At the time of a start-up, it's good to have experts on the spot to offer tips and assistance. Check on the effectiveness of the training. Have trainers stay around to make sure everything is understood.
- Consider a 24/7 help desk that is bilingual, if needed.
- Some plants have really odd shifts, so you have to think the training plan through thoroughly and devise it so that it accommodates all of the variables.

Above all, have a training plan and execute it. Lack of training is one of the biggest problems with the implementation of new IT systems; all too often it's only an afterthought. People foolishly neglect to spend the time and money and pay for it later. All of the money spent on the system goes down the drain if people don't know how to use it. In our experience, it's impossible to spend too much time or too much money on making sure the users know how to use the system and why it's there.

Test the Project and Review Regularly

There's a lot to be gained from thoroughly testing a newly installed system. It's highly unlikely that a new software package will run perfectly the first time out. Testing helps smooth out many of the kinks right away, so that you're not having a series of headaches on a daily basis when everyone starts using the system. In order to be thorough, the testing process should be formalized and fully documented. Define early on how the testing will be done. You want everything to be traceable to the requirements at every stage of the process.

In one case, a company had a legacy application that it wanted to replace with a module of its ERP system. The ERP vendor assured the company that the module would handle the requirements perfectly, so the company's IT specialists worked with the ERP vendor to install and configure the system. The people in charge of the project declared it ready one day, so the legacy system was turned off and the new ERP module was turned on.

It was a complete disaster. Nothing worked the way it was supposed to work. They'd neglected to test anything before they started it up. No one was involved with the project other than the technology specialists. There should have been tests done in a lab environment for starters. Then they should have devised a way to incrementally bring the new system on line, while at the same time incrementally shutting down the legacy system.

You'll also want to chart your progress. If you do your homework, you'll have a clear schedule for each stage of the implementation. Set up regular intervals, perhaps monthly, where you review the status of all aspects of the project. You'll be able to see how the actual work compares to your plan and to adjust your plan accordingly.

Stay Flexible

The one certainty of any implementation is that it will evolve over time. Most projects take a reasonably long time to be completed and over that time, things will change. New people will come in and others will go, and ideas about the project will come and go with them. The system that gets installed is never exactly the same one that you first envisioned. The smart approach is to anticipate change, instead of resisting it. You need to have a process in place for managing the changes that will inevitably occur. One of the primary dangers is that the project will veer away from the initial goals. Keeping a clear and distinct sense of the ultimate goals and outcomes is the key to staying the course. While knowing the requirements is clearly important, knowing the intent behind the requirements is even more important. If requirements change, make sure they stay aligned with the underlying goals.

SUPPORT

Once you have completed the implementation, there remains one stage to the project lifecycle: Support. It's easy to feel like you are done once the implementation is over, but without support for your systems, problems will certainly arise. Ultimately, no IT project can claim to be successful if this final stage is slighted or neglected. It turns out that "support" means much more than many people think. The focus in this section is on the essential elements of establishing and maintaining support.

The Essential Elements of Support

Success with an IT project is an ongoing process. Even if the implementation goes perfectly according to plan, everything will not continue to run smoothly unless efforts are made to provide top quality support. Projects vary tremendously, so support will vary accordingly. In general, however, there are several essential ideas that should be examined. Those ideas are:

- Maintain a broad perspective on support
- Create support documentation
- Use an application "health monitor"
- Provide support to the user community
- Ensure that training evolves
- Keep a review process in place

We will look at each of these ideas so that you can see how they might apply to your specific situation.

Maintain a Broad Perspective on Support

Support is often misunderstood. Many people have a concept of support that's overly simplistic. They are focused on keeping the system running, keeping the software working, keeping revisions up to date, keeping the servers working, and fixing the bugs. In this mindset, support is all about maintaining the status quo of the systems that are in place. There can be no disputing that all of this is important, but support shouldn't stop there. The fact of business life is that change is occurring more rapidly than ever. Manufacturing processes change, business processes change, market conditions change, and as a result, business drivers change. Support in the broader sense means constantly reevaluating your requirements to ensure that your IT solutions are continuing to fulfill the functions demanded by your business. The idea here is that support should be viewed as more than simply keeping the systems running. It should encompass keeping the business requirements functioning and that can involve more than just maintaining the systems already in place.

Here is an example that involves CMMS. A look at companies that have used maintenance management systems over the last 20 years reveals that virtually all of them have seen a lot of change in the software they are using. One aspect of this is that many companies have sought to improve their maintenance practices and as their practices matured, they outgrew the system they had been using. One common change is going from the practice of maintaining work instructions on paper to maintaining them electronically. So they move on to a system that provides a better fit for the company they have become.

Create Support Documentation

The creation of manuals, installation guides, troubleshooting guides, help desk information, and other similar materials is fundamental to the support process. Whenever you're debating whether to upgrade, extend, or replace an existing system, the support documentation library can be a valuable resource. Use these materials to help you analyze the situation and to develop requirements.

Use an Application "Health Monitor"

An application "health monitor" performs diagnostics on IT systems. You can use a health monitor to check critical and noncritical information about the IT systems, and it can be set to do this weekly, daily, or hourly. By checking such things as application events, disk space, performance, availability, and alarms among others, a health monitor helps support people catch problems quickly, before they become critical. This can be the difference between taking a few minutes to address a problem and having a line or even an entire plant shut down for hours because the problem wasn't found in time.

Provide Support to the User Community

Users are central to the success of any project and they need a sustained source of support. The new technology you just implemented may be remarkable, but if users have trouble with it, you'll have trouble achieving the payback you anticipate. There are various ways to structure user support, such as offering it locally in each plant or making it available in one central place for the entire company. You have to find the way that best suits your organization. The point is to provide clear and concise information that addresses the needs of the users. Toward this end, it can be extremely beneficial to track problems and record the type and nature of the help that's needed. This information facilitates efforts to spot trends and discover recurring problems, thus supporting continuous improvement efforts.

Ensure That Training Evolves

Companies evolve in terms of their personnel, their products, and their practices. Training has to keep pace with this evolution. Good training programs will make use of the information gathered by user support about the most common problems. This way, training programs can be changed to address these problems and help users become more proficient from the start. As upgrades or other specific changes are made to various systems, there may be the need for one-time training sessions. Keeping an eye on the ever changing IT environment is the key to maintaining a good training program.

Keep a Review Process in Place

Keeping a review process in place will protect the long-term return on your IT investments. You need good processes in place that ensure two things. One is that you're getting the documentation you need, and the other is that you will regularly review this documentation. The lifecycle costs for any application don't stop with the initial capital expense. In some cases, the costs of maintenance, repair, and labor support can exceed the costs of an alternative solution. Do I fix this system by enhancing it or upgrading it, or do I get a new one? It is similar to deciding when to fix your old car or buy a new one. Sometimes it's unwise to put extra money into an old car, when the same amount of money could get you a better car. In other cases, it does make sense to repair the car you have.

It's a Journey, Not a Destination

Through all of this, keep in mind that making manufacturing IT projects a success in your company is a never ending process. The more you do, the more you'll find to do. If you succeed in one area, you'll want to transfer that success to other areas. If you're tempted to conclude that the end of an implementation means you're finished with that system, you're starting down the path to all kinds of problems. Support is the final stage of the project lifecycle, but it's also more than a stage. It's an ongoing process of continuous improvement that will lead to more success as you continue your pursuit of business solutions.

CONCLUSION

Implementations can be nightmares, but they don't have to be. If you follow all of the prescriptions here that apply to your situation, you'll greatly increase your chances of success. But after the implementation is complete, your work is still not done. No project can sustain success if the Support stage is neglected. Support can also be seen as encompassing the challenge of handling problems. So in the final chapter, we turn our attention to the many pitfalls that can beset IT projects.

11

PITFALLS

Every project has hidden dangers and difficulties. By definition, a pitfall is something camouflaged or not easily recognized. Drawing upon 20 years of seeing people succeed and fail in all aspects of everything described in this book, we present our list of the pitfalls that have beset project after project. If you can keep a sharp eye out for pitfalls, you may be able to avoid falling into them. We start with a list of the 10 most common project pitfalls. We also explain why they occur and we give you examples of each. After that we provide a longer list of potential pitfalls, offer some advice about dodging all of these problems, present a list of why projects succeed, and then explain some techniques for getting out of a pitfall, if you should fall in. We end this chapter with our "Seven Habits of Highly Effective Manufacturers." Here we present our ideas for creating a corporate culture that is supportive of and conducive to successful IT projects.

THE 10 MOST COMMON PITFALLS

1. The Project or System Requirements Are Disconnected from, or Not Driven by, the Business

The importance of defining requirements should be clear to everyone, yet people sometimes give this task only meager attention at best. Companies undertake information technology projects to improve their performance. The purpose of any project should be clearly defined by its requirements. If you want a recipe for a project failure, start it without a clear understanding of its purpose. The project's requirements should be clearly aligned with the business drivers for your company. If you don't understand precisely why you're pursuing the project and what value you expect to gain from it, you can't expect the finished product to solve the problems you want solved.

This pitfall manifests in a variety of ways. One example is when the project is managed by a corporate IT department that doesn't have a good understanding of the plant's needs. Another example is when a project is too narrowly focused and as a consequence it offers solutions that serve only a part of the business. In this case, the overall needs of the business may not be met. The ERP-mania has led some people to decide to implement full ERP systems without any clear conception of what they're trying to achieve. There are people who come back from trade shows convinced that they must have one of the products on display, not because it's the right product at the right time, but just because it dazzled them at the show. The same phenomenon can occur at any time if a vendor is particularly persuasive. It's easy to end up with something you don't really need if you take all of a vendor's claims to heart. Finally, don't fall for the "everyone else is doing it" line of reasoning. If everyone else is doing it, you should certainly investigate it, but make an informed decision based on the specific circumstances your company faces.

2. The End Users Aren't Sufficiently Involved in the Design and Implementation Process

The gulf between the needs of corporate IT and the needs of plant operations can present all kinds of pitfalls. A good example of this is when a system is designed or implemented without firm involvement of the end users. It's easy for the people in charge of a project to presume that they know exactly what the plant needs, but it's rarely the case that they're completely accurate. Even if they devise solutions that serve 80% of the user community, that still leaves a full 5th of the users ignored. You need to talk to the people who'll actually be using the system and ask all kinds of questions: What's needed? What's wanted? How is it going to be used? What operations are involved?

Don't forget the lesson of ERP implementations. Remember how the ERP project implementations turned plant operators into data entry clerks? The people who are specifically trained to run the equipment that produces the goods were asked to spend valuable time doing something they weren't trained to do. If they'd been consulted ahead of time, you can be sure they'd have let it be known that extensive data entry would make them less productive.

Good communication with end users includes training. New systems often mean significant changes in the way people perform their jobs. In order to have successful training programs, make use of the input from the people who will undergo the training. This will help you define the nature and scope of the training, and it helps you devise the best way of scheduling it.

Finally, don't think of user involvement as a one-time encounter. Instead, recognize that it's an ongoing process and make it part of your change management program. This is important not only because some aspects of any project may change, but also because communication is always prone to difficulty. You may have solicited input from end users, but as the implementation proceeds, you find out that there was a misunderstanding: "I know that's what I said, but it turns out that's not actually what I really need." Effective communication is best achieved through a dialogue that stays open.

3. The Functional Requirements Are Misunderstood Because They're Poorly Documented

Expecting to get the system you really need from poorly written requirements is like expecting to have a beautiful house built from sloppily drawn blueprints. Nevertheless, it's rare to encounter requirements documents that are solid and clearly written. Most people just don't spend the time and effort needed to do the job right.

There are any number of reasons why this happens. For starters, this task is regarded by some as a solitary endeavor. The job is assigned to one person, who is supposed to hole up in an office for a day or two and grind out a requirements document. Rule 1: If you don't talk to other people about the requirements, you're going to have a lousy requirements document.

But getting input from others guarantees nothing, because another common problem is failing to distinguish between needs and wishes. It's common to wish for things because they are attractive, not because they are essential to your goals. Rule 2: A requirement is something truly integral to improving the way things work, not just something that sounds appealing.

There's also the danger of taking shortcuts. Sometimes, no effort is made to learn about all the solutions that are available, so the requirements listed are confined to what's already known, even if that doesn't begin to adequately describe what is really needed. Another shortcut happens when you focus only on the vendors' solutions. This can lead you to lose sight of your company's problems. Some requirements documents are nothing more than a list of features taken from the Web sites of various vendors. In other cases, someone will decide in advance that the company must have a specific system, so the requirements are written to be biased toward that solution. If you have already decided to get that system, why bother to write the requirements up at all? Rule 3: Learn about all the solutions available, but write your requirements based on your actual needs, not on what the vendors offer.

4. The Project Is Over Budget Because the Project Plan Hasn't Been Developed Correctly and Accurately

Budgets come under pressure from all sides, so it will always be a challenge to devise them accurately. This is part of the reason why good project plans are so critical. If it's not in the project plan, then it will not be in the budget, but that doesn't mean you won't have to implement it. For example, some plans fail to include the design phase or the requirements phase, but these can't be avoided and they do cost money, at least in terms of time spent by personnel working on them. Of course, this is a complicated process. There may be pressure to set the entire budget before the requirements are defined and the design is worked out. In this case, you are shooting in the dark. You may get lucky, but you also risk the possibility that you will come up with a design that costs more than you have budgeted.

There's also a list of common, budget-busting mistakes that can occur in the project plan. For one thing, any project has a certain amount of risk involved. A good plan addresses this and incorporates contingency plans for handling the risks. Likewise, the budget should account for these potential problems as well. Another aspect of a project that frequently gets downplayed in planning is the amount of work involved in managing everything. Double-checking invoices, getting project status reports, sitting on the phone scheduling meetings, deciding on reviews — all of these things take time, and it's easy to expect them to be handled with the minimum of effort, when they actually can become a full-time job. Similarly, it's rare to overestimate the amount of time it takes for training and startup. Look at your own experience or ask around: Can anyone report that startup was actually completed in less time than the project plan allotted? One other difficulty arises when there's also a disconnect between the schedule in the project plan and the schedule that's actually followed. A reasoned pace of implementation often allows for certain cost-reduction efforts. This can mean that pushing up the schedule will substantially increase the costs. A good plan makes it clear that schedule changes can ruin the budget.

5. The Project Is behind Schedule Because of Poor Planning

It doesn't take an Einstein to realize that a substandard project plan will undermine any attempts to make deadlines. What may not be so obvious are the essential steps that should be taken to stay on schedule.

Step 1: *Complete the requirements and design phases before you lock in the implementation schedule.* There may be legitimate reasons to devise a schedule from the start, but make it clear that such schedules are preliminary. They will necessarily be amended after the requirements are documented and the design is finalized.

Step 2: *Set milestones so that you can closely monitor your progress.* Don't allow the project plan to remain vague about scheduling by establishing only a final deadline. Break the project down into stages and have deadlines for each stage, so that you have a sense of what should be accomplished each week or month.

Step 3: *Make sure the resources needed for each stage are available.* Too often, people have an excellent plan, but they underestimate the amount of muscle required to make it all happen. When this happens, things get bottlenecked and the schedule is shot.

Step 4: *Stay ever vigilant about coordinating all participants in the project.* "Look, I'm ready to go with my part, but I can't get started until Bob gets done." A project manager is bound to hear some version of this at some point, but it can be kept to a minimum with good planning and diligent efforts at communication.

Step 5: *Incorporate risk and change management into your project plan.* Nothing ever goes completely according to plans, so it's essential that you be prepared for the inevitable bumps along the way. While you can't explicitly put the unexpected into your schedule, you can include some wiggle room as a matter of course.

6. The Project Is in Danger Because Scope Creep Hasn't Been Managed Well

Scope creep is a truly insidious foe that lurks around every phase of a project. The most powerful antidote to this potential problem is a solid plan with well-articulated goals and requirements. If the scope of the project isn't clearly defined in the first place, how can you even tell when the scope is expanding? Once you've defined the scope, keep an eagle eye on the project's boundaries. Scope creep is aptly named, because it routinely begins as something small and insignificant, then grows gradually. "This is no big deal, so why don't we include it in the project?" Indeed, it may well be that some minor adjustments can be made without any major harm to the budget or the schedule. There are two problems, however. One is that some changes are not as insignificant as they may appear at first glance. Every change should be thoroughly evaluated not only for its local impact, but also for its potential to have ramifications in seemingly unrelated areas. Small changes can have big consequences, so it's important to examine all efforts to alter the original plans. The other problem is that the changes that really are rather small start stacking up. A good way to counter this is to insist on using the change order process even for minor adjustments. This ensures that everything is documented and it helps you track the changes. Once your change orders begin accumulating, you can spot the scope creep more easily and manage it appropriately.

7. The Business Environment and Requirements Have Changed during the Course of the Project

There's not much you can do when the ground shifts under your feet. Mergers and acquisitions have been the undoing of even the best-laid plans for projects. If the merger is suddenly approved, the company may very well turn all of its attention to the merger details, and any current IT projects will be postponed for the time being. There's nothing you can do to prevent this, but if a merger is on tap, you can at least approach the IT project with your eyes wide open. Should your project get sidelined as the company handles its new situation, be sure to keep good records of all that has occurred. You may need these details if the project is revived later on.

There are less severe ways that businesses change, and these changes can also pose problems for projects. One is simply the turnover of personnel. Let's say that you go to a lot of trouble consulting the end users and really nail the requirements as a result. But before you finish the implementation, you discover that none of the end users you consulted are still employed and the end users that are don't approve of the requirements you wrote up. This is an extreme situation, but it does happen. The only solution is good communication. Stay on top of personnel changes and make sure new people are given a chance to provide input as soon as they come on board.

Another problem is the pace of change in some industries. Changes in technologies, fashions, markets, and other areas can mean that a business faces substantially new challenges every 6 months. If your implementation schedule is set for a 2-year period, you could be in trouble. It may be best to structure the design and implementation so that the project can be handled incrementally and adjusted as needed after each phase. Doing this will be difficult, but it's better to choose to do something that isn't easy than to choose to do something that will necessarily be a failure.

8. Conventional Wisdom Is Being Followed Even When It Conflicts with Common Sense

By conventional wisdom, we mean the ideas that become popularly accepted by a wide group of people. In fact, there can be a great deal of validity to these ideas. Any number of trends in business occur because the concepts actually make sense. So, our point isn't that conventional wisdom should be rejected.

Rather, we're pointing out that each situation is unique, so you have to use some common sense to decide if the general trend applies to your business. Don't fall into the trap of following the crowd blindly. Don't presume that you need to have every new technology that comes onto the scene. Don't take your vendor's word as gospel and automatically buy every upgrade that's released. Don't let the top vendor persuade you that it knows more about what you need than you know. Don't pursue technology for technology's sake — make sure there's a good reason for it. In short, use your head to evaluate conventional wisdom in light of your particular circumstances.

9. Dominant Personalities on the Project Team or in the End User Community Are Hijacking the Project

Interpersonal dynamics is an entire topic unto itself, but one aspect worth mentioning is the phenomenon of people who seem driven to be in charge, or at least desire to be. These people are particularly a problem when they have a personal agenda that is at odds with the goals of the project. For example, at times someone will try to use a special project as a stepping stone to a promotion. To this end, these people have to make their presence known in some dramatic fashion, usually either trying to take over the management of the project or boldly presenting their insight into how the project is fatally flawed.

The way to rein these people in is by having roles and responsibilities clearly defined from the beginning. Also, keep a clear picture of lines of authority. Know who reports to whom and don't allow people to overstep their bounds. Finally, make sure the project's stated goals are kept in plain view, so that everyone is regularly reminded what the real agenda is.

10. A Vendor or Consultant Is Diverting Your Attention from What You Actually Need and Getting You to Focus on What It Has to Sell

There are some amazing products out there today, but the most remarkable software in the world is worthless if it doesn't help you solve a problem. The fanciest, most powerful, cordless electric drill is not so impressive if what you really need is a hammer. Given how wonderful some of today's software is, and given how persuasively it's presented by many vendors, it's not surprising that many people fall into this trap. The solution is simple concentration. Focus on *your* situation, *your* problems, *your* requirements. Then look for products that clearly meet *your* needs.

AN EVEN LONGER LIST OF PITFALLS

- Lack of clear goals and objectives
- Fundamental lack of understanding of the business processes
- Lack of buy in
- No champion
- Insufficient funding
- No real business reason or justification
- Misunderstanding of technology
- Technology-driven solutions
- Weak project planning and project management
- Continual reorganization of the company
- Unclear, incompatible, or contradictory standards
- Lack of commitment
- Assuming the solution before understanding the requirements
- Poor vendor selection
- Nonaligned people, processes, or organizations
- Misunderstanding of assumptions or constraints
- Poor requirements definition or analysis
- Lack of expectation management
- Solution is too complex, too hard, too big, too difficult, or requires too much change
- Lack of change management
- Lack of alignment with the business strategy
- Too much reliance on heroes

DODGING PITFALLS

The first step to dodging pitfalls is to simply know what they are. The next step is to make specific efforts to avoid them. Here are seven specific ways that you can proactively work to prevent problems from occurring.

1. Align Your Project with the Business on Day 1 and Keep It There

If the project isn't aligned with the business from the outset, it's certain to have problems. But even if it starts out aligned, keeping it there requires diligence. It's critical that there be some way to measure the impact of your project on the business. Keep in mind what it is that you're trying to achieve and set up checkpoints for reviewing your accomplishments. The requirements are key. Stay focused on the requirements; make sure that they're traceable back to the business and that the project is traceable back to them.

Execute the project in steps and look for business benefits at each step. At the same time, be prepared to do mid-course corrections throughout the project. If you plan to implement a project at several plants and it doesn't go smoothly at the first plant, learn from your experience. Get feedback and make adjustments for the next plants. If your aim is to do reporting for the EPA and it changes the rules after you started your project, you'll need to change the project to adapt. Through it all, maintain ongoing contact with the key stakeholders so that the project objectives can be reviewed regularly.

2. Get the Functional and Technical Requirements Right

Carpenters have an expression: "Measure twice, cut once." Though the amount of time spent measuring is doubled, fewer mistakes occur. The fundamental idea is simple — spending extra time and money up front can save time and money later by preventing problems. This is 100% true when it comes to defining requirements and finding the right technical solution and architecture. Give these initial matters your full attention and you'll completely sidestep all kinds of nasty pitfalls.

3. Control Technology and Product Selection So You Don't "Get Sold" the Wrong Thing

Make the effort to fully grasp all of the requirements so that you know exactly what the technology should do and also what it shouldn't do. This puts you in the position to thoroughly evaluate the products you're considering. You need to know what they can do and what they can't do. To this end, don't simply rely on what your vendor tells you. Talk to other people who have used the product. Any reputable vendor will be happy to provide you with the names of satisfied customers. The main point is to compare the features of the software with your requirements and see which product provides the best solution and actually solves the problems you need solved. If you don't have a firm understanding of your own requirements or if you don't get more information than is contained in a vendor's simple demo, then you're in danger of buying the wrong product.

4. Plan the Project with Particular Focus on the Scope, the Schedule, the Resources, and the Risk

Planning is both everything and nothing. It's everything in the sense that it's unthinkable to attempt any project without it. But it's also nothing in the sense that even the most carefully thought out plans never survive reality intact. The point is that in addition to planning from the start, you must also adjust your plan as the project proceeds. The scope will change, the schedule will change, the resources will change, and the risk will change. Don't skimp on the time and money required for thorough planning both at the start and throughout the life of the project. It will pay off in the end.

5. Follow Good Project Management Practices — the Basics

It never fails to amaze us how many people tend to neglect the fundamentals. Think of the ideas that would be part of a Project Management 101 course and make sure you use these ideas. *Manage the scope, the schedule, and the budget. Measure your progress. Update your plan as things change. Manage the project risks.* Maybe the reason the basics get ignored is that they do take time and effort. But the fact is, these are the practices that will keep your project on track. It only takes one bad experience with a big project to convince most people that time spent attending to these fundamental tasks is time well spent.

6. Keep the Key Stakeholders Up-to-Date as the Project Proceeds

The stakeholders are, by definition, the people who have a significant investment in how the project comes out. There's the possibility that they will be either really satisfied or really disappointed when the project is complete, and good communication can be the determining factor here. Keep these people informed of the project's progress and of all changes that occur. But don't view this as a one-way street. Don't just tell them about what is going on; ask them for feedback as well. Feedback helps you be certain that they are keeping up with the information you provide, and it helps you make the right decisions along the way.

7. Implement a Few Program Management "Best Practices" for Larger Projects

Here are some best practices that should be common sense, but aren't commonly used:

- Establish simple, clear, open, and easy lines of communications and authority.
- Have an empowered project champion.
- Keep the stakeholders involved.
- Work closely with the end user community.
- Follow the basics of project management.
- Have key milestones and reviews throughout the life of the project.

A LIST OF WHY PROJECTS SUCCEED

- Clear business objectives
- Clear business need
- Good project management
- Good people
- Clear communications
- Training — early and often
- Good financial planning
- Setting the right expectations
- Empowered champion
- Good requirements and design process
- Good buy in from all stakeholders
- Good metrics and incentives
- Dividing the project into manageable pieces
- Clear lines of authority and responsibility
- Clear ownership
- Having the right vendors
- Having vendors whose goals are aligned with yours

CLIMBING OUT OF PITFALLS IN FIVE STEPS

If you follow the advice already given, there's a good chance you'll be able to avoid each and every pitfall mentioned. Nevertheless, it's possible that at some point, you'll find yourself in the middle of a serious problem. Here is a simple process for handling difficult situations:

1. The first step to getting out of a pitfall is recognizing that you fell in. Be prepared to make an honest and thorough assessment of the project at every milestone.
2. If you do fall in, take stock of your situation. Don't just reflexively start scrambling to get out. It probably took some time to get into the pit and now it may take some time to get out. Think about why it happened and what it's going to take to correct the problem. Start with small steps and gradually move forward.
3. Remember to focus on the basic goals of the project and how they are aligned with the business needs. Always keep the following question in mind: Is this project delivering value to the business?
4. Get support from the project sponsors and from the key stakeholders. If you've established consistent communication with these people, they'll want to help in any way they can. Plus, if you've been getting their feedback on a regular basis, you probably won't be that deep into the pit in the first place. However, if you've

neglected to keep them informed as the project has progressed, you may be in for some difficult negotiations as you attempt to correct the problem.

5. Invest the time and energy needed to get the project back on track. In the end, there's no getting around it — correcting problems takes time and focused attention.

Finally, share what you've learned with others. After a project is done, conduct reviews so that other people can benefit from your experience. You'll have the benefit of hindsight, and this puts you in a position to make valuable suggestions for the way future projects are managed.

SEVEN HABITS OF HIGHLY EFFECTIVE MANUFACTURERS

One of the most important ways to provide support concerns corporate culture. Up to this point we have limited our focus to the technology and the mechanics of making IT projects successful for your organization, but there's a big idea that hasn't been addressed yet. You have to consider whether or not your organization has certain behaviors and attitudes in place which will allow you to get the full benefit of your project.

This is actually a subject for an entire book by itself, but we want to share a few ideas with you. We've seen that certain practices are effective in terms of the way behaviors and attitudes go hand-in-hand with supporting IT implementations. These ideas can be highly beneficial to the success of any project. You might want to think about making these ideas part of any cultural changes that will happen along with your implementation. These are not the only ones and you don't have to use them, but we have seen them work time and time again. Borrowing from Stephen Covey, we call them the "Seven Habits of Highly Effective Manufacturers."

Habit 1: They Manage the Business Based on Goals

They start by defining a vision and a mission for the business as a whole, for each business unit, for each department, and for each individual. Out of this comes goals for the business as a whole, for each business unit, for each department, and for each individual. This information is communicated to every person in the company so that everyone knows his or her mission and goals and can see how these goals contribute to the goals of the entire company.

The goals must be *SMART*: simple, measurable, achievable, reasonable, and timely. Everything is done with the aim of achieving the goals. But they also realize that goals are not an end unto themselves. Business is a process, not a destination.

Habit 2: They Measure against Their Goals

Having a business goal is great, but it becomes meaningless unless you measure your success. Each person, each department, and each unit in the company is measured both quantitatively and qualitatively, and every measurement is designed to track back specifically to the business goals.

But this isn't a static process. It's possible to meet your goals and still fail as a business, so the goals themselves must be continuously redefined as the business changes. This means that the measurements need to change along with the goals.

Habit 3: They Make a Cult out of Quality

The only number that matters to them is zero — zero customer complaints, zero recalls, zero defects, zero problems with regulatory agencies, zero breakdowns, and zero failures. It's not that adherence to specifications doesn't matter; it's that it doesn't take it far enough.

Quality can be defined as black or white or it can be defined as a value. In different situations, customers define it either way and the customer is king. As Sam Walton said, "The customer can fire everybody in the company, from the CEO right on down, just by shopping somewhere else." In order to please the customers, quality must be paramount. One small failure can ruin thousands of good things. One product failure can cause tremendous damage. The point is to create an environment where high quality is inevitable. This is the essence of quality assurance.

Habit 4: They Strive to Reduce Costs in a Smart Way

To reduce costs, they use world-class measures, understand their suppliers and work collaboratively with them, eliminate processes that don't add value, and expect their customers to work with them.

Everyone wants to cut costs, but there are smart ways and not-so-smart ways to reduce costs. It takes money to make money. For example, a smart way to reduce costs is to get the best people possible and pay them fairly for the skill and knowledge they provide. Another way is to buy the best quality raw materials. You should invest heavily in your people, your processes, and in new ideas.

Habit 5: They Work to Continuously Improve the Business

They know that business is a process and that change is the only constant, so they're seeking continuous improvement. But they realize that improvement is made in steps. So they're always looking for the breakthroughs that will take them to the next level.

They also realize that breakthroughs require significant change and there's always the risk of losing ground, but this is the only way to make breakthroughs, so they embrace the challenge and take the risk associated with it. Only by continuously improving can you make big breakthroughs.

Habit 6: They Understand the Importance of People

In the 1980s, Lights Out Manufacturing was the fad of the day, but it turned out to be a massive failure. The lesson can be summed up by a quote from Henry Ford, "You can take my factories, burn up my building, but give me my people and I'll build the business right back again."

Computer systems aren't creative, flexible, and able to learn new things. People can learn new things and they can find ways to do things differently. The lights are back on in manufacturing today and people are an integral part of the process. Let computers do what they do best and let people do what they do best. People can create new solutions, find new breakthroughs, and solve difficult problems. Highly effective manufacturers understand that people are their greatest asset.

Habit 7: They Use the Right Tools for the Job

They know that technology changes rapidly, so picking the right tools is no simple matter. The challenge is to get the right tools at the right time in the right place, which means they have to have *know-how*, *know-where*, and *know-when*.

They know that fighting technology is not the answer. Instead, they look at problems from a business point of view. They make sure they understand the goals, so they can determine which tools will work to reach those goals.

But they also do not get too caught up with tools. They remember that a tool is only as effective as the person who wields it. They also keep in mind that when all you have is a hammer, everything begins to look like a nail. And they resist buying a new tool just because it's the latest fad. They focus on the business problem, find the right tools, and give these tools to the people who need them.

CONCLUSION

All projects come with problems; that much is certain. But if you know what to anticipate, you should be able to keep minor irritations from becoming major headaches. An awareness of the pitfalls others have fallen into will make it easier for you to avoid them. And one of the best ways to reduce the occurrence of all kinds of problems is to create a corporate culture that supports success in every aspect of your business. We hope our Seven Habits contribute to this effort.

12

CONCLUSION

There's one thing to be emphasized. *This is real. Manufacturing companies have achieved measurable and sustainable success using the ideas in this book.* We know this to be true because we've personally witnessed it. The book you just finished reading is not full of speculative theories about what *should* work. Every bit of information is based on our observations of what actually *does* work. The tools and methods we describe have already worked in manufacturing plants around the globe, and they can work in your plants as well.

It won't be easy, but it will be worth the effort. Diligent efforts applying these ideas will produce a solid reward. The work will involve extensive research and planning so that you can sort through the endless claims from competing vendors about the value of their products. You will need to give careful attention to each step in the process, because there are dangerous pitfalls at every turn that can undermine your endeavors. IT projects require a tremendous amount of work, but when done properly, they bring tremendous advantages to the company.

It may be helpful to see the project lifecycle as a series of calls to action. Your first task is to develop a strategy that both defines what you will attempt to accomplish with information technology and spells out what benefits you expect to gain. This will be the roadmap for using IT to support your business and operating goals. Next, use your strategy to create the framework for achieving your IT objectives. In this stage, you will hammer out the details of the business process changes, the application software architecture, the budget, and the expected financial returns. After the project has received funding, it will be time for the implementation. The intelligent use of industry best practices can make a world of difference here, so be diligent about applying the wisdom learned by others. After the new systems are up and running, support is critical. This final stage musn't be neglected if you want you to keep your IT investment in tune with your business and the changes that lie ahead.

We encourage you to use the information in this book to help your company find its own path to IT success, because there are as many paths to success as there are companies. Remember, however, that successful organizations share certain traits. Above all else, our experience shows us that the companies that derive the most benefits from their IT applications are those that are striving for continuous improvement. While no single program or philosophy can be the true religion that everyone should follow, it's clear that the companies who have a culture geared toward continuous improvement are the ones who always get a payback on their IT investments.

If this isn't already your orientation, we urge you to adopt it. The potential for using information technology in manufacturing companies today is immense, and the opportunities will only increase in the years ahead. If you feel behind the curve, don't worry; you're not alone. The daily challenge of getting products out the door leaves many managers with little time for conducting research on new technologies.

But now is the time to start learning more. Take it one step at a time, but think of it as a never ending process. The point shouldn't be simply to get the best new technology and be done with it. That attitude, in fact, is a recipe for failure. Change is our constant companion, so there'll always be new systems, new technologies, and new applications to learn about and consider. With a concerted and continuous effort, you can help your company succeed in the years ahead.

We wish you luck!

Appendix A

STANDARDS

In Chapter 9 we mentioned the following as examples of standards that have sunk below the horizon:

- DECnet
- IBM® SAA® (System Application Architecture)
- OSF and OSF/1
- MAP/TOP and IEEE-802.4
- X-Windows
- PowerBuilder® software

To give you a better idea of how standards come into being and how they pass out of existence, we want to describe these standards as examples in more detail. For each one, we will answer the following four questions:

1. What type of standard is it?
2. What was it trying to accomplish?
3. Why did it fail?
4. What is its legacy?

DECNET

A vendor standard from Digital Equipment Corporation (DEC), DECnet was created to address how computers should talk together using the network. It sought to define how computers should talk to each other, how terminals should talk to each other, and how computer programs talk to each other. It made it easier, more efficient, and less costly for computers to interface.

It failed because all of the software was proprietary. It allowed all DEC computers to work together, but it didn't help a DEC computer talk to an HP computer. DEC lost thought leadership and price leadership. It clung to its standard and charged a premium for it. Its legacy is that it spawned new standards, which have evolved into the ubiquitous networking that we use today. The idea was so beneficial that others decided to make it universal. Eventually an open standard (nonproprietary) took over. DEC itself was finally forced to adopt the new, emerging open standards, and DECnet has fallen completely out of use. Digital Equipment Corporation has since been purchased by Compaq Computer Corporation, which in turn has become part of Hewlett Packard.

IBM SAA

SAA was a vendor standard from IBM that was intended to provide a set of rules for developing software. It applied to all software and all computers. It was conceived around 1984 to 1985 and died around 1988. In an attempt to drive the development of software, IBM wanted corporations to adopt the standard as a corporate standard. Such an idea was not well received by companies like HP.

The adoption of SAA obviously would give a huge advantage to IBM, so all of its competitors were in favor of open software. There has always been a tremendous amount of inertia and infighting between platforms within IBM and they couldn't really agree about how to do it, so it failed. SAA was one of the many standards that IBM was pushing to the marketplace. Other companies couldn't have survived a failure of this magnitude, but IBM was in a position to spend enough money on other research to keep the company going. SAA's legacy is that it actually pushed forward the development of the Open Software Foundation, the opposite effect that was desired. IBM hedged its bet on SAA by also putting money behind the Open Software Foundation and gradually embraced open systems architecture and standards. SAA is now a faint memory, even for seasoned IT professionals who have spent many years working in an IBM environment.

OSF (OPEN SOFTWARE FOUNDATION)

OSF was a technical industry standard. At the time, there were four or five versions of UNIX, so the idea was to create one version and at the same time avoid paying AT&T for a license. Vendors like DEC, HP, IBM, SUN, Oracle plus large buyers like Boeing got together to create the foundation. The idea was to make a level playing field, but the project never really got off the ground. Everyone paid lip service to the product, but no one wanted to sell it. All of the vendors wanted to push their own product, so that clients would be dependent on them. Vendors would have it as an option, but did everything possible to discourage their customers from buying it. The market was screaming for this product, so the vendors responded, but they didn't really want to sell it. Boeing bought it and the government bought it, because it did serve a purpose. Companies could use computers and programs from different vendors. It failed because you have to have a revenue stream to support the effort to continually upgrade it. Since no one was really pushing OSF, it never developed the needed revenue stream. Its legacy is that vendors started standardizing nondesktop operating systems. Although both the OSF operating system and its sponsoring organization have died, their fundamental goals live on in the open source movement's work with Linux.

MAP/TOP

A technical industry standard, MAP/TOP was almost exactly like OSF. It was Boeing, GM, automation and computer vendors (DEC, HP, IBM, Rockwell, Foxboro) that wanted to develop a standard that came to be called Manufacturing Automation Protocol and Technical and Office Protocol. The idea was to create one universal standard for the factory, so that everyone can talk to each other, and they did it. There was a trade show that came to be dominated by the MAP effort. Technically it was successful.

The problem was they created a standard (802.4) that was tremendously expensive. It required a broadband network in the plant, which was expensive to install and maintain, and it was slow compared to Ethernet. Plus, the components each vendor had to sell to get you on it were very expensive. At the same time, DEC had come out with DECnet, but the people behind MAP/TOP didn't want everyone to have to run DEC. These two standards were competing visions, like VHS and Beta, but in the end, neither one won.

Originally DEC's vision was very limited and focused only on helping the big computers communicate — the minis, the mainframe, and maybe some PCs. The MAP/TOP vision was taking a computer over here, a PLC over there, a DCS over there, and making all of this into one system — the backbone of the CIM Pyramid. It would run through the entire factory and everyone would be plugged into it. It was in response to this that DEC extended DECnet to PCs.

But everyone else wanted a third solution — nonproprietary Ethernet — the hardware that makes DECnet cheap, but software that doesn't belong to anyone. To see why it didn't work, consider what one paper mill experienced. The paper mill spent $500,000 in the mid-1980s to put in a broadband system and was spending $100,000 a year on maintenance. Then the mill ripped it out and put in an HP Ethernet system for only $100,000. The MAP/TOP solution was elegant, but it cost so much that no one ever implemented it. It was a wonderful idea, but ultimately it was just too expensive. The theory was that it would become cheaper over time and the originators (GM and Boeing) had plenty to spend, but as smaller companies started looking at it, it became clear that many companies would never choose to spend the money on it.

Its legacy is similar to DECnet. DECnet was helping the computers in the computer room communicate. The idea of MAP/TOP was for plant computers and the legacy was to extend the Ethernet around the plant. It promoted the principle that networking was needed in the plant. Outside of governmental use, MAP/TOP never achieved any practical market penetration due to its complexity and costs.

X-WINDOWS

This technical industry standard was an attempt to come up with a graphical standard like Microsoft® Windows, but one that ran on a dumb terminal. A dumb terminal has no hard drive, only a mouse, keyboard, and a green or amber screen. They are much cheaper than PCs, but people really liked the flexibility of a PC. The idea was to make dumb terminals function like PCs without having to buy PCs. Dumb terminals are also tougher. They don't need fans, they can withstand the harsh chemicals in the plant, and they don't have hard drives that fail. Because of its appeal, X-Windows was widely adopted. A lot of people wrote their software with it and many implemented projects with it. It was truly a great idea.

But two things happened. One is the advent of the browser, which will run on most hardware platforms and is free. The other is that PCs now cost $600, instead of $5000. So X-Windows lost its competitive edge. We have come 360° since the 1970s. Things were centralized at that time, then they became distributed through the rise of the PC, but now everything is being centralized again. The use of the browser connects everyone to a central processing point. The legacy of X-Windows is having graphical user interfaces on the shop floor. Commercial market pressures forced everyone to find a replacement for X-Windows, and character terminals now are a thing of the past.

POWERBUILDER

A vendor product standard from Powersoft, PowerBuilder was a software development environment that did something called client server and object-oriented programming. It basically was trying to take advantage of the computing power of having a PC on everyone's desk and to use this power to create software in a new way. Tools came out that were new programming languages, and they took advantage of these two new paradigms. PowerBuilder really won in the market for a time, having maybe over half of the market share. Powersoft shot to the moon. You could use PowerBuilder to go from the green character screen to something that looked like Windows.

First and foremost, it was a software development tool. Second, it was a development tool on the Windows/Intel® platform, in contrast to applications that were on mainframes. It allowed the focus to shift from the mainframes to the desktop in a developer-friendly environment. It allowed the proliferation of small systems development. You just didn't write a quick application for anything prior to PowerBuilder. Before, if you wanted to do anything, you needed at least 6 to 8 weeks to get it written. With PowerBuilder, you could do it in 2 weeks.

Imagine that someone in the front office needs an application to keep track of all the staff coming and going. There has to be a component on each staff person's PC where the data gets put in, a component on the office manager's PC where the data can be read, and a database on the company's server. This is a perfect PowerBuilder application. Instead of waiting for someone to make this, you can do it yourself in a couple weeks. If one staff member wants mileage to be included in the program, PowerBuilder's object-oriented ability makes it easy to reuse elements already in the program. You can take the screen and tweak it a little bit by reusing the code you wrote originally.

PowerBuilder succeeded in part because of its independence. It was nonproprietary. It became the market leader and de facto standard for client-server development — the PC is the client and the database lived on a server. You write the program that runs on the PC and talks to the database in the server. Entire cottage industries and half the world started training on PowerBuilder. PowerBuilder development was everywhere. Half the corporations in America had PowerBuilder going on.

Technically it's still not dead. You can still buy it. But people eventually saw that writing all of this software created a huge maintenance problem. You could find yourself with thousands of programs to be maintained and supported. Then, when Microsoft® upgrades Windows to 95 from 3.1, you have to go update every copy of every program on every PC. It was a maintenance nightmare. People discovered that a browser could do everything if you write it all on Java, which is free and runs anywhere.

The programming can all be housed on the server, and you don't have to worry about changing everything on all the PCs. If you have 1100 programs, you can maintain them all on your server and not worry about all of the copies distributed everywhere on countless PCs. In contrast, with PowerBuilder's client/server solution, if your corporation has 3000 machines and just two applications, you have 6000 instances of these applications on the machines. If one word was misspelled, you have to fix it using an army of 20 people, each with eight disks, taking 3 months going around to each of those 3000 machines and installing the change.

This was a worst-case scenario. PowerBuilder developed automated ways of doing this, but there was risk involved. Think of a national insurance company with agents spread over the entire country. Updates meant shipping 3000 disks out and hoping they got installed. Now, with the browser, it's instantly available to everyone. Ultimately, Powersoft was completely blindsided by the combination of the browser and Java. The part of their model that didn't work was the "fat client" — programs installed on each PC. It was replaced by the "thin client" — host-based applications running on a browser. PowerBuilder's client/server model ran its technological course.

The legacy of PowerBuilder is that it initiated the complete use of the graphic interface for business applications, just like X-Windows did for the plant floor. Everyone started using object oriented programming, which is much better for developing applications. Everyone started using rapid application prototyping and client-server development. All of these things came about because of PowerBuilder. The idea of how desktops work today is pretty much the way PowerBuilder set it up. Powersoft has since been purchased by Sybase and the PowerBuilder development suite has migrated away from client-server technology.

Appendix B

MODELS

NINE IMPORTANT MODELS

We said in Chapter 9 that models have always had an important role to play in helping people come to grips with IT strategies and architectures for manufacturing. This appendix presents nine of the most important models, past and present, which pertain to manufacturing IT. We describe these models by focusing on answers to the following four questions:

1. What type of model is it?
2. What does it seek to do?
3. How does it succeed?
4. What are its drawbacks?

Computer-Integrated Manufacturing (CIM) Pyramid

The CIM Pyramid (see Figure B.1) was an attempt to depict various levels of computing architecture. Before the model was created, there were two environments that didn't interface — plant controls and the business system environment, which included accounting, inventory, purchasing and such. CIM came into existence when someone thought, "If I could measure these things over here, I could update the inventory automatically." There needed to be some reference to describe how that would take place, and CIM was the first model that attempted to bring discipline to that pursuit.

It was developed around the same time that everyone in the technical and engineering world went through a hierarchical modeling phase and ISO came out with its model for networking standards, so the five layers made perfect sense. Here's how the levels were envisioned: You go out to a line and see a PLC attached to the line — that is Level 1; walk over

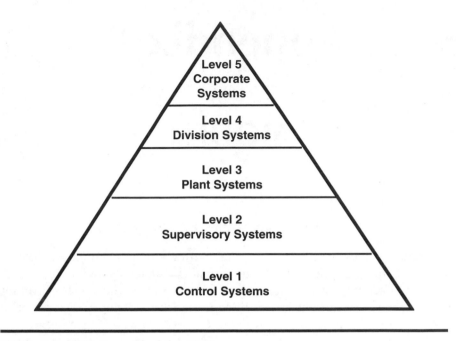

Figure B.1   CIM Pyramid of the 1980s

to the enclosure and open it and there's a PC with a SCADA system running on it — that is Level 2; you go into the computer room and see a minicomputer running some program — that is Level 3. The shape is based on the idea that Level 1 involves many different computers and Level 5 was a single mainframe.

The CIM Pyramid sought to provide a reference framework so that people could have a conversation about requirements. People used it to think about what they needed or what was missing in their systems. There was the idea of a "CIM gap," as in, "You don't have a Level 3 system." It succeeded by raising awareness of what could be done. It was a model that allowed people to communicate. It provided a place for a vendor to hang his hat — "My product is for Level 2."

The main drawback of the CIM Pyramid was that it was purely architectural, so it had no real mechanism for making changes. It was purely a hardware model and that led people to order hardware based on the model instead of on their functional requirements. It didn't address business problems or IT functions. There was no industry tailoring, just a broad general idea. There were no data flows. CIM was made by engineers who saw the need for it, but corporate IT completely ignored it because corporate IT saw IT architecture from a dramatically different perspective where Level 1 had much greater detail.

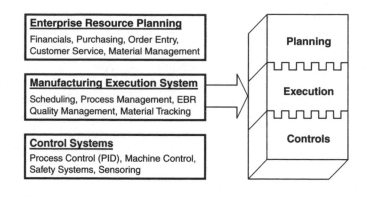

Figure B.2 AMR 3-Layer Model (Source: AMR 1992. Used with permission.)

AMR 3-Layer Model

The AMR 3-Layer Model (see Figure B.2) was a business function model that was intended to be an improvement over CIM. It moved away from a hardware architectural model into a business function model, but it still remained hierarchical, with three levels emphasizing business processes, without emphasizing hardware. It was an attempt to make things more generic and to concentrate on the manufacturing space. "Planning" did not mean how to plan payroll or how to plan a merger. It meant how to plan actual production. So all of the other corporate matters were cut out. This was in the early 1990s, so it was pre-supply chain. Although it did move away from CIM's strict hierarchy, it still tended to have people looking at each computer and classifying it to one of the three layers. The interlocking edges indicate that there is some awareness of boundary blurring. Vendors may have tried to exploit this in terms of not being restricted to any one layer.

The AMR 3-Layer Model succeeded by getting people to start thinking about what data had to flow from one layer to the next, and it provided a reference point for discussions. It was more about how to do things, instead of which hardware was needed. It was focused on manufacturing; it drew some boundaries around functions by listing them within the layers. As a result of CIM, there were now products available and the AMR3 helped you evaluate them. It also helped people see the benefit of open systems.

The biggest drawback of the AMR3 was that the execution layer had the "then a miracle occurs" element to it if you tried to draw a diagram of all the data flows. By this we mean that it failed to address all of the complexity of manufacturing reality. It was overly simplistic; realistic data flows came later. It created the expectation that you could have a product that would handle each of these layers. In fact, this was possible with controls, but not with execution and planning. It also had the drawback of promoting silo thinking by delineating the layers.

One other problem was that, by defining the marketplace, it fostered the creation of industry groups that defined what was going to exist in that marketplace. This isn't necessarily a drawback, but it turns into one if the scope of products on the market become artificially contrived and as a result they don't naturally fit what companies are doing. The AMR 3-Layer Model has been superceded by a more sophisticated model from AMR, the REPAC model, which is described later.

MESA Model

The MESA Model (see Figure B.3) was a functional model that took the middle layer out of the AMR 3-Layer Model and broke it down into a list of functions. Thus it sought to focus entirely on execution. It succeeded in that it moved away from the hierarchical structure, and it provided a good checklist of functions that needed to be considered.

The model's drawback was that it didn't provide much more than a checklist. The drawing was almost pointless. It was put together not by people doing manufacturing, but by people selling software, so the boundaries of what falls into each category was decided in large measure by what products they were trying to sell. The model was driven by software, instead of having software developed in response to a model showing functional needs. The drawing also gives no indication of how things might fit together into business processes.

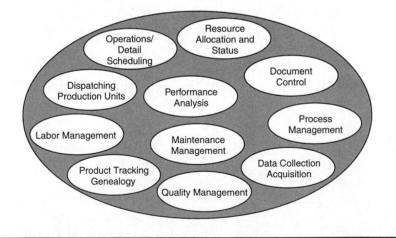

Figure B.3   MESA Functional Model (Souce: MESA. Used with permission.)

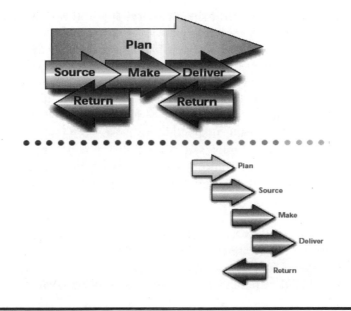

Figure B.4 Supply Chain Operations Reference (SCOR) Model (Source: Supply-Chain Council, Pittsburgh, PA. Used with permission.)

Supply Chain Operations Reference (SCOR) Model

The SCOR model (see Figure B.4) is both a business process model and a project execution model. It was created by business process experts, not engineers. It provides a big picture and a breakdown into many parts, because it seeks to create a model with varying levels of depth to show typical business processes. First, it presents a broad view of every business process in the company; then it carries the focus down two layers where businesses find themselves doing things in common ways. It seeks to be a platform for people who take it to the next layer and talk about how those processes are implemented in their company. It is really useful as a tool for a company that wants to build a framework of its own business processes and use that framework as the basis for improvement, changes, reengineering, and understanding. It helps you see what you are doing now and what you are trying to do.

The SCOR model is a terrific starting point. It has defined the things that are common to business processes. It has created a comprehensive model from beginning to end, producing a great methodology. One of the SCOR model's successes is that it finally documented the fact that the whole company mattered. It addressed business problems and gave you a map for handling them. You couldn't do that with any of the former models. It handles many details at the various levels of the model by providing you with a detailed map for everything you do. Everything that is done in your company can be connected to a part of the model. If you have parts of the model that are left blank, you may want to consider whether or not you need to add these elements. It works as an example, a checklist, and a framework. If you have sourcing problems, delivery problems, or production problems, you can find a way to look at them through the SCOR model. It is well thought out and clearly took a lot of work to produce. It was the first model to address the supply chain.

As good as the SCOR model is, it still will not carry you to the promised land all by itself. It's only a starting point and unless you immerse yourself in it and follow the methodology, you're not going to get any value out of it. Not enough people make use of the entire model. Given that it is a supply chain model, many people tend to focus on sourcing, delivering, and planning, but neglect the "make" part. "Make" is the hardest. It's the most difficult, the most intractable, and the most diffuse from industry to industry. Supplier relationships and customer relationships are really not that different, but the manufacturing part is totally different.

REPAC Model

This business process model is a big step forward in terms of showing business processes (see Figure B.5). It sought to examine what manufacturing was trying to accomplish, not just show what it was doing. It

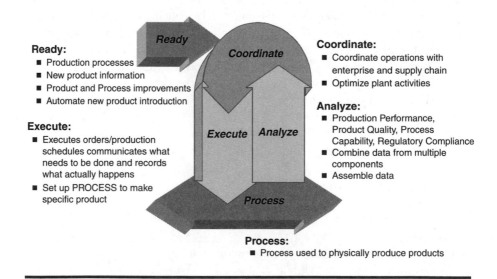

Figure B.5 AMR REPAC Model (Source: AMR 1988. Used with permission.)

recognized that the objective was to get products out the door, and it succeeded in defining certain business functions.

The drawback of the REPAC model is that it's still too high level and too abstract. It doesn't actually describe things in ways that people can identify with. No one has a "Ready" department. It is disconnected from the common parlance of manufacturing. Plus, the very name "REPAC" conjures up notions of product failures, because repackaging implies things weren't packaged right in the first place.

New Manufacturing Model

The New Manufacturing Model (see Figure B.6) is a conglomerate, using SCOR, REPAC, and AMR 3-Layer Model. By taking the elements of these three models and joining them together, it is trying to be all encompassing. The point is to make sense out of all the models and to show how different models fit together. So it promotes the idea that no one model should be used exclusively. It is also an attempt to address the difficulty of "make." It succeeds by giving a context to a project proposal, but its drawback is that it is a forced fit. It has all of the weakness of its component models.

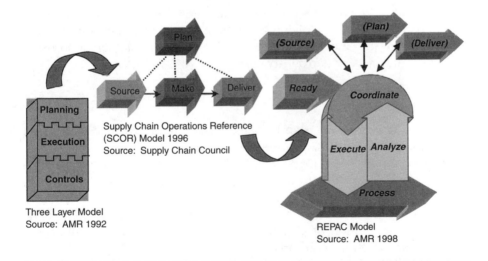

Figure B.6   The New Manufacturing Model (Source: AMR 3-Layer Model, AMR 1992; SCOR Model, Supply-Chain Council 1996; REPAC Model, AMR 1998. Used with permission.)

ISA-88

ISA-88 is a standard that is based on a model of how companies manage batch execution and batch processes. It seeks to establish some common terminology. Companies engaged in batch process manufacturing need a common set of definitions for controlling, organizing, and communicating between systems about batches. ISA-88 is trying to define the basic terminology, the basic structure of information, and the basic hierarchy for this manufacturing environment. It establishes guidelines for how you perform a batch, how you define a batch, and how those elements interact. There's an equipment hierarchy and a process model hierarchy. The standard defines what each of the levels of the hierarchies are and what the interactions between them are.

Before, there was no standard about how you documented or defined equipment, steps, phases, lines, or process cells. ISA-88 will allow you to change vendors and have the same definitions in your new product. ISA-88 is like a dictionary, which is very useful. It addresses the problem of how a set of materials is transformed through the batch process to the product that you're selling.

If someone wants a batch system that's ISA-88 compliant, it means that the equipment model follows the modeling standard laid out in the ISA-88 model (see Figures B.7A through B.10). When you model your batch process, it's organized in the same fashion as the ISA-88 model is laid out. The model documents how the equipment and the process interact.

ISA-88 succeeded by solving a problem. It was the right thing at the right time, but the drawbacks are that it leaves the implementation up to you and it has a very narrow focus.

ISA-95

ISA-95 is a multiple part standard, the first part of which establishes a model for manufacturing processes (see Figure B.11). This makes it a manufacturing business operations model, and it also turns out that it is an IT-type model coming from an engineering organization. ISA-95 establishes the essential features for a manufacturing enterprise. In effect it says, "These are the things that have to be done." It describes the general functional organization of a manufacturing operation and how the operation interacts with an enterprise system.

The goal of ISA-95 is to model data and information flow, as opposed to modeling business processes, as the SCOR model does. It clearly delineates which things are in the model and which things aren't in the model. It defines interfaces between what is in and what is out, it gives data flows, and it shows functional relationships of the things that are in the model. For example, it says what project scheduling should look like.

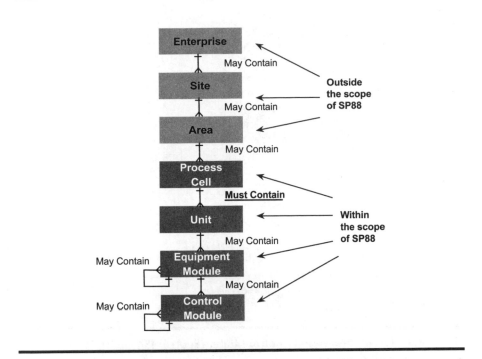

Figure B.7A ISA-88 Physical Model (Source: ISA-88.01-1995, © ISA 1995. Used with permission.)

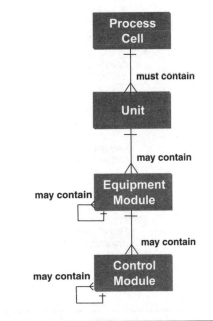

Figure B.7B ISA-88 Physical Model (Source: ISA-88.01-1995, © ISA 1995. Used with permission.)

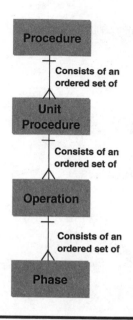

Figure B.8 ISA-88 Procedural Control Model (Source: ISA-88.01-1995, © ISA 1995. Used with permission.)

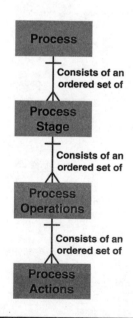

Figure B.9 ISA-88 Process Model (Source: ISA-88.01-1995, © ISA 1995. Used with permission.)

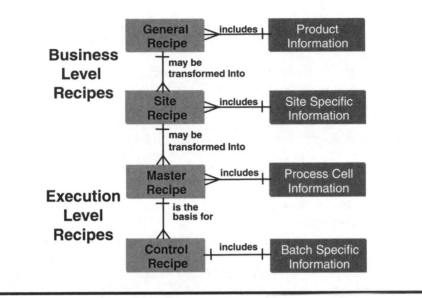

Figure B.10   ISA-88 Recipes (Source: ISA-88.01-1995, © ISA 1995. Used with permission.)

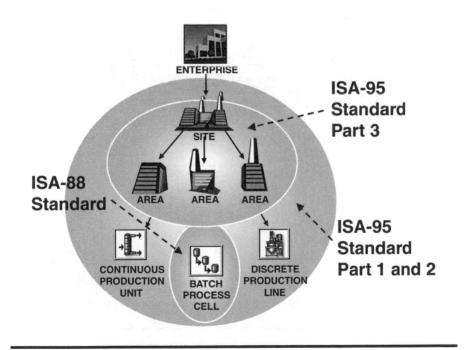

Figure B.11   ISA-88 and ISA-95 Standards Scope (Source: ISA, Portions of this illustration © ISA 1995, 2000. Used with permission.)

It also defines how a lower-level system will interface with an ERP system to get the data needed for various functions, one example being inventory monitoring.

Before ISA-95, there were different interface designs according to vendors. ISA-95 doesn't care how interfaces are implemented; it just describes the data that needs to go back and forth (see Figures B.12 and B.13). The context to this is that ERP had established a huge presence in the IT architecture of manufacturing companies, and the solutions for how to send data back and forth were all over the map. People were coming at the problem from every conceivable angle, so there was no uniformity whatsoever. ISA-95 draws a boundary around ERP and says where it stops. It says to ERP, "You stop here and you send this information to this application over there."

ISA-95 succeeds by showing processes apart from departments. Data flows are defined in ways that make sense and are comprehensive and thorough (see Figure B.14). A significant drawback is that it's an evolving standard. It's new, so it hasn't been widely accepted yet. It's too early to tell if there are any conceptual flaws, because it hasn't been thoroughly put to the test through extended actual usage. Because it's from ISA, people will start asking for an ISA-95 compliant system, but that isn't

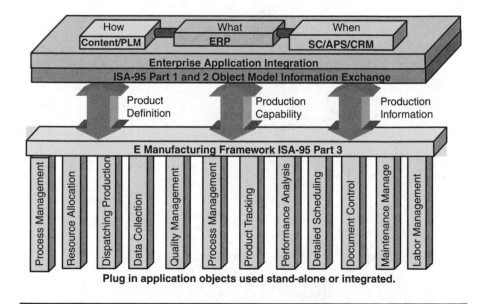

Figure B.12   ISA-95 e-Business Architecture (Source: ISA, Portions of this illustration © ISA 1995, 2000. Used with permission.)

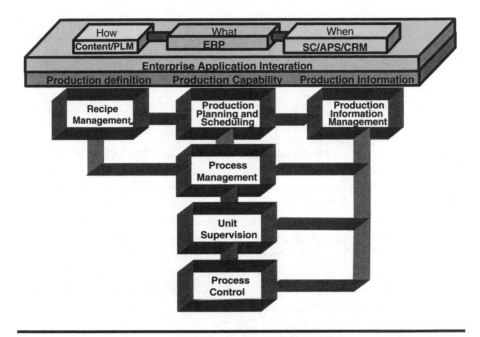

Figure B.13   ISA-95 and ISA-88 e-Business Architecture (Source: ISA, Portions of this illustration © ISA 1995, 2000. Used with permission.)

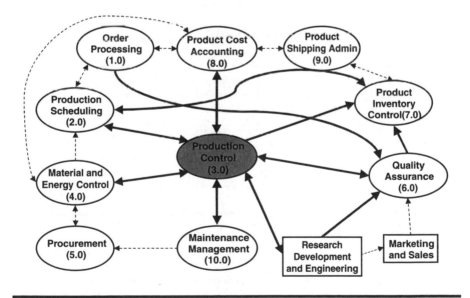

Figure B.14   ISA-95 Enterprise Control Model (Source: ISA-95.00.01-2000, © ISA 1995. Used with permission.)

feasible. The arena is just too complex. It would be great if the ERP vendors would make an interface available according to ISA-95 specs. This would make it easy for them to be compatible with a number of vendors, but it's unlikely this will happen because they still think that they can do it all.

Manufacturing Performance Model

The Manufacturing Performance Model (see Figure B.15) is a benchmark model and as such it seeks to provide a test for measuring your company's performance by providing five levels that are applied to various areas. It explains what to do to improve and it also spells out the benefits of making the changes. The point is to use it in an ongoing fashion, so that you can check your progress as you move toward your performance goals. It succeeds through its flexibility and its broad range of applicability. It doesn't insist that you do things in any particular way. How you use it is up to you. You may be perfectly happy being at Level 2 in some areas, but it helps you see where you are. Its strength can also be seen as its drawback. It's not a model that shows you how things should be, so it doesn't guarantee that you will improve anything. It's also not widely used or known.

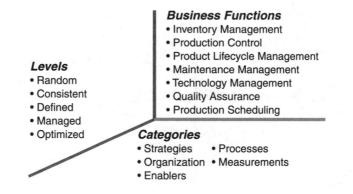

Figure B.15   Manufacturing Performance Model

Appendix C

GLOSSARY OF ACRONYMS

ANSI American National Standards Institute, ANSI is a standards body working to help coordinate and define a wide range of standards in a variety of areas.

AMR AMR Research is one of the leading global industry analysts in the IT arena. AMR has distinguished itself since its founding with in-depth analysis of the use of information technology in manufacturing companies.

API Application Program Interface is the term used to describe the part of an application software package that is dedicated to communicating with external software applications.

APICS American Production and Inventory Control Society is the leading industry professional association for materials and manufacturing management.

APS Advanced Planning and Scheduling is the function performed by application software packages that use some degree of intelligence, logic, or heuristics to help schedulers produce schedules.

BOM Bill of Material is the term used to describe the list of items, usually parts, that are the components of any manufactured product, including the quantity required for each item.

BOMP Bill of Material Processor was a simple computer with hard-wired logic, used in the early days of corporate computing to calculate the total quantities of various parts required to produce a certain number of end products.

CAD Computer-Aided Design or Computer-Aided Drafting both refer to the use of computer systems to replace the traditional pen and paper methods of conducting engineering design and drawing those products and their components.

CAM Computer-Aided Manufacturing refers to the use of computer controlled equipment in work centers that use digital and numeric inputs to drive the process instead of manual dials and manual movement by a human operator to conduct machining operations.

CFR Code of Federal Regulations are the published body of governmental regulations and rules written by the agencies responsible for those regulated environments.

CIM Computer-Integrated Manufacturing was a term coined in the 1970s and popularized in the 1980s to describe early visions and architectures for using computers in the manufacturing environment.

CMMS Computerized Maintenance Management System refers to a software application that is designed to help in the planning and execution of maintenance activities and the management of maintenance resources.

COA Certificate of Analysis is a statement that declares the performance of the raw material or product in any number of areas, including chemical analysis, stress test results, microbiological test results, taste tests, or almost any other measurement or criteria needed to assure the receiving manufacturer that the material has passed all necessary testing. Sometimes a COA represents test results received from an outside testing lab on product or raw material sent by the manufacturer.

COTS Commercial Off-The-Shelf is a term used to describe software that is prepackaged, offers specific functionality out of the box, is usually configurable for specific uses, and is sold on a "license to use basis" by software vendors.

CRM Customer Relationship Management. CRM encompasses all aspects of interaction that a company has with its customers, whether it be related to sales or service.

DB/400 A relational database management system product offered by IBM.

DCS Distributed Control System is a commercially available system designed to perform regulatory physical process control, which can be installed incrementally with components and programmed for its intended application.

DDE Dynamic Data Exchange. An interprocess communcation method used in Microsoft® Windows and OS/2. DDE allows two or more programs that are running simultaneously to exchange data and commands.

DEC Digital Equipment Corporation was one of the pioneering computer vendor companies in the era of minicomputers.

DECnet A propriety networking system based on Ethernet technology that was offered by DEC to connect all DEC computers and allow them to interoperate over the network.

DSS Decision Support Systems are computerized systems that gather and present data from a wide range of sources. They help people make decisions based on data that is culled from these sources.

EDI Electronic Data Interchange refers to the process of transmitting and receiving data between two computer systems based on a mutually agreed upon definition of electronic data formats.

EPA Environmental Protection Agency, an arm of the U.S. government.

ERP Enterprise Resource Planning refers to the class of commercial off the shelf application software products designed to run the commercial and financial operations of a company.

FDA Food and Drug Administration, a regulatory arm of the U.S. government.

FTE Full-Time Equivalent is the amount of labor or number of work hours expected from one full-time employee over the period of time in question, usually a year.

HMI Human-Machine Interface is the name given to specifically programmed graphical computer display screens that are designed to interact between humans and the functions of a computer program. HMI is often used to describe the portfolio of screens used in a process control application.

HP Hewlett-Packard, a leading computer vendor.

HP MPE Hewlett-Packard's proprietary commercial operating system used on the HP 3000 family of minicomputers in the 1980s and early 1990s.

HPWS High Performance Work System is a specific combination of human resource practices, work structures, and processes that maximizes employee knowledge, skills, commitment, and flexibility in the work environment.

IBM International Business Machines, a leading computer vendor.

IRS Internal Revenue Service, the tax collection arm of the U.S. government.

ISA Instrument Society of America is the leading professional association for the field of process control engineering.

ISA-88 Instrument Society of America's standard for describing batch management.

ISA-95 Instrument Society of America's standard for describing a framework for the integration of an enterprise's business systems with its manufacturing operations and control systems functions.

ISO International Organization for Standardization is an international standards body responsible for the development and promotion of standards in a number of arenas.

IT Information Technology refers to all things related to the deployment and use of computers.

JIT Just-In-Time is a manufacturing operations philosophy that stresses coordination and scheduling to reduce the inventory levels required to operate a manufacturing enterprise.

KPI Key Performance Indicator is a specific measurement or metric used to give some sense of status or performance for the activity or process being monitored.

LIMS Laboratory Information Management Systems are the application software systems used to integrate all of the functions of testing laboratories.

MAP Manufacturing Automation Protocol was a computer networking software and hardware standard that was developed in the mid-1980s.

MAP/TOP Manufacturing Automation Protocol/Technical and Office Protocol was an iteration of the MAP networking standard aimed at creating a uniform networking architecture for the back office and the plant floor.

MES Manufacturing Execution Systems are application software systems used to manage and control production and other functions in a manufacturing plant.

MESA Manufacturing Enterprise Solutions Association was formerly the Manufacturing Execution Systems Association, a trade group founded in the early 1990s to promote awareness and education for MES and now a broader array of applications in manufacturing.

MRO Maintenance, Repairs, and Operations.

MRP Material Requirements Planning is a planning process that defines the raw material needs for production and identifies the sources of those materials. It is also used as a slang term to refer to the broader class of application software products used to support these functions.

MRP II Material Resource Planning was distinguished from Material Requirements Planning by the Roman numeral II so they could share the MRP acronym. It refers to a broader set of manufacturing functionality that includes MRP and was frequently packaged this way in the 1980s.

NASA National Aeronautics and Space Administration, an arm of the U.S. government.

OEE Overall Equipment Effectiveness is a key performance indicator or calculated metric used to evaluate manufacturing performance.

OEM Original Equipment Manufacturer refers to a product or a product supply relationship where one finished product is purchased from a manufacturer and bundled or assembled into a larger manufactured product by another.

OS/400 IBM's first operating system for the AS/400 family of minicomputers.

OSF Open Software Foundation was a corporate entity founded and funded by computer hardware and software companies to produce and promote a standardized UNIX system in the 1990s.

OSHA Occupational Safety and Health Administration is a regulatory arm of the U.S. government.

PC Personal Computer.

PDA Personal Digital Assistant is small handheld portable computer typified by the Palm Pilot.

PDM Product Data Management refers to a software application designed to manage all information about specifications, usage, components, and all history of revisions of any manufactured product.

PLC Programmable Logic Controller is a simple programmable microprocessor based computer capable of reading from instruments and sensory devices, sending signals to control external physical devices or actuators. It's intended for use in process control applications.

PLM Product Lifecycle Management is a term used to describe software application systems that are designed for the management of all information and associated processes related to any product during its life journey in a manufacturing cycle from development through production.

PM Preventative Maintenance is the work performed in an effort to prevent the future breakage or other failure of equipment.

R&D Research and Development.

RCM Reliability Centered Maintenance is a philosophy used to guide maintenance management planning and work processes.

RDB Relational Database is a software program designed to manage large amounts of data and organize it in a way that it can be input, archived, retrieved, and used by application programs or reporting programs.

REPAC (AMR) Ready, Execute, Produce, Analyze, Coordinate. REPAC is a functional model for manufacturing operations and systems created by AMR Research.

RF Radio Frequency is a shorthand or slang term for devices that use radio frequency communication to transmit and receive data.

RFID Radio Frequency Identification refers to the products and technologies used to create and use mobile electronic tags that can store information written and read from a distance via RF.

ROI Return On Investment. A general concept referring to earnings from the investment of capital, where the earnings are expressed as a proportion of the investment.

SAA Systems Application Architecture was an IT applications architecture strategy developed and promoted by IBM in the late 1980s.

SCADA Supervisory Control and Data Acquisition is a class of applications software dedicated to interacting with PLCs and other devices controlling or measuring physical processes and human operators who oversee those physical processes through the system.

SCOR Supply Chain Operations Reference model is a multilevel standardized business process model maintained by the Supply-Chain Council and its members. It's often used as a starting point for business process mapping exercises.

SKU Stock Keeping Unit is a term that's often used to refer to part numbers or item numbers that reference the identity of a part or product.

SPC Statistical Process Control is a set of online, offline and at-line mathematical tools used to determine and monitor the level of statistical control demonstrated by a production process.

SQC Statistical Quality Control is the application of statistical techniques to control quality.

SQL Structured Query Language is a programming language used to interact with relational database management systems.

TOP Technical Office Protocol (see MAP/TOP).

TPM Total Productive Maintenance is a maintenance management philosophy.

UNIX A multiuser computer operating system that runs on a wide variety of hardware.

USDA United States Department of Agriculture, an arm of the government.

VMS Digital Equipment Corporation's proprietary operating system for its VAX line of minicomputers.

WIP Work in Process refers to the materials and components used to manufacture a product during the time they are in the manufacturing process, but before the finished product itself has been produced.

Y2K Shorthand for the year 2000, but the term became slang for the sometimes massive projects and programs companies undertook to ensure that their computer systems were prepared to deal with the date rollover event at the turn of the century.

INDEX